GW00656846

Diversity Management

Diversity Management
Triple Loop Learning

Robert L. Flood
and
Norma R.A. Romm

JOHN WILEY & SONS
Chichester · New York · Brisbane · Toronto · Singapore

Other Wiley Editorial Offices

John Wiley & Sons, Inc., 605 Third Avenue,
New York, NY 10158-0012, USA

John Wiley & Sons, Inc., 7222 Commerce Center Drive,
Suite 240, Colorado Springs, CO 80919, USA

Jacaranda Wiley Ltd, 33 Park Road, Milton,
Queensland 4064, Australia

John Wiley & Sons (Canada) Ltd, 22 Worcester Road,
Rexdale, Ontario M9W 1L1, Canada

John Wiley & Sons (Asia) Pte Ltd, 2 Clementi Loop #02-01,
Jin Xing Distripark, Singapore 129809

Library of Congress Cataloging-in-Publication Data
Flood, Robert L.
   Diversity management : triple loop learning / Robert L. Flood,
   Norma R. A. Romm.
      p.   cm.
   Includes bibliographical references and index.
   ISBN 0-471-96449-2 (cloth)
      1. Comparative management.   2. Organizational behavior.   I. Romm,
   Norma R. A.
   HD30.55.F55   1996
   658—dc20   96–14671
                                                                  CIP

British Library Cataloguing in Publication Data

A catalogue record for this book is available from the British Library

ISBN 0-471-96449-2

Typeset in 10/12pt Palatino by Footnote Graphics, Warminster, Wilts
Printed and bound in Great Britain by Bookcraft (Bath) Ltd, Midsomer Norton
This book is printed on acid-free paper responsibly manufactured from sustainable forestation,
for which at least two trees are planted for each one used for paper production.

To
Mandy and Ernst
♡

And castles made of sand
Slip into the sea
Eventually...

Jimi Hendrix Experience
Axis Bold As Love, 1969

$\mathcal{C}$ ontents

Book Preface   xi

PART 1   CONCLUSION

CHAPTER 1
Diversity Management: Triple Loop Learning   2
1.1   Introduction   2
1.2   The Research Program   2
1.3   Summary and Conclusion   11

PART 2   DIVERSITY MANAGEMENT
Preface to Part 2   14

CHAPTER 2
Metatheory, Philosophy, and the History of Knowledge   17
2.1   Introduction   17
2.2   The Enlightenment   17
2.3   Thomas Kuhn   18
2.4   Jürgen Habermas   20
2.5   Methodenstreit   22
2.6   Postmodernism   24
2.7   Summary and Conclusion   27

CHAPTER 3
Metatheory, Theory, and Methodology   29
3.1   Introduction   29
3.2   The Natural Sciences   29
3.3   The Social Sciences   30
3.4   Summary and Conclusion   35

CHAPTER 4
Metatheory and Systems Thinking   36
4.1   Introduction   36

4.2 Cybernetics   37
     4.2.1 Introduction and Summary   37
     4.2.2 Discussion   37
4.3 Systemic Interpretivism   40
     4.3.1 Introduction and Summary   40
     4.3.2 Discussion   40
4.4 Critical Systemic Modernism   41
     4.4.1 Introduction and Summary   41
     4.4.2 Discussion   42
4.5 Postmodern Critique   47
     4.5.1 Introduction and Summary   47
     4.5.2 Discussion   47
4.6 Summary and Conclusion   51

CHAPTER 5
Contours of Diversity Management   53
5.1 Introduction   53
5.2 Diversity Management   53
5.3 Summary and Conclusion   57

PART 3 TRIPLE LOOP LEARNING
Preface to Part 3   60

CHAPTER 6
Typology of Power   62
6.1 Introduction   62
6.2 Typologies of Power   63
6.3 Structuralism   65
     6.3.1 Opening Remark   65
     6.3.2 Parsonian Discourse   65
     6.3.3 Marxist-oriented Discourse   65
     6.3.4 Implications for Practice   66
6.4 Intersubjective Decision Making   68
     6.4.1 Discourse   68
     6.4.2 Implications for Practice   69
6.5 Might–right Management   71
     6.5.1 Discourse   71
     6.5.2 Implications for Practice   72
6.6 Summary and Conclusion   75

CHAPTER 7
Loop 1. Design Management: How?   76
7.1 Introduction   76
7.2 About Design   76
7.3 Organisational Design   78
     7.3.1 Introduction   78

7.3.2   Bureaucracy: Traditional Hierarchy   79
7.3.3   Circular Organisation: Democratic Hierarchy   87
7.3.4   Organic Organisation   91
7.3.5   Viable System Organisation   97
7.3.6   Community Organisation   104
7.3.7   Postmodern Organisation   106
7.3.8   Concluding Comment   110
7.4 Process Design   111
7.4.1   Introduction   111
7.4.2   Quality Management   112
7.4.3   Business Process Reengineering   120
7.4.4   Concluding Comment   124
7.5 Summary and Conclusion   124

CHAPTER 8
Loop 2. Debate Management: What?   127
8.1 Introduction   127
8.2 About Debate   127
8.3 Action Learning   131
8.4 Action Research   134
8.4.1   Introduction   134
8.4.2   Participatory Action Research   136
8.4.3   Action Science   140
8.5 Systems Approaches   145
8.5.1   Introduction   145
8.5.2   Strategic Assumption Surfacing and Testing   146
8.5.3   Soft Systems Methodology   154
8.5.4   Concluding Comment   160
8.6 Postmodern Debate   161
8.7 Summary and Conclusion   166

CHAPTER 9
Loop 3. Might–right Management: Why?   169
9.1 Introduction   169
9.2 About Might–right   170
9.3 Might–right and the Question of Interests   172
9.4 Options for Might–right Management   172
9.5 Vitalising Educational Practices   173
9.5.1   Introduction   173
9.5.2   Dialogical Intervention Strategy   174
9.5.3   Critical Systems Heuristics   177
9.6 Nurturing Self-reliance   183
9.6.1   Introduction   183
9.6.2   Collaborative Inquiry   184
9.6.3   Self-reliant Participatory Action Research   188
9.7 (Re)Consideration of Social Relationships   194

9.8   Protest   198
      9.8.1   Introduction   198
      9.8.2   Right in Protest Through Communicative
              Rationality   199
      9.8.3   Might of Strategy in Protest   201
      9.8.4   Novel Protest   203
      9.8.5   Concluding Comment   204
9.9   Summary and Conclusion   205

CHAPTER 10
Loop 3 Continued. Enhancing Emancipatory Practice   **207**
10.1   Introduction   207
10.2   Dilemmas for Triple Loop Learning   209
10.3   Current Responses to the Dilemmas   210
10.4   A New Response to the Dilemmas   212
10.5   Two Examples of the New Response   212
       10.5.1   Introduction   212
       10.5.2   Oblique Use of Cybernetics   213
       10.5.3   Oblique Use of Soft Systems   215
       10.5.4   Concluding Comment   218
10.6   Moral and Theoretical Justification   218
10.7   Enhancing the Process of Choice   221
10.8   Summary and Conclusion   223

CHAPTER 11
Contours of Triple Loop Learning   **225**
11.1   Introduction   225
11.2   Triple Looping   225
11.3   Summary and Conclusion   230

PART 4   BEGINNING

CHAPTER 12
Closing Remarks   **232**

References   **235**

Index   **247**

Book Preface

This book is about diversity management and triple loop learning.[1]

Diversity management is about managing the increasing diversity of issues that confront humankind[2] in contemporary organisational[3] and societal affairs. Initially this meant people managing the increasing diversity of issues they confronted by increasing the diversity of types of model, methodology and theory available to address those affairs. Diversification, however, created a brand new issue to be managed – how to choose between the models, methodologies and theories. Consequently, the emphasis in diversity management switched to people managing the increasing diversity of models, methodologies and theories that continue to come to the fore, thus improving management of the increasing diversity of issues confronted. Diversity therefore means that more choices are made available for people to manage organisational and societal affairs. Management means that these choices, which after all have to be made, are thought through intelligently and made responsibly. Intelligence and responsibility are the defining features of triple loop learning.

Triple loop learning is the dénouement of single loop learning and double loop learning. There are three types of single loop learning each with a different centre of learning. There are specific questions asked respectively for each centre. The first centre of learning asks, Are we doing things right? This assumes that choosing things to do is not problematic. A second type of single loop learning accepts that identification of things to do is often problematic and makes this its centre of learning. It asks, Are we doing the

---

[1] *Diversity Management: Triple Loop Learning* presents the desired mentality and deeper consciousness of *Solving Problem Solving* (Flood, 1995a). The *Solving Problem Solving* book title contains its own irony. The book says there are no problems or solutions. The circular title says this too.

[2] Issues of humankind to us refer to physical, biological and social cares. That is not to say that the physical and biological worlds are there for human exploitation. For example, ecological issues may be issues to be cared about not solely in terms of human needs. No matter how these issues are seen, humankind must take some responsibility for their care.

[3] By organisation we mean a set of activities organised around purposes or themes that observers highlight in the process of setting organisational boundaries.

right things? A third form of single loop learning centres the issue that rightness is often buttressed by mightiness, and mightiness by rightness, resulting in very little learning at all. The question here is whether mightiness is acting as too much of a support for definitions of rightness or conversely any presumed right way is becoming too forceful (i.e. fanatical). It makes this its centre of learning and asks, Is rightness buttressed by mightiness and/or mightiness buttressed by rightness? The first two loops consider this third one problematic because it is regarded as ideologically based and not scientific. Each loop is dominated by the task-oriented quest to achieve an answer to *its* question. The centres of learning are in conflict and are not reflexive.

Double loop learning attempts to interplay the first two centres of learning. These two are most easily reconciled since they both share a grave concern that the last centre of learning is too ideologically based. It asks, Are we doing things right and are we doing the right things? This is a bid to de-emphasise the task-oriented nature of intervention. Interventionists are then not committed solely to one loop and its task. Intervention thus moves a step forward in a reflexive direction by facing up to choice between the two centres at any one time. There is a new consciousness as interventionists loop between the two centres of learning.

Triple loop learning is about increasing the fullness and deepness of learning about the diversity of issues and dilemmas faced. It is about ways of managing them. It wants to establish tolerance between all three centres of learning and preserve the diversity therein. It does this by bringing together the three centres of learning from the three loops in one overall awareness, Are we doing things right, and are we doing the right things, and is rightness buttressed by mightiness and/or mightiness buttressed by rightness? Triple loop learning links into a triple loop the three centres of learning. Triple loop learners loop between these three questions. In this way triple loop learners are reflexive and are able to operate more intelligently and responsibly. Their whole consciousness becomes more than the sum of its parts, encouraging awareness of dilemmas involved when addressing issues such as those introduced above.

Triple loop learning is represented in Figure P1. In the figure you will see that there are three loops. Each loop represents one of the centres of learning that are discussed above. The loops link through C, which represents the interventionists' consciousness. By consciousness here we mean awareness of all three centres of learning each encircled by a loop. The dots give C access to each centre of learning. They point to consciousness of the provisional character of answers to the questions raised in each centre of learning.

This book, *Diversity Management: Triple Loop Learning*, is for theoreticians and interventionists. The book introduces diversity management and triple

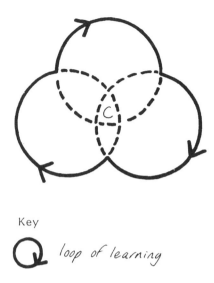

Key

Q *loop of learning*

Figure P1

loop learning in the opening chapter but is split into two main parts thereafter; one for theoreticians about diversity management (Part 2) and one for interventionists about triple loop learning (Part 3).

If you approach this book as a theoretician; then read the opening chapter followed by Part 2, Chapter 11 (where we elaborate on triple loop learning), and then the closing remarks. If time and interest prevail then read the whole of Part 3. In Part 3, models and methodologies from each of the three loops of triple looping are introduced, cases are provided that illustrate their application, and a discourse for learning about each loop is extended. This will help you to see metatheoretically how ideas presented in Part 2 are applied, thus helping you to understand much better our (meta)theoretical ideas.

If you approach this book as an interventionist; then read the opening chapter followed by Part 3 and then the closing remarks. If time and interest prevail then go on to read Part 2. In this section you will find a more detailed account of theoretical dilemmas that need to be dealt with practically.

We wish to make the following acknowledgements. For thought-provoking discussions we thank staff and affiliates at the Centre for Systems Studies at the University of Hull, namely, Mandy Brown, Claire Cohen, Peter Dudley, Phil Green, Wendy Gregory, Gerald Midgley, John Oliga, Gillian Ragsdell, Néstor Valero-Silva, Werner Ulrich, Jennifer Wilby, and Zhu Zhichang. Thanks to Gerard Fairtlough for helping in the formulation of words about creative compartments. We have also enjoyed and benefited from discussions with our colleagues at the University of Los Andes in Mérida,

Venezuela, through several exchange visits funded by the British Council. Thanks also to Martin Spaul. Much thanks to Ernst Onkenhout for his meticulous editing work on our manuscript. Finally, we acknowledge gratefully the contribution of Norma's friendly neighbour James Martin Hewitt who provided necessary food for the final few months of this project.

Robert L. Flood
Norma R. A. Romm
January 1996
Hull, UK

PART 1
Conclusion

Diversity Management: Triple Loop Learning

1.1 INTRODUCTION

Chapter 1 provides a background to our research program and the conclusions drawn in this book. It summarises the meaning we wish to invoke
when employing the terms diversity management and triple loop learning.
To begin the story, we take the reader back 200 years to one of the great
turning points in human thought.

1.2 THE RESEARCH PROGRAM

Until the eighteenth century the Christian Church in Europe determined
the nature of knowledge of the world and the position of people within
society. The Church elevated a religious philosophy based on theological
speculation that generated ideas which cannot be proven or disproven. A
literal faith in the Scriptures was called for, for the good of all people.

In the eighteenth century the counter-project of Enlightenment was
launched. Enlightenment theorists argued that human thought, independent of the Scriptures, is able to understand and/or control the world.
Enlightenment for the most part was built on a mode of thought termed
critical scientific rationalism. The idea of critical scientific rationalism was to
seek out scientific truth that would support human progress and hence lead
to emancipation. The human condition would be improved through human
reason (rationality) and human experience (empiricism). Reason and
empirical science would facilitate the rational organisation of society.

As the project of Enlightenment progressed, ideology critique took up a leading position in social science research. It was argued that ideas serve the interests of power and that this led to there being a ruling class with ruling ideas. "The ruling ideas of each age have ever been the ideas of the ruling class" (Marx and Engels, *Communist Manifesto*, 1888, English translation). For Marx and Engels, the promise of rational scientific inquiry was to disclose truths that lay behind false conceptions of the past (cf. Simons and Billig, 1994). Marx and Engels' critical interest in Enlightenment urged laying bare and challenging dominant ideology and hence became liberatory in this sense too.

In recent times much doubt has been cast over the feasibility of rational scientific thought and ideology critique. Commentators pointed out, for example, that Marx and Engels' contribution to the project of Enlightenment was subject to its own ideology, one that "put an innocent trust in the power of reason and an optimistic faith in modernity" (Simons and Billig, 1994: 2). New studies continued the search for a sound, stable, and fair modern world. Recently, the concrete foundations of castles of modernism have worn away, crumbling into sand as they are weathered by a postmodern critique.

The postmodern critique of modernism undermines the idea of truth by raising dilemmas, doubts, and suspicions about all truth statements, and maintains that it is not possible to lay open ideological chimera. It paints the dark side of modernism. It is not possible, through modernism, to emancipate people from whatever system dominates their lives, be it Scriptures or ideas of a ruling class (which in some cases are the same thing). The project of Enlightenment had "failed". In a short-lived victory, postmodernism seemed to conclude that the crux of emancipation is, "anything goes". With this goes solidity of thought, leaving a fluid and diverse world of many equally valid truths. Ironically, then, choices in a postmodern world can easily be colonised by the ruling class or its equivalent. It is this whimsicality and dark side to postmodern thought that provides modernism with a second chance; a chance to come up with a reworked account of ideology critique that provides a retort to an unfettered postmodern critique. The reworked account, however, will not be a reinstatement of modernism. The critique will tack its course between modernism and postmodernism, succumbing to neither.

Of course, there is great depth and breadth in, and between, the modernist and postmodernist positions, not touched upon here, that we take into account in succeeding chapters. From what has been said, however, it is possible to design and paste up two headline posters that we reckon must feature in any contemporary social theory:

- diversity in types of model, methodology and theory, and
- emancipatory practice.

The question is, (how) can these two poster features be designed within one scheme of thought? There are perhaps four main styles of response in answer to this question: pragmatism, isolationism, imperialism, and complementarism (cf. Reed, 1985).

Pragmatism. In practice with pragmatism, little, if any, reference is made to inferable underlying theory, or methodological or model-based rules. There is barely reflection over which theory, methodology or model is likely to be relevant, when, or why. Practitioners' command over these tools is based on experiential knowledge about them gained through a process of trial and error. Models and methodologies can be mixed, but without concern for the way mixing is done, whether or how mixing could be justified, and why some parts of models and methodologies (rather than others) are being chosen for the mixing pot. This kind of trial-and-error pragmatism is sometimes called eclecticism. It is a weak heuristic approach. Choice of this sort of pragmatism, if followed literally, may lead to unfortunate social repercussions resulting from heuristic *in vivo* experimentation on social affairs, running the risk of unnecessary levels of damage and distress to people. Furthermore, a preconceived, prestructured appreciation of affairs is likely to prevail giving rise (effectively) to predetermined solutions. In this way a pragmatic approach is likely to maintain or even increase the power of select groups, and hardly represents fair emancipatory practice (how ever defined).

Isolationism. There are two forms of isolationism. *Theoretical isolationism* comes to be noticed when clear philosophical beliefs are held, are consistently subscribed to and, in fact, firmly protected against perceived extraparadigmatic enemies. *Methodological and model isolationism* occurs when a single methodology or model is permanently in interventionists' service. In the academic world, typically, gurus author and promote a favoured approach. In the commercial world consultants employ an in-house methodology or model. With choice of isolationism, a number of key issues may bounce back and impair the balance of interventionists. Perhaps the most concerning impairment is a lack in variety so that they cannot possibly be balanced. Societies and other forms of organisation are far too rich and diverse for serious interventionists to remain content with limited options. At a theoretical level the restriction is not so bad, limiting interventionists to act within a paradigm, for which several methodological and model expressions are possible. Yet the limitations are significant enough to raise concern because adherence to one theory confines explanation of organisational and societal affairs and therefore restricts options for managing them. Furthermore, in terms of emancipatory practice, promotion of one way by definition means demotion of others, which is one way of being totalising and oppressive.

Imperialism. Imperialism is like isolationism except that some recognition is given to ideas from other theories, yet recognition is achieved in imperialist terms. Imperialism comes in two forms. Analysis is given below for types of theory but the same can be said of types of methodology and model. *Imperialism by annexation* is one way of managing dissonance about anomalies in a preferred theory that surface when recognition is given to other theories. The option chosen is to patch up anomalies by annexing ideas from other recognised theories. Annexation, however, is contracted in terms of an imperialist's favoured theory. *Imperialism by subsumption* ensures new theories are totally subsumed (also) in terms of an imperialist's favoured theory. Concern about imperialism therefore mirrors concern expressed about isolationism.

Complementarism. Pragmatism is a form of non-reflective eclecticism. Isolationism and imperialism will not entertain the near total lack of theoretical, methodological and model content that characterises pragmatism. Yet their solutions limit theoretical, methodological and model content. Complementarism is an attempt to preserve diversity in these three spheres of thought and action. Preservation of diversity enhances opportunities people have to manage intelligently and responsibly the most exacting issues that arise in organisational and societal affairs. The question for complementarism is, How can theoreticians and interventionists find a way that satisfactorily allows us to theorise and act with *different notions of the world* while at the same time maintaining overall emancipatory practice? How can we have diversity management? While apparently still grappling with this hanging difficulty, complementarism offered some promise of avoiding the dark side, keeping alive optimism and breeding diversity for its potentially non-repressive nature.

Complementarism takes on several guises, but we see it as a discussion about the possibility of commensurability as a starting point for managing diversity of types of theory, methodology and model.[1] A leap from isolationism to *commensurability* was therefore a calculated move that we tried to make. It promised to hold in the frame many different theories, methodologies and models. It also posed a dilemma for practically minded researchers like us.

The dilemma begins with the question, On what basis can choice be made between theories, methodologies and models? All answers to this question are contingent on the meaning they ascribe to commensurability. One seemingly reasonable assumption on this score defines commensurability in terms of measurement by a common standard; or, in other words, the reconciliation and integration of different spheres of thought and action.

---

[1] The methodological bases we define are the point of action where theoreticians and practitioners act in terms of theoretical underpinnings that specify ways forward in terms of principles and purposes (cf. Flood, 1995a: 182–185).

Integration, however, carries more than a suggestion that the spheres must end up denatured, being reduced in meaning to comply with determining factors set in the measurement standard. Action is possible following choice of measurement standard, but this, it seems, immediately starts a process of slipping back, down a muddy bank into isolationism (through imperialism).

The dilemma gets more complicated on further investigation. Footholds can be found that indicate a route up the muddy bank. *Incommensurability* is the goal of the climb. Incommensurability, of course, means that there is no common measurement standard, no possible way of comparing theories, methodologies and models. They are fundamentally different and that is that. Action following choice of theory, methodology or model, therefore, can result in only one thing if practice is not to be contradictory. The result of choice appears to be a somewhat arbitrary adherence to a preferred theory, methodology or model. The *irony* is that the footholds work a way back to isolationism and to the very bottom of the muddy bank.

What we see here is a "triangle of dilemma" for action-minded researchers (see Figure 1.1). No matter which pole of the triangle interventionists try to hang their action on, sliding down the muddy bank cannot be halted. In a modernist world theoreticians and interventionists attempt to solve this dilemma by appealing to some version of commensurability to compare theories. In a modernist world, as we have hinted at above, theoreticians and interventionists are trapped by this dilemma, trapped in a pit bounded by the triangle.

How do things look in the postmodern world? Things shape up uncannily like the "triangle of dilemma". The postmodern world is characterised *inter alia* by dilemmas and differences.[2] The difference between modernists and postmodernists on this matter, however, is that the former attempt to solve dilemmas while the latter want to live by them.

Living by dilemmas creates a rather confusing world of disorder if taken literally. This stance of naive postmodernism eradicates the possibility for choice. It shies away from measurement standards, believing that standards remove diversity and consequently oppress thought and action. It sees standards as a force of the dark side. Everything, therefore, should be contradicted and remain relative. Dilemmas rule, OK.

And yet relativism means it is not possible to make choices. Relativism is very depressing news for practice-oriented researchers. Relativism is gloomy. As if in C. S. Lewis's *Shadowlands*, whichever way a relativist turns

---

[2] Some have argued that what characterises the postmodern age is its quality as a post-industrial information society, where the explosion of information in all spheres of social life has implications for the way social relations are pursued (cf . Wexler, 1987: 111). Others concentrate more on the postmodern world as a movement which is constructed as a critique of the modern ways of constructing knowledge and living accordingly (cf. Hassard, 1993: 124). Postmodernism as an intellectual movement implies a loss of faith in dominant systems of thought and a quest to delineate possible ways of thinking that are not guided by the search for representational or consensual forms of knowing.

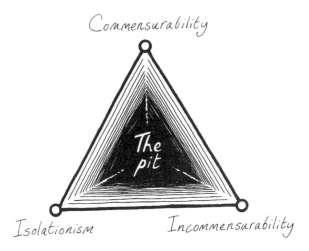

Figure 1.1 (Reproduced by permission of Plenum Press.)

s/he never leaves the Shadowlands, never feels or senses the optimism of sunny (theoretical) spaces. No choice is perceived possible, so no change in commitment is actually possible. Relativism tends toward conservativism. Ironically, relativism is another victory for the dark side.

Take Cummings's (1994) view that an apple is an apple, an orange is an orange, and apples and oranges cannot be compared. This can be challenged. People in attempting to compare them will talk for ever, Cummings says, drawing a metaphor between apple–orange comparison, and choice between different theories. There are no grounds, no measurable standards on which we can compare unlike theories (different fruits) and make choices. People can only carry on talking, and it seems that they primarily will talk past each other.

In our view there are grounds on which comparison can be made between apples and oranges from which we can make choices. It is a matter of setting out locally relevant grounds for discussion. In this way it is possible to measure comparatively apples and oranges in terms, say, of sweetness and make a choice. A disabled person with limited use in one arm can assess how easy each one is to prepare for eating and (perhaps) choose the apple because an orange is hard for them to peel. The mode of production of these two particular fruits can be investigated and a choice made on their relative environmental friendliness. Or the mode of production can be assessed in terms of relative exploitation of the workforce (say according to value of their remuneration) and choice made on this basis. Each choice, it should be remembered, can only be made using locally generated criteria informed by wider considerations (in our examples, about taste, disability, environmental friendliness and exploitation as possible factors worthy of consideration).

Also of value to complementarism is the irony in Cummings's claim, by use of metaphor, that unlike things cannot be compared. The irony arises because Cummings's tool, metaphor, by its very nature contains comparison of one thing to another where it is not literally applicable. Again, it is a matter of setting out locally relevant grounds for discussion. And another irony for relativism is that no choice is a choice. It is a choice to carry on doing things in the same old way, even if this means talking forever without taking direct action. Inaction is a choice. We cannot escape choice.

So, where can theoreticians and interventionists find sustenance? There have been several attempts to keep choice and action alive, to prevent slow death and burial at the bottom of the pit (e.g. papers in Simons and Billig, 1994, in particular Brown's). Our proposal is reviewed below.

We have recently labelled our effort that responds to the above debates diversity management. We choose to be optimistic, but not naively optimistic as were (understandably) early Enlightenment thinkers. Our optimism sticks with argument, but only where choices are made and responsibility for choices accepted, as patterns of action or even apparent inaction are followed.

Our argument goes back to the commensurability versus incommensurability triangle of dilemma (see Figure 1.1). In full awareness of the potential danger of slipping into the pit in Figure 1.1, we choose to speak of incommensurability. Now, however, we add an important proviso. We suggest that tension between different theories, methodologies and models, as modes of knowing and intervening in organisational and societal affairs, needs to be kept in consciousness and their radical differences acknowledged. Keeping radical differences (and tension) in consciousness allows us to reformulate the relationship between the apparently incomparable options they equip people with. The term incommensurability, therefore, is useful only insofar as it allows us to keep in consciousness diversity and the radical differences in position, which open up a wide set of choices. To highlight this feature of choice making we now speak of *(in)commensurability*. When choosing theories, methodologies and models, we place brackets within the word incommensurability.

Choice of theories, methodologies and models cannot be absolutely defended on the grounds that they have been agreed or that they are in tune with what the situation calls for. This is because at the moment of action there may still be competing choices for both inquiry and intervention. This is why we do admit a degree of incomparability between options and why we place a bracket in the term incommensurability. There are no universal or absolutely standardised ways of comparing. Choices can be defended on the grounds that they incorporate a degree of sensitivity to other options as well as an effort to encounter these without thereby subsuming them in a prefavoured one. This, of course, is our own notion of defensibility of choices – a proposal about what constitutes better choice making in the face of diversity, without slipping into the pit identified in Figure 1.1. We also have our own standard arising from this view of choice making.

The *standard* we wish to measure by is: the chances people have to make widely informed and locally contingent choices in the process of managing issues and dilemmas that characterise organisational and societal affairs through triple loop learning. This standard contains five core themes that thread through this book: diversity management, triple loop learning, managing dilemmas, the process of critique, and complementarism and emancipation. Each is sketched out below.

Diversity management is about managing the increasing diversity of issues that confront humankind in contemporary organisational and societal affairs. Initially this meant people managing the increasing diversity of issues they confronted by increasing the diversity of types of model, methodology and theory available to do the job. Diversification, however, created a brand new issue to be managed – how to choose between the models, methodologies and theories. Consequently, the emphasis in diversity management switched to people managing the increasing diversity of models, methodologies and theories that continue to come to the fore, thus improving management of the increasing diversity of issues confronted. Diversity therefore means that more choices are made available for people to manage organisational and societal affairs. Management means that these choices, which after all have to be made, are thought through intelligently and made responsibly. Intelligence and responsibility are the defining features of triple loop learning.

Triple loop learning is the dénouement of single loop learning and double loop learning. There are three types of single loop learning each with a different centre of learning. There are specific questions asked respectively for each centre. The first centre of learning asks, Are we doing things right? This assumes that choosing things to do is not problematic. A second type of single loop learning accepts that identification of things to do is often problematic and makes this its centre of learning. It asks, Are we doing the right things? A third form of single loop learning centres the issue that rightness is often buttressed by mightiness, and mightiness by rightness, resulting in very little learning at all.[3] The question here is whether mightiness is acting as too much of a support for definitions of rightness or conversely any presumed right way is becoming too forceful (i.e. fanatical). It makes this its centre of learning and asks, Is rightness buttressed by mightiness and/or mightiness buttressed by rightness? The first two loops consider this third one problematic because it is regarded as ideologically based and not scientific. Each loop is dominated by the task-oriented quest to achieve

[3] The allusion is to Plato's *The Republic* (1987: 19–20) where the question is asked whether might is right.

an answer to *its* question. The centres of learning are in conflict and are not reflexive.

Double loop learning attempts to interplay the first two centres of learning. These two are most easily reconciled since they both share a grave concern that the last centre of learning is too ideologically based. It asks, Are we doing things right and are we doing the right things? This is a bid to de-emphasise the task-oriented nature of intervention. Interventionists are then not committed solely to one loop and its task. Intervention thus moves a step forward in a reflexive direction by facing up to choice between the two centres at any one time. There is a new consciousness as interventionists loop between the two centres of learning.

Triple loop learning is about increasing the fullness and deepness of learning about the diversity of issues and dilemmas faced. It is about ways of managing them. It wants to establish tolerance between all three centres of learning and preserve the diversity therein. It does this by bringing together the three centres of learning from the three loops in one overall awareness, Are we doing things right, and are we doing the right things, and is rightness buttressed by mightiness and/or mightiness buttressed by rightness? Triple loop learning links into a triple loop the three centres of learning. Triple loop learners loop between these three questions. In this way triple loop learners are reflexive and are able to operate more intelligently and responsibly. Their whole consciousness becomes more than the sum of its parts, encouraging awareness of dilemmas involved when addressing issues such as those introduced above.

Managing dilemmas is about managing insoluble issues otherwise tagged dilemmas. Confounding the long scholarly search for rightness is the insoluble character of dilemmas it meets. Dilemmas plague societal, organisational and, indeed, individual's affairs. For example, our standard is our way of managing the haunting dilemma about what emancipation means in societal affairs.[4]

The dilemma is a play between rightness and anything goes. Ironically, rightness is oppressive because it forces a system of thought and definition of emancipation that may suit some but never suits everyone. Watching TV or listening to radio debates that deal with this issue is the only reminder we need that the issue is insoluble – it is a dilemma. Ironically, the ultra-liberal experiment with this dilemma, that anything goes, runs smack into another dilemma. Freedom to define for oneself what emancipation means is full of tension and easily undermined by exposure to power play. Difference

---

[4] Shotter (1993: 49) points out that what he calls "dilemmatic themes" are intrinsically present in the common sense of a society. Opposing words, images, maxims, etc., abound in the discourse of everyday life. These oppositions point to moments of uncertainty when addressing issues that arise. Shotter warns that researchers must be wary of over-systematising theoretical categories in a way that seems to deny the relevance of the dilemmatic themes of everyday life. The suggestion in this book is that researchers need not deny such everyday dilemmas, but can still offer ideas about managing them.

may become divisive. It may lead to negative exchanges so that benefits of tension that is encouraged are lost to destructive forces. The tension may then be resolved through power play. Alternatively, divisiveness may lead to people talking past each other, where decisions do not appear to be made. Conversation loses all integrity. Decisions are likely to be made through power play.

Our standard manages the irony that rightness or anything goes both lead to oppression, yet choices still have to be made. Our standard chooses a liberal stance, that decisions about emancipation, and all other issues, are locally decidable – it wants diversity. Our standard chooses an argumentative stance, that decisions about emancipation, and all other issues, are widely informed, and made intelligently and responsibly – it wants management through triple loop learning. Diversity management through triple loop learning thus incorporates management of dilemmas.

The process of critique is the process of being systemic. Being systemic to us means creating and managing diversity and tension rather than the traditional idea of manufacturing harmonious, perfect wholes. Reflexivity as a process of critique provides a means to maintain diversity and tension. Our methodological clarification given in Part 3 is nothing more than a process of critique directed at managing organisational and societal affairs.

Complementarism and emancipation are identified in this chapter as two headline posters that must feature in any contemporary social theory, including our own. The question we posed is, (how) can these two poster features be designed within one scheme of thought? A dilemma faced here is that a strong commitment to either commensurability or incommensurability lead straight into the pit in Figure 1.1. Our tentative (in)commensurability solution is found in our standard, in its expression of core themes just summarised, and throughout the book as we follow the threads.

1.3 SUMMARY AND CONCLUSION

Perhaps the most productive way of rounding off this introduction to our research program and the conclusions drawn in this book is to summarise the meaning we wish to invoke when employing the terms diversity management and triple loop learning. This we do in the form of bullet points.

- Diversity management is about people managing the increasing diversity of models, methodologies and theories that continue to come to the fore, thus improving management of the increasing diversity of issues confronted in organisational and societal affairs.
- A choice has been made in this endeavour to promote the optimistic and demote the dark side of modernism and postmodernism. The dark side brings forward totalising theory and naive relativism respectively. Optimism

promotes argument and diversity, also respectively. This statement needs to be qualified carefully. In any circumstance there is always choice and action (even in the form of inaction). Because there is diversity there is choice. Since we cannot escape choice, every effort must be made to ensure that choice is made thoughtfully, through argument. Argument, however, is not the standardised tool of validation control suggested by modernist rationality. Argument is carried out in the light of the following point.

- Choice making is locally decidable, temporally ephemeral and widely informed. Because diversity management is a theory, it must take into account wider ongoing theoretical debates. Because diversity management is about action, it must also take into account wider matters of contemporary concern.
- The standard of measurement is: the chances people have to make widely informed and locally contingent choices in the process of managing dilemmas that characterise organisational and societal affairs through triple loop learning. This standard contains five core themes that thread through this book: managing diversity, triple loop learning, managing dilemmas, the process of critique, and complementarism and emancipation. The two most central themes are summarised once again below.
- Diversity management states that tension between different theories, methodologies and models, as modes of knowing and intervening in organisational and societal affairs, needs to be kept in consciousness and their radical differences acknowledged.
- Triple loop learning operates intelligently and responsibly by looping between three centres of learning by asking the following three questions:
  - Are we doing things right?
  - Are we doing the right things?
  - Is rightness buttressed by mightiness and/or mightiness buttressed by rightness?

  Triple loop learning when invoking these questions does not imply a search for harmonious consensuality in society but it does recognise that we are implicated in each other's lives.

Part 1 of this book provides a background to our research program on diversity management and triple loop learning. The remainder of the book adds detail to what has been sketched out. Part 2 for theoreticians (and interventionists), coming up next, establishes an understanding of diversity management as a form of complementarism in terms of metatheory. Part 2 explores issues raised on metatheory in social philosophy and social theory, and concludes with a summary of our defence of complementarism. Part 3 for interventionists (and theoreticians) then follows, examining triple loop learning through types of methodology and model as options for taking our theoretical findings into action.

PART 2
Diversity Management

Preface to Part 2

The philosophy of the social sciences will surely record a tensionful debate coming to prominence in the last quarter of the twentieth century, between modernism and postmodernism. Has there been an epochal transformation to a postmodern society? Or are we witnessing what Giddens (1990) calls late modernity, where postmodernism is an expression of stresses associated with the modern world? In this confusion the current condition of the debaters has become paroxysmal; experiencing fits of triumph, fits of depression, and fits of playful exchange. The fullness of these moods, however, will become apparent only as the debate matures, and its complexities and tensions become better understood.

Nevertheless, as we see it, a handful of vital issues are beginning to gel. One such issue is a concern for diversity management: the management of diversity in types of theory, methodology and model. The challenge for action-based researchers is knowing how to manage diversity and dilemmas in each of these spheres of thought and action.

Diversity in types of theory, methodology and model improves chances of meaningfully tackling unyielding issues experienced in human organisation by widening choices about the means to tackle them. For this reason, it is argued, diversity is essential to the continued well-being of practice-oriented endeavours. There is wide, although far from exclusive, agreement in contemporary writings in social science research that diversity is *desirable*, yet debate burns on because complementarity is not obviously theoretically *feasible*. It is our intention in this book to put forward a new position on complementarism, called diversity management, that we argue goes some way toward managing apparently insoluble theoretical issues that continue to cast doubt on its feasibility.

The way we approach this theoretical issue is first to establish an understanding of complementarism in terms of metatheory. Metatheory is initially explored in the context of philosophy and the history of knowledge. This exploration in effect takes us through modernist and then postmodernist forms of metatheory, in terms of their bearing on the issue of complementarism.

Our next task is to investigate and position disciplinary theory and methodology within the metatheoretical literature, assessing progress at this level, and looking for ways forward for complementarism. This is repeated for systems thinking from where (surprisingly!) we launch our own initiative. Our brand of systems thinking bears little resemblance to the commonly held understanding of systems theory – save for its commitment to holism, now understood to mean complementarism. Quite how different our brand is from its logico- and empiricist–positivist, and more recently interpretivist, predecessors, however, is clear in its antithesis that holism means creating and managing diversity and tension, rather than manufacturing harmonious, perfect wholes.

Overall, our analysis of complementarism through theory yields an approach that applies necessary theoretical and methodological diversity to organisational and societal affairs. This encourages people to explore choices which enhance chances of managing issues, some insoluble, in human organisation. This is what we mean by diversity management. This is why we need triple loop learning. The way our research program is reported in Part 2 about diversity management as a form of complementarism is set out in the following abstracts of the chapters it comprises.

Chapter 2   Metatheory, Philosophy, and the History Of Knowledge

In Chapter 2 metatheory is explored in the context of philosophy and the history of knowledge. Exploration takes us through various modernist and then postmodernist forms of metatheory in terms of their bearing on the issue of complementarism.

Chapter 3   Metatheory, Theory, and Methodology

In Chapter 3 disciplinary theory and methodology are positioned within the metatheoretical literature, assessing progress at this level, and looking for ways forward for complementarism.

Chapter 4   Metatheory and Systems Thinking

In Chapter 4 systems thinking is positioned within the metatheoretical debate put together in the previous two chapters. A number of modernist approaches are reviewed. A postmodern critique of these that draws upon findings from Chapters 2 and 3 yields the essential ideas of diversity management and the embryo of triple loop learning.

Chapter 5   Contours of Diversity Management

Chapter 5 picks up where Chapter 4 leaves off. It draws out the contours of diversity management. This rounds off theoretical work and clears the way for triple loop learning in Part 3.

The path to diversity management and on to triple loop learning begins in Chapter 2 to which we now turn our attention.

Chapter 2

Metatheory, Philosophy, and the History of Knowledge

2.1 INTRODUCTION

With an introduction to our research program secured in Chapter 1, we now begin a detailed theoretical investigation into metatheory. The purpose of this is to lay out motivation and justification for our brand of complementarism, that is, for diversity management and triple loop learning. Overall, Part 2 secures understanding of complementarism as such in terms of patterns of metatheory, surveying issues in social philosophy and social theory drawn out by the patterns. To start with, in Chapter 2, metatheory is explored through the subject matter of philosophy and the history of knowledge. The survey here casts our mind over modernist and then postmodernist forms of metatheory conditioned by their bearing on complementarism.

2.2 THE ENLIGHTENMENT

The philosophy of the Enlightenment is often understood to present a (meta)theoretical dictum. Enlightenment as mentioned in the last chapter came to the fore in the eighteenth century. The aim was laudable; to free people from unreason, from the idols of their mind, specifically, from the dogmas of tradition and religion, so that rational understanding of the world could ensue. The Enlightenment fought for rational analysis, seeking to identify natural connections between empirical events and, further to this, to make predictions about future events. It opened up ways for people to rethink their hitherto traditional relationship to the world.

However, the Enlightenment has been (ab)used to justify scientific developments and discoveries by grounding them in a supposed absolute foundation for knowledge construction. It was linked to a strong belief that it is necessary to adjudicate with reference to known criteria, which the Enlightenment defines. In this sense it became a metatheory that sought to provide and impose an overarching scientific methodology for theory development. The Enlightenment has a dark side.

Our lobby room for discussion entertains tension between the Enlightenment and speculative theology. Attendance in the lobby room enables researchers to confirm the profoundly different ways in which people do come to relate to their world. This corroboration was exploited by Thomas Kuhn whose metatheory about scientific progress is discussed in the following section.

2.3 THOMAS KUHN

Many intellects, ranging from Frankfurt School authors such as Horkheimer and Adorno, to postmodern writers such as Foucault and Lyotard, have pointed out that the Enlightenment tradition became associated with forms of positivism. Positivism promised ingredients that would make concrete knowledge. The positivist belief in scientific progress toward concrete knowledge was challenged radically in Kuhn's famous and much quoted book *The Structure of Scientific Revolutions*. We incorporate Kuhn's argument in our story because it has a particular bearing on our brand of complementarism.

Kuhn cast new light on the so-claimed relentless progress of science. He argued that progression realises modes of doing science and, consequently, of understanding the world, that constitute incommensurable paradigms. He offered a metatheoretical solution to the diversity of modes of approach, arguing that through scientific revolutions new paradigms become dominant in a recurring cycle of normal and extraordinary science.[1] Normal science is where a dominant paradigm progresses in sophistication. Extraordinary science is where anomalies found in a dominant paradigm, often discovered in the process of sophistication, are exploited in a revolutionary process that dislodges the normal science paradigm from dominance and replaces it with a new one. Another period of normal science ensues as the new paradigm progresses in sophistication.

Ultimately, for Kuhn, there is no Archimedes point from which to judge

---

[1] Kuhn's commentary refers largely to theories generated by empirical natural scientists. However, he also offers a brief commentary (Kuhn, 1970: 164–165) on the way that students of social science face a diversity of perspectives. The diachronic existence of a diversity of perspectives in social science has implications for the notion of evaluation. Kuhn does not elaborate on what these implications may be – but we pick up on some of these issues below.

superiority of paradigm. Competing paradigms employ languages and criteria of assessment to judge validity that are incommensurable. Kuhn (1970: 148) states his point as follows: "The competition between paradigms is not the sort of battle that can be resolved by proofs." Although proponents of a new paradigm may claim that they are able to solve theoretical crises which they see as characterising the old paradigm, the issue, Kuhn continues, is not hereby resolved. It cannot be resolved when "the issue is which paradigm should in the future guide research on problems many of which neither competitor can claim to resolve completely" (Kuhn, 1970: 157). Hence "a decision between alternative ways of practising science is called for ". Kuhn suggests that this decision cannot be resolved by simply assessing the comparative ability of the paradigms to address issues agreed to constitute problems, for one of the issues at stake is how the problems should be addressed. As he puts it: "If there were but one set of scientific problems, one world within which to work on them, and one set of standards for their solution, paradigm competition might be settled more or less routinely by some process like counting the number of problems solved by each" (Kuhn, 1970: 147). For Kuhn, there is no one set of scientific problems, no one world, and no one set of standards for deciding between paradigms. Nevertheless, Kuhn holds out, this does not make proponents of old paradigms entrenched in a process of normal science completely deaf to arguments advanced by those proposing new types of science.

Kuhn's incommensurability thesis is not a statement to the effect that researchers working in one paradigm are naturally deaf to arguments from researchers of other paradigms (Kuhn, 1970: 152). Deafness, he seems to think, is an example of excessive "pigheadedness"; a characteristic he leaves largely undefined. In the context in which he describes it, pigheadedness implies a propensity to close off one's thinking entirely and to resist indefinitely any thought of entertaining an alternative way of seeing or doing things. This propensity may be related to "productive careers" of researchers committed to an established tradition of normal science. And so, Kuhn argues, it is sometimes necessary for established and resistant opponents to die before a new generation of thinking can be fully brought to bear on the scientific enterprise (Kuhn, 1970: 151).

Interestingly, although Kuhn refers to incommensurability between different research traditions, he still speaks of progress in the process of doing science (Kuhn, 1970: 170–171). In keeping with his focus on the paradigmatic nature of discovery, he argues that progress does not imply progress toward the truth about the world. This is not possible since he insists that the world is paradigmatically defined. However, Kuhn hints, there are other ways of assessing progress. One criterion, for example, is whether forms of science help the community of scientists to evolve their knowledge and appreciation of research issues.

Kuhn is clear, then, that the best he can do with his incommensurability thesis is hint at the need to consider alternative views of scientific advance. He was reluctant to "specify in any detail the consequences of this alternative view of scientific advance" (Kuhn, 1970: 171). Consequently, many people have laid siege to his argument because it is regarded as simply relativistic. The theory of scientific revolutions seems to conclude that since there are no common standards by which to assess the relevance of paradigms, there are no standards at all. Yet, Kuhn may not have to surrender his argument so quickly, as we find a route of escape in a reference to the process of social science (Kuhn, 1970: 164).

When contrasting natural and social science, Kuhn concludes that in the latter enterprise the process of solving problems takes on a new meaning. He observes that social scientists "often tend, as the former [natural scientists] almost never do, to defend their choice of a research problem – e.g., the effects of racial discrimination . . . – chiefly in terms of the social importance of achieving a solution". What is considered important is contentious indeed. Consequently, in the social sciences revolutionary switches to new paradigms are less likely to be able to destroy traces of old paradigms. Thus a student of social science is faced with a diversity of paradigms and "has constantly before him [sic] a number of competing and incommensurable solutions that he must ultimately evaluate for himself" (Kuhn, 1970: 165).

Kuhn's statement is significant. He recognises that in the social sciences people are called upon to make choices whenever they address social issues. With Kuhn's route of escape we show in following chapters how the apparent relativism of his metatheory can be revised to lend credence to an enhanced process of choice making by researchers evaluating competing solutions.

We have paid special attention to Kuhn's argument because it provides a useful backdrop to our brand of complementarism. We believe as stated in the opening chapter that the term incommensurability is useful insofar as it allows us to keep in consciousness diversity and radical differences in position, which open up a wide set of theoretical choices. This alerts researchers to the nature of theoretical alternatives as alternatives and encourages researchers to encounter theoretical differences in choice making.

Our complementarist stance is also informed by other researchers interested in the philosophy and history of knowledge. We continue our narrative by referring to such researchers, beginning with Jürgen Habermas.

2.4 JÜRGEN HABERMAS

Casting new light on Kuhn's argument, that understanding is *theory based*, Habermas's (1971) *Knowledge and Human Interests* sets out to demonstrate that knowledge is *value based*. Habermas contends that knowledge is a feature of people's existence that cannot be divorced from their values. He argues that knowledge and action are inextricably connected because knowledge is always tied to some purpose. Taking stock of the whole project of empirical–analytical science, applied to both the natural and social worlds, Habermas detects that the project is rooted in values and, he expresses with concern, that values are tied to the administrative apparatus of control and its purpose. The purpose of this apparatus is to use science to predict and control natural and social processes. The result is that empirical–analytical science controls people and reduces the human species in its potentialities. Empirical–analytical science operates within and suffers from restrictions inherent in its mode of doing (social) science research.

Habermas contends that counter efforts to operate an interpretive approach slip into an empiricist outlook. They make meanings objects of investigation in an attempt to encase and to grasp given meanings.[2] They fail to recognise, however, that social suppression of discursive communication fixes a casing around meaning. They fail to engage in quests to remove the casing. And they fail to address the question of standards of discursive engagement. The practical purposes which Habermas associates with both early and contemporary interpretive theory are linked to an agenda unable to question its own interests and purposes in the social arena. Interpretive theory has a dark side.

Habermas's metatheoretical solution in his *Knowledge and Human Interests* makes provision for the exercise of different human interests under the control of critical and conscious self-reflection. We must take control of our historical destiny through discursive reflection on goals being sought in the process of knowledge construction. The quest is to engage consciously and discursively in human interests.

Habermas's (1984, 1987) later work on the ideal speech situation continues, although from another angle, his suggestion that the human species has the potential to develop its historical path through discursive encounter. Here, however, he raises more starkly the uncertainty of the tension between a "system" which seems to be buttressed by scientific technological knowledge construction and a "lifeworld" where people are able

---

[2] We have not included in our narrative the interpretive argument – popularised by Weber in the social sciences – about the distinctiveness of the subject matter of the social sciences. Since Weber's seminal writings around the start of the twentieth century, the so-called interpretive tradition has been operative in various forms of phenomenology and ethnomethodology in social theory. Its metatheoretical account of the relationship between different theories largely followed the rationale that better theoretical accounts could be determined with reference to their ability to account better for meaning constitution in social reality. In this sense the interpretive argument still bears the mark of Enlightenment roots, with the quest for better understanding grounded in reality. What is relevant for our narrative is that the interpretive school highlighted another distinct way of doing (social) science. What is also relevant is the way that certain authors such as Brown, Gouldner, and others cited in Chapter 3, drew on the interpretive argument, while reconstructing its theoretical underpinnings so that the endeavour to uncover meaning could be redefined.

to raise continually the question why specific foci for knowledge construction are chosen. Habermas (1993: 94) argues, albeit ambivalently (see Chapter 9), that it is possible in discursive encounter to reach consensus about values to be pursued and priorities to be set. He also suggests that such consensus seeking may be trammelled by the force of administrative technical standards of rationality and knowledge creation which can come to colonise the "lifeworld" (see Habermas, 1993: 168–170; Brand, 1990). This implies that the tension between valuation of standards is likely to be a continuing one as people attempt to engage with what he calls the project of modernity (Habermas, 1981).

How ever Habermas's metatheory is interpreted, it is relevant to our complementarist endeavour because it recognises and differentiates between different human interests and purposes. An important question remains, however. How can we make choices between interests and purposes while remaining accountable? Habermas accepts tension will enter the process of choice making, but places accountability firmly in a process of consensus seeking. But, can choices always be made by consensus? The reader's everyday experience demonstrates that it is rare for everyone to agree on purposes to be pursued. This is true even if consensus is sought in a critical rather than regulative way. Habermas (1993: 94) admits this but, it seems to us, leaves the issue hanging in the air. People's defence of choices that are not consensually grounded, then, appear to have no grounding at all. It is on this score that we take issue with Habermas later in the book by juxtaposing his position with that of postmodernism.

The status of positivist empirical–analytical science and its ability to offer progressively better, objective representation of the world, was questioned from yet more angles. The late 1960s and 1970s saw a proliferation of texts positing different answers to the metatheoretical questions raised above. This led to considerable debate between those advocating forms of positivism and their challengers. One such debate known as *Methodenstreit* is briefly reviewed in the next section.

2.5 METHODENSTREIT

German social scientists entered a debate known as *Methodenstreit* (cf. *The Positivist Dispute in German Sociology*, 1969, edited by Adorno *et al*). This debate characterises some of the points of tension surrounding social science research. Tension sparked between those who argued for a positivist, value-free methodology adopted from the natural sciences,[3] and those who

---

[3] The definition of positivism used here and indeed by those criticising its premises in the *Methodenstreit* embraced versions of inductivism as well as (Popperian) hypothetico-deductivism. The inclusion of Popper under the positivist category by non-positivists in the dispute – such as Habermas – was later followed up by other critics of the position. These included

believed the social sciences should develop its own methodology that acknowledges the influences of values on theoretical interpretation. In one sense it can be claimed that positivists won the dispute. The dominant epistemological position subsequently expounded in the social science literature was and remains positivism. Positivism reduced metatheory to justification of forms of empiricist approaches to doing science. Empirical evidence came to be seen in most circles as the ultimate arbiter between theories.

An interesting commentary on the victory raises new issues for metatheory. The commentary says that the victory hardly came about because of the strength of the better argument. A more plausible explanation might be located in direct and indirect tactics and strategies of institutional forces where vested interests in maintaining positivism as dominant come in to play (Bourdieu, 1975; Bleicher, 1982; Ashley and Orenstein, 1985). For example, applications for grants to support social science research are in the main handled and vetted by researchers whose reputations are built on published work of a positivist ilk. Picou *et al* (1978) identified funding structures as a cause of theoretical closure and methodological monism. Editors of many, if not most, key journals are researchers of the same type, whose preferences for referees, and papers to publish, are influenced by a commitment to positivism. Morgan (1984) talked about academic institutional constraints that prevent innovation.

These factors and others may be responsible for the positivist content of much of today's social science literature. The influence of these forces are of great importance to metatheory because they force a paucity of theoretical options. Furthermore, the idea that these forces are of significance adds another dimension to both Kuhn's[4] and Habermas's arguments. Tactical and strategic dimensions demand tactical and strategic solutions, ones that we introduce in the next section.

---

people from the so-called Marxist realist camp, such as Benton (1977) and Keat and Urry (1982). What the Popperian position added to the discussion about science, was that specific statements could never be verified with certainty – but only tentatively corroborated (cf. Romm, 1991: 38–39). What he argued though, is that we can know when a set of statements (a theory) is better than another in offering a truer representation or explanation of reality. (This is linked to his assertion that false statements can be weeded out.) He insists that we know when some theories are better than others in their representation of external reality (cf. Romm, 1991: 40). Popper also elevated empirical studies as the foundation (basis) of science – even though he admitted that any particular empirical statement could not be proven. He believed that the public character of empirical observation was what allowed science to develop theories that could be known to be better than others.

[4] Kuhn does mention issues such as career-linked adherence to paradigms, but he does not make a play on this. Instead he concentrates on how conversion to new ways of thinking may occur (Kuhn, 1970: 155–159).

2.6 POSTMODERNISM

Postmodernism challenges the foundations of modernist thought. The post-modern critique of modernism undermines its idea of truth and fairness through reason by raising dilemmas, doubts, and suspicions about all truth statements. Forerunners of postmodern thought include Feyerabend and Quine. Challenges such as those propounded in Feyerabend's (1975) widely cited *Against Method*, and Quine's (1964) *From a Logical Point of View*, managed to gain some momentum, at least in lobby rooms where the philosophy of natural science and social science were being debated. They helped to keep alive a critique of the positivist view of science and metatheory.

Feyerabend's shocking metatheoretical contention stated that in the realm of methodology, anything goes. He highlighted a number of core developments to support his case.

- Already in 1975 Feyerabend was struck by the proliferation of theories that gave rise to much theoretical diversity.
- A consequence of theoretical diversity was recognition in some quarters of the importance of non-rational factors in the development of science.
- Another consequence of theoretical diversity was a need to reject the empiricist criterion of cognitive significance, because of incommensur-ability between modes of understanding our experience.

Western science ignored such issues in its relentless quest for objective knowledge. Feyerabend thus concluded that, ultimately, Western science has become a new form of dogmatism. Furthermore, he criticised Western science for being over-intellectual and hence elitist. Western science has a dark side.

Feyerabend's metatheoretical solution did not go as far as rejecting science or scientific practice(s). He did, however, criticise the elevated status of science. He aimed to sensitise scientific interventionists and other members of society to the danger that science is a potential instrument of coercion. This will always be a concern if science continues to be seen as a process of antiseptically discovering truth by testing theories against evidence. The shockwaves of Feyerabend's understanding of modern science kindled debate about the possibility of doing science in the light of, what he argued to be, the impossibility of adjudication between theoretical and method-ological choices. Quine had pre-empted this debate.

Quine challenged the distinction between so-called synthetic (empirically grounded) and analytic statements. He argued that any empirical piece of evidence can be accounted for in a theory by altering the pattern of the web of concepts that make up the theory (cf. Quine, 1964; Quine and Ullian,

1978). Webs of belief can be respun to account for supposed evidence.[5] The credibility of the positivist idea of using evidence as a way of testing theory was therefore strongly challenged by Quine.

So, Feyerabend kept alive debate in natural and social science research by shocking the dominant empiricist view, saying, when it comes to method, anything goes. Quine also kept the debate alive by writing shocking accounts of logic. Both contributions are relevant to our debate for this reason.[6]

It is relevant to indicate at this point that certain so-called (self-named) realists (e.g. Bhaskar, and also Keat and Urry) entered the dispute about positivism by developing what they considered to be an alternative logic to explain the relation between theory and evidence. Their accounts gave credence to the idea that theories could neither be verified or falsified with reference to (supposed) evidence. They still argued, however, that evidence can be used, though never in a foolproof way, to help assess theoretical statements. The argument was that empirical assessment serves to ensure that scientific theorising is gradually improved. Because of their belief that the truth of statements is linked to representational accuracy, their argument came under the attack of Marxist nonrealism as well as postmodernism. Postmodernists, as we shall see below, in turn attacked not only Marxist realism alongside all other quests for representational knowledge, but also Marxist nonrealism, particularly in its Habermasian form, the latter being castigated on grounds that its narrative of emancipation was too grand in character.

The challenge known as postmodernism, as stated, raises queries about the project of modernity, which it links to the Enlightenment and many subsequent writers. Postmodern thought[7] characterises modernism as a failed attempt to ground the search for knowledge in some absolute foun-

---

[5] Thus, for example, even the so-called deduction that the apparent observation of a black swan falsifies the statement that "all swans are white" is not clear-cut. Observation that it may be a swan is already imbued by theoretical conceptualisation. We can adjust the web of theory to account for, say, the existence of this creature, no longer called a swan, or we can incorporate black swans into the category of swans. It thus becomes unclear whether the statement "all swans are white" is a so-called synthetic (refutable) one or an analytic one. The time-honoured analytic/synthetic distinction was thus challenged in Quine's formulation.

[6] As pointed out above, positivists did not relinquish their elevated status in society, nor did they compromise the quest to ground theoretical statements with reference to evidence. Consequently many if not most scientists and philosophers of science continue in their privileged positions to ground their quest for good and sound theorising in a narrative that offers criteria for choosing between theories. Responsibility for choice can then purportedly be placed in the hands of the scientific community.

[7] There are many definitions and strands of postmodern thought. In this chapter we consider both Foucault's and Lyotard's arguments to help map the postmodern mentality. We focus on their contributions to highlight the narrative character of knowledge and the problem of absolutism which, they argue, is linked to the terror of political domination. See also Leroke (1994) for an account of the links between Foucault's postmodern position – grounded in post-structuralism – and Lyotard's postmodernist position as a critique of the project of modernity.

dation. Postmodern writers argue that absolute foundations are illusory, involving an infinite regress. Modernism leads to dangerous practice where actions are justified by reference to presumed foundations of knowledge that is used to support the actions.

The postmodern critique of grand narratives, as it saw the modernists' contribution, extended to Marxist-oriented thought that relies on its own theoretical knowledge to legitimate recommended forms of activity. Action motivated in this way fails to make provision for a toleration of incommensurable theories (cf. Foucault, 1984: 382–385; Leroke, 1994: 389–391; Readings, 1991: 109). The postmodern critique targeted Habermas on this score, tagging his work as yet another grand narrative. Habermas's so-tagged grand narrative does make provision for the exercise of different human interests, but presumes that a standard for generating knowledge about human interests can be formulated (or at least can be found in principles of human speech).

Two researchers often referred to for this sort of criticism are Foucault and Lyotard. Foucault's extended program of research on the connection between power and knowledge uncovers ways in which knowledge becomes constituted within power relationships in social networks. Unhappy with the implications of his discovery, Foucault wanted to subvert both the self-understanding of scientists and legitimation of social activities in terms of so-called scientific backing (cf. Foucault, 1973: XIV).

Lyotard echoed Foucault's concerns, repeating that theorising is the legitimation of domination, with a resounding account of the "terror" associated with grand narratives (Lyotard, 1984). He located the limited and transient status of all knowledge claims in an effort to prevent people idolising the narratives that they construct – be they political, moral, mythical, religious, or indeed scientific narratives. Lyotard insists on propounding an incredulity toward any metanarrative aimed at securing firm criteria for knowledge construction.

For postmodern thinkers, thought can be defined as "that which allows us to step back from this or that way of acting or reacting, to present it as an object of thought and question it as to its meaning, its condition, its goals" (Foucault, 1984: 334). Thinking encourages toleration of incommensurable and adversarial positions.[8] Thinking defines a relationship with other people that is not grounded in an attempt to reach consensus. Ethical and intellectual integrity cannot be gained by justification of actions through mandates from religion, law, science, or indeed social agreements (cf. Dreyfus and Rabinow, 1982: 121). A similar concern is epitomised in Lyotard's

---

[8] Foucault (1984: 378–379) insists that the ideal of consensus must not become a regulatory principle, though it could be a critical one in the sense that it emphasises patterns of domination built in nonconsensuality. Lyotard (1990: 340) wishes to remind us that any consensus is based on the playing of the present players and reflects only a provisional contract.

(1984) insistence that knowledge and action formulated and legitimated with reference to metanarratives is totalising thought best linked to social totalitarianism (cf. Readings, 1991: 109; Hassard, 1993: 124). Postmodern incredulity with metanarrative provides a refreshing account of living with and making sense of diversity although it does have its own dark side explored in Chapter 1 (cf. Hassard, 1993: 69–75; Gergen, 1992: 222–223; Jackson and Carter, 1991: 110–111; Spaul, 1993: 151; Taket and White, 1993: 737).[9,10] It has strongly influenced our theory of diversity management and our methodological principles of triple loop learning.

2.7 SUMMARY AND CONCLUSION

To conclude this chapter we summarise our findings in four bullet points below.

- The Enlightenment can be understood as implicated in metatheory in that it sought to impose overarching scientific methodology as a way of defining the development of scientific theories and adjudicating between theories.
- Kuhn's metatheory about the structure of scientific revolutions argued that understanding is inextricably theory based. Our difficulty with Kuhn's metatheory is that it appears in the main part to lead to relativism. With no common language or criteria of assessment there seems to be no grounds for choosing which theory to operate with, when, or why. Kuhn provides a novel account of how scientific progress occurs but the contours of this are left open to (re)definition. Furthermore, he leaves open the question of how choice making can be made in the face of diversity arising from diachronic existence of multiple paradigms. This leaves management out of diversity management.
- Habermas's metatheory casts new light on Kuhn's thinking, arguing that

[9] Postmodernists often shy away from using terms such as theory and metatheory. For postmodernists they imply metanarrative. But we are not averse to either theory or metatheory and we do not take issue with people who construct them, as long as they do not then take the construction too literally. Without theory, we argue, one cannot make considered choices. Some postmodernists admit that their project is not anti-theoretical – for example, Hassard, Gergen, and others, who argue that new theoretical visions may help provide cultural resources to allow us to move forward (e.g. Hassard, 1993: 135). Huyssen (1990: 271) also shows that these efforts are linked to a critique of tendencies to associate postmodernism with an "anything goes" attitude. Jackson and Carter (1991) offer some theoretical guidelines for embracing emancipation, now locally defined.

[10] Freundlieb (1989) points to a difficulty raised by the postmodern suggestion that argument itself takes place in terms of criteria that may not be agreed by the players. He notes that it is unclear how this reservation about argument relates to their own proffered arguments. Postmodern writers themselves offer arguments in support of their statements (e.g. their statements concerning the textual character of social reality; the necessary deferment of all meaning construction; and the importance of preserving variety).

knowledge is value based. His metatheoretical solution makes provision for different human interests under the control of critical and conscious self-reflection. Habermas's metatheory is relevant to our complementarist endeavour because it recognises and differentiates between different human interests and purposes. However, there are issues that are not fully explained, such as how choices can be made between theories, and how consensus between theorists, as well as between them and the wider community, may be defined. The management in diversity management is sought through an elusive consensus.

- Foucault concentrated on the connection between power and knowledge. He highlighted the way in which knowledge becomes constituted within power relationships in social networks. Lyotard went further, arguing that knowledge and action formulated and legitimated with reference to metanarratives is totalising thought which may become linked to social totalitarianism. Enlightenment-oriented thought and Habermas are criticised in this way. Foucault and Lyotard are linked to the postmodern project. Attempts at metatheoretical accounts of living with and making sense of diversity are evoked by the postmodern project, which gives us clues toward possible ways of realising management in diversity management. It hints at triple loop learning.

In Chapter 2 we have explored metatheory in the context of philosophy and the history of knowledge. Exploration has taken us through various modernist and postmodernist forms of metatheory in terms of their bearing on the issue of complementarism. In the next chapter, disciplinary theory and methodology are positioned within the metatheoretical literature, assessing progress at this level and locating further ways forward for complementarism.

Chapter 3

Metatheory, Theory, and Methodology

3.1 INTRODUCTION

In Chapter 2 we carried out a recce on metatheory, pointing to philosophy and the history of knowledge. Discussion tracked through modernist and postmodernist forms of metatheory, locating each one's point of view on complementarism. In Chapter 3 we turn our attention to disciplinary theory and methodology and how these are positioned within the metatheoretical literature. The purpose of this is to develop further the theoretical context for our brand of complementarism, that is, for diversity management and triple loop learning. This chapter does not, incidentally, provide scope for a detailed mapping of the disciplinary theory that we cover. Rather, theories are discussed only to the extent that they contribute to our interest in metatheory and complementarism.

3.2 THE NATURAL SCIENCES

Metatheory in the natural sciences arguably has its roots in Bohr's complementarity theory (Bohr, 1932). Its most famous exposition is in physics and deals with theory of light. At one time light was a little-understood phenomenon. Physicists brought forward an explanation of light by drawing parallels between the behaviour of light and the behaviour of water waves. From this parallel came the wave theory of light. This parallel, however, provided only a partial explanation. Some properties of light do not conform to the theory of water waves. A second parallel was drawn between light and moving particles. Some of the behaviour of light, not explained by the wave theory, was explained by the moving particle theory. So two analogies/theories had been drawn. The first analogy/theory reasoned that light behaved like waves. The second analogy/theory reasoned that light behaved like moving particles. Bohr called this dual analogy/theory "the wavicle theory of light" and from this was born in the natural sciences the idea of complementarity between theories.

Similar lines of thought have been advanced in other domains of science such as biology. For example, Manier (1969) reckoned that, to capture the real flavour of biological science, researchers should refuse to be satisfied with analysis of singular paradigms, no matter how lucid. Favouring paradigms, Manier claimed, results in theoretical reduction, reducing chances of theoretical explanation of complex phenomena. Manier made reference to pioneering work in genetics, in particular T. H. Morgan's success, and attributed this to Morgan's willingness to entertain patiently theoretical alternatives. Manier then turned to Wm. Bateson, another leading geneticist, who was unwilling to accept the utility of theoretical diversity which, Manier goes on, led to theoretical closure and rejection of evidence that ultimately gave fame to the powerful chromosome theory of the gene.

In Bohr's and Manier's works, complementarist arguments are formulated that support the sentiment of holistic thinking, vindicated by the benefits of consciously recognising value in diversity of viewpoints. Their arguments, however, are couched in terms that imply criteria for scientific progress can be established and that it is feasible to know when better theories are contrived. In the previous chapter scientific progress of that kind was challenged on various scores relevant to our final argument. For example, it implies progress toward the truth about the world which we, ironically, cannot tolerate in our theory of diversity management. The irony is toleration of the intolerable.

Our brief foray into the natural sciences turned up little supplementary support or otherwise to our argument. However, the issue appears much stickier in the social sciences. As Kuhn pointed out, there is a social importance to solutions and what is important is contentious indeed (see Chapter 2, page 20). This gummyness has led to a much more wide ranging debate about complementarism in the social sciences.

3.3 THE SOCIAL SCIENCES

Picou et al (1978) researched the theories and methodologies of rural sociology. Historically, they argue, rural sociology has been atheoretical.[1] The

---

[1] Which in terms of our argument presented above is not possible because on reflection any research program will be found to have assumptions that indicate a theoretical position. A more insightful observation we believe is that historically rural sociology has been non-reflective in regard to its premises.

first metatheoretical inquiry they encountered was Bealer (1975). Bealer talks in terms of Kuhnian theory discussed in the last chapter. The normal science dominating rural sociology at that time was structural functionalism. Disciplinary theory of rural sociology was subject to theoretical closure and methodological monism. For Bealer, this suggested a crisis of discipline stasis with all problems being forced rigidly into the mould of a structural functionalist paradigm. To escape from this stasis, Bealer suggested a new rural sociology founded on theoretical and methodological diversity. Here Bealer endorses diachronic existence of multiple paradigms, that Kuhn identified as a feature of social science, rather than pushing for a revolutionary shift to a new perspective in which scientists would again practise uni-paradigm normal science. The theory-centred research lead was to develop diversity with the following aims.

- To cover the changing structure in rural societies (diversity).
- To mirror the many dimensions to the concept "rural" (diversity).
- To build into it a critical discipline of self-analysis (management).

Bealer does not take into account forms of resistance introduced in the last chapter capable of putting a stranglehold on his call for diversity. Resistance is most likely to originate from those wedded to the structural functionalist option. Career prospects and research funding prospects are often tied to the dominant option. This might involve micropolitical forces such as the ones Foucault identifies. Reflection on this sort of explanation suggests ways open for intervention other than the theory-centred one which Bealer offers here. Being aware that "might" can be embroiled in monolithic research programs adds insight into tactics that can be employed to nurture diversity.

In a review of theoretical diversity in organisational analysis, Nurse (1988) sensed a political statement in the way Burrell and Morgan (1979) deliberated about choice of theory for conducting research. He minuted with favour Burrell and Morgan's aversion to integrated consensual approaches. The co-workers encourage analysts to step outside of their favoured theoretical position and from there piece together a richer appreciation of what other theories have to offer. Following Driggers (1977), Nurse believed that it is possible then to harvest a plentiful crop of theoretical development by purposely confronting opposing perspectives with each other.

Continuing along these lines, Nurse worked out ways of posing questions about organisations, work, the production of relations in society, and of generating knowledge about these phenomena. He called for different theories to study the different phenomena and the kinds of (insoluble) issues they generate. There is, he argues, value in theoretical diversity because it leads to differing conclusions about organisational realities and is of practical significance because it broadens options for organisational intervention.

Morgan (1980) too is keen that organisational theorists recognise the existence and validity of rival modes of research practice. The research process, he says, belies assessment in terms of neutral criteria and always proceeds in the image of some metaphor that excludes other images.[2] Yet all studies involve some choice making precisely because of the exclusionary nature of metaphors (theories). The quality of research choices, that are inevitable, improves in line with researchers' ability to recognise the partial character of any study. Morgan (1980: 612) argues recognition of that kind "cautions against excessive commitment to favoured points of view". The aim is to prevent "premature closure" to alternatives (Morgan, 1980: 613). As Jackson and Carter (1991: 116) recognise, Morgan here accepts and indeed hopes that divergent theoretical perspectives will exist in perpetuity and that the tension between them will never be dissolved.[3] Reed (1985) wanted to wrap a methodology around these ideas encouraging diversity to strike a sensible balance between incremental conceptual integration (tension dissolution) and theoretical proliferation (tension generation). His outline of options available, discussed in Chapter 1, bears witness to his concerns (i.e. pragmatism, isolationism, imperialism, and complementarism).

Also writing about organisational studies, Gergen (1992: 215) argues that it is incumbent on theorists to entertain a sense of ludic humility in their judgements. This reminds theorists of the constructed character of their insights. They are constructors of narratives. Awareness of this retains in the minds of all concerned a mindfulness that insights are not constructed on "vindicating foundations" (Gergen, 1992: 215). Hassard (1993: 127) also points to this need for self-reflexivity, continually retaining a "suspicion of our own intellectual assumptions", so that our own discourse will then not serve to suppress "the possibility of a multitude of alternative voices" (Hassard, 1993: 128).

Gergen's paper is one of 15 in an edited book by Reed and Hughes (1992). Other contributions included Aldrich (1992) which re-examines three approaches to understanding organisational change popular in the 1980s: population-ecology, institutional, and interpretive approaches. He argues that the complementary mien of their relationship far outweighs their points of conflict.

[2] The metaphorical nature of theory and the implications for theory construction are examined by Morgan (1984) and has informed his account of the diversity of approaches to organisational analysis (see also Morgan, 1989).

[3] Jackson and Carter (1991: 120) argue that a simple acceptance of diversity is likely to lead to a position where a middle ground option becomes the favoured one. They are worried about the implicit assumption of equality of power between the discoursers. Their concerns relate to questions of micropolitics that have been raised by Foucault and that we follow up later in the book.

Aldrich (1992: 17) pins complementarity across the three approaches because "they treat similar problems at a different level of analysis". Although they make different assumptions about their subject matter, each one casts different light over issues (Aldrich, 1992: 27). Since this leads to glowing results, Aldrich (1992: 26) takes up position against a simple advocation of paradigm incommensurability, that is, if incommensurability insinuates that there are no fruits to be gained by juxtaposing positions one against another. He argues that juxtaposition is likely to generate a salutary discomfort where discomfort is a possible source of insight generation.

Aldrich supports his reasoning with examples. He shows how different imaginative insights of agency in organisational life can be juxtaposed. He offers various accounts of how theorists may connect to the variety of insights. One account gives credence to researchers proceeding by "not taking seriously the stream of contradictory research findings" (Aldrich, 1992: 36–37). This would seem to imply that they find a way to avoid discomfort. Another account pictures researchers being impelled to "stretch their minds" to cope with apparently contradictory views: the multiplicity of perspectives is at least a mind stretcher (Aldrich, 1992: 37). Another account firmly persuades a view that scientists in the research process become geared to seeing the world through coloured lenses. From this point of view "paradigms should be chosen to match researchers' purposes" (Aldrich, 1992: 38). However, in all of this Aldrich fails to register how researchers can make choices and manage rising discomfort.

Ackroyd (1992) is another contributor who appreciates the reality of institutionally located theoretical conflict and controversy. He stands firm against a paradigm mentality. This type of mentality leads to polarisation which debilitates efforts to improve the calibre of organisational knowledge. It leads to fragmentation. It fractures knowledge into a competing set of theoretical factions. Unity must not be forced, however. Instead, Ackroyd plays his hand, there should be a limited synthesis between competing approaches and empirical research projects to correlate relevance of approaches to improved organisational practice.

Ackroyd (1992: 116) admits that there are points of intellectual as well as moral tension when riding the pro-diversity bandwagon. However, this does not mitigate against the relevance in riding with such research practice. On the contrary, he notes, "A case can be made that growth areas in social science have always centred on points of intellectual as well as moral tension, and it is this that gives vitality to schools of thought." Ackroyd thus reinforces Aldrich's taste for the invigorating quality of tension, an issue which we latch onto later in the book.

Of further interest to us is Ackroyd's secured focus on the principle of practical relevance. Our brand of complementarism also has a practical strain. Part 3 is a testament to that. Only, we lend even more credence to tensions involved in demonstrating relevance. We concentrate on exploring tensions by linking them to a quality of reflexive research coupled to widely informed local decision making.

Gouldner (1973) in *The Coming Crisis of Western Sociology* called for reflexivity in the field of sociology. His time-honoured theory has strongly shaped our appreciation of reflexivity. Gouldner judged that a quality reflexive approach looks

> . . . to the deepening of the self's capacity to recognise that it views certain information as hostile, to recognise the various dodges that it uses to deny, ignore, or camouflage information that is hostile to it, and to strengthening of its capacity to accept and to use hostile information. In short, what Reflexive Sociology seeks is not an insulation but a *transformation* of the sociologist's self, and hence of his [sic] praxis in the world. (Gouldner, 1973: 495)

Gouldner likens the process of getting to know the world as a continuous process of self-discovery. In Gouldner's process theorists discover miscellaneous dodges that they use to avoid information hostile to how they prefer to know the world. Wanting to dodge the dodges, Gouldner schemed what he called knowing as awareness. Knowing must include an awareness of the fragility and anomalous character of theoretical and attendant moral judgements.

Other sagacious commentaries assume different angles on reflexivity.

Brown (1977) in his *Poetic for Sociology*, using poetic terms, deliberated over the use of irony as a way of avoiding excessive theoretical commitment to singular points of view. Irony, Brown (1977: 173) suggests, serves a "critical and self-reflective function for professionals". He isolates a number of forms of irony, all of which involve juxtaposing apparent opposites to nurture a grasp of unexpected yet valued associations that may result (Brown, 1977: 174).

Wexler, operating in the field of education, launched his own offensive to secure the potential in diversity. Potential can be secured from the moment that researchers recognise disjunction in all theoretical accounts of organisational and societal affairs. He wants to install a mentality where people can reconfront their starting position with cognitive armoury issued by different interpretations. It is this self-encounter that may prevent reification of theory into fixed signs and solidified consciousness (Wexler, 1987: 179).

Reflexivity has thus been championed in many disciplines in the social sciences, although not necessarily in their mainstream! The purpose of reflexivity is to question in deliberate fashion the relevance and consideredness of unchallenged yet favoured points of view. It enables and prepares theoreticians and interventionists for the enriching process of confronting alternatives. Reflexivity is indeed a means by which disciplines are able to retain and encourage diversity and tension. This is the main contribution that disciplinary theory offers our endeavour. Still, other than calls to reflexivity there has been little work done on isolating ways of managing diversity. This is where triple loop learning registers its credentials, as we shall see later on.

3.4 SUMMARY AND CONCLUSION

The findings of this chapter are now summarised in the same style as previous chapters by using bullet points.

- Metatheory in the natural sciences has its roots in Bohr's complementarity theory and its most famous exposition in physics termed the "wavicle theory of light". Similar lines of thought have been advanced in other domains such as biology. The argument, however, is couched in terms which imply that criteria for scientific progress can be established and that it is feasible to know when better theories are created. Discussion in Chapter 2 raises serious doubt about the contribution of the natural sciences understood in this way.
- A review of the literature from a number of quarters in the social sciences surfaces a recurring theme: the existence and validity of rival modes of research practice. Few of the researchers, however, indicate how or even whether choice making and hence diversity management is possible.
- Reflexivity provides a means for disciplines to retain a necessary tension between rival modes of research practice. A metatheory that takes seriously a call for reflexivity must aspire to and accept the following. It must locate diversity of, and irreducible differences between, theoretical positions. It must accept that there can be no objective adjudication between theories via criteria of adjudication which assumes an Archimedean viewpoint. Other than calls to reflexivity there has been little work done on isolating ways of managing the resulting diversity. Triple loop learning squares up to this task.

In Chapter 2 we outlined some developments in philosophy and the history of knowledge, exploring implications for metatheory with special reference to complementarism. In Chapter 3 we extended our inquiry into disciplinary theory to see how far things have progressed there. We have seen that considerable thought has been applied to the issue, especially in terms of complementarity. A key feature is the strong desire among several bands of social science researchers to preserve diversity, because diversity promises some kind of improved future for disciplines. Little is said about diversity management. Further preparation for diversity management and triple loop learning is now made by getting up to date in Chapter 4 with developments in systems thinking from where, as we have previously stated, we surprisingly launch our own brand of complementarism.

Chapter 4

Metatheory and Systems Thinking

4.1 INTRODUCTION

Chapter 4 bridges the metatheoretical findings of Chapters 2 and 3 to our theoretical end result (for now!) of Chapter 5. Chapter 4 draws attention to systems thinking and the way that holistic thought can mix a fresh solution that provides a holding matrix for metatheoretical dilemmas so far encountered. Chapter 4 in this way brings together contemporary systems thinking with the dilemmas of metatheory.

Systems thinking emerged as a popularised discipline[1] in the 1950s.[2] It declared as its original intent the unification of science. It was, therefore, pitched in the domain of metatheory right from the start. Since its emergence, systems thinking motored on relentlessly, making major tracks and dust storms in methodology practice while, increasingly in recent times, undertaking self-critique of those tracks and dust storms using social theory. The critique has blown away some of the fall-out of methodology practice and mapped its tracks onto theory about society and organisation. This chapter follows four main tracks: cybernetics, systemic interpretivism, critical systemic modernism, and a postmodern critique (represented in Figure 4.1). Each track is introduced with a summary. The summary is extended into a discussion of patterns that make up the tracks when the patterns relate to metatheory, the theme of this chapter.

---

[1] Often referred to as interdisciplinary in the way it traverses other disciplines.
[2] There are incidentally many publications that are claimed to be forerunners of systems thinking and the systems discipline. We take the 1950s as a starting point because it was at this time that systems thinking took on an identity of its own and, to some extent, became popularised.

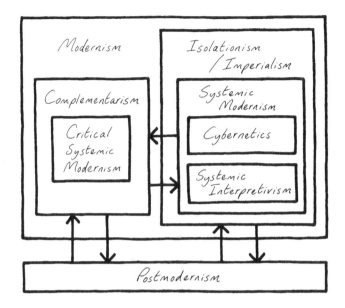

Figure 4.1

4.2 CYBERNETICS

4.2.1 Introduction and Summary

Cybernetics is a form of systemic modernism which supposes that modern societal and organisational systems are a product of science and technology. Society is organised around scientistic and technocratic knowledge. The theory advocates social control by large-scale technical systems. This cybernetic thinking conceives complexity in terms of a system of causal laws, of many interacting variables which are subject to co-ordination and control in order to achieve set goals. Once goals have been set (and these must be set within the limits of the known causal laws) it is possible to determine optimal actions in social contexts. Performance is a key concern. It has its source of legitimation in the system's technical capability to reduce complexity and to increase certainty. Control and performance require individuals to adapt their actions for the benefit that the system offers, so that their actions become compatible with the system's goals. Rational action requires individuals to submit to the laws of organisational life, which working scientists are geared up to establish.

4.2.2 Discussion

Cybernetics broadly speaking incorporates General Systems Theory (GST).

GST was the first popularised approach to systems thinking. It was launched by a disparate group of scholars in the mid 1950s. Bertalanffy, whose interests were in the domain of biology, is considered to be the prime mover. In 1955 Bertalanffy published a key reference paper called "General Systems Theory". His main worry was that increasing specialisation in science would lead to a breakdown in science as an integrated realm. "Specialists are encapsulated in a 'private universe', and it is difficult to get word from one cocoon to another" (Bertalanffy, 1955: 75). It is necessary, he argued, to prevent research from being carried out in an isolated fashion. The way forward is to identify a system of laws and generalised theories that unify all sciences.

To this end, Bertalanffy proposed a theory of universal principles – GST principles. There were three main ones.

- Look for isomorphies[3] that demonstrate general system properties, and transfer these models across different fields (do not employ vague analogies!).
- Employ a general theory of organisation that deals with organised complexity[4] (cf. Weaver, 1948). The general theory includes concepts like organisation, wholeness, directiveness, teleology, control, self-regulation, and differentiation.
- Physical systems, organisms, and societies, as examples of systems, are not all the same – the laws of behaviour are isomorphic but the essence of each system is different.

The aims, then, are clear. There should be integration of sciences, natural and social. This integration should be centred on a general theory of systems. Centring of efforts may yield an exact means to build an exact metatheory in the natural and social sciences. An exact metatheory will establish unifying principles running through universes of individual sciences, bringing us nearer to the unity of science.

Another seminal paper by Boulding (1956) called "The Skeleton of Science", extended the aims and scope of GST. Disciplines, Boulding argued, are separate bodies of theory that correspond to a segment of the empirical world. Each discipline develops theories that have a particular applicability to its own empirical segment. Disciplines carve out for themselves elements of the experience of humans and develop theories and research that yield

---

[3] Isomorphic means exactly corresponding in form and relations.
[4] In a well-referenced article, Weaver (1948) identified three ranges of complexity: organised simplicity, organised complexity, and disorganised complexity. Organised simplicity is where there are said to be a small number of significant factors and a large number of insignificant factors. Disorganised complexity occurs when there are many variables that exhibit a high level of random behaviour. Each range is slim and the two occupy positions at opposite extremes of Weaver's three ranges. This leaves organised complexity that sits between the two (Flood and Carson, 1993: 35).

satisfaction in understanding appropriate to their special segment. GST as a metadiscipline accordingly explores the empirical world of disciplines, progressively coming to understand and develop a theory about the systems that it comprises. In this way GST will ultimately unify science, that is, it will produce a unified approach that explains all forms of discipline and system.

Interestingly, Boulding predicted that a most advanced form of GST would surrender a system of systems that may perform the function of a Gestalt in theory construction.[5] Like other Gestalts, the system of systems might be of value in directing the attention of theorists toward gaps in theoretical models, and might even be of value in pointing them in the direction of ways of filling them. Ultimately, Boulding admitted that he was not wholly clear at this early stage about what was being "promised and brewed".

GST as a metatheory, then, wished to unify sciences, but in some way maintain diversity in the form of, for example, a system of systems with theoretical models relevant to different chunks of an empirical world. We can detect an underlying urge to establish more meaningful diversity in theories. GST nudged at the door of diversity, but the door remained firmly closed by the lock of positivism. We can elaborate on this last remark.

GST falls to many of the criticisms in Chapter 2 levelled at empiricism and positivism. Quine's critique would picture GST as an empirical endeavour whose evidence can be accounted for as alterations to the pattern of its web of concepts, for example, by invention of a new isomorphy to justify otherwise unexplainable evidence. In terms of Feyerabend's inquiry, GST fares as follows.

- In a way GST wanted to proliferate theories.
- But GST stuck to rational factors in its development.
- And GST accepted wholeheartedly empiricist criteria of cognitive significance.

Accordingly, a Feyerabend type critique identifies GST as another dogma. It is a totalising theory unable to question its own foundations. It seems that the brew Boulding talked of did not produce the substance that we seek in this book. The realisation of diversity in theory and methodology was shut away from systems thinking by its original isolationist premises, not to be revived until a theoretical metamorphosis had occurred.

GST was the forerunner of wide ranging research into cybernetics that is still actively pursued today. These efforts do not enter our discussion here. However, it may be noted that cybernetic reasoning underpins the great majority of designs that make up Chapter 7.[6] We now jump tracks onto systemic interpretivism.

---

[5] By Gestalt we mean a perceived organised whole that is more than the sum of its parts.
[6] As will be shown in Part 3, the way that we deal with the issue of design is by locating cybernetics as a form of design and by locating design management as one way of reflecting on human coexistence. In this way we position the potential isolationism of cybernetics.

4.3 SYSTEMIC INTERPRETIVISM

4.3.1 Introduction and Summary

Systemic interpretivism is a second form of systemic modernism. It supposes that modern society and organisations are a product of human interpretations and actions leading to knowledge production. The theory, informed by a conception of intersubjective accommodation of viewpoints in the social sphere, assumes desirability in social management of interpretive actors who perform actions within cultural systems. This interpretivist position conceives complexity in terms of interrelations between human interpretations, actions mediated by social rules and practices, and constitutive meaning that makes the rules and practices meaningful. It has an internal source of legitimation in the cultural system's power to manage complexity of issues and to increase consideredness of action. It has no external source of legitimation. System manageability requires people to adapt their actions so that they may be compatible with the rules and practices that become developed as shared symbols.

4.3.2 Discussion

With interpretive modes of thought "system" took on a new meaning. "System" was understood to be a conceptual structure, a structure to explore issues of human organisation; especially in terms of social rules, social practices, and underlying constitutive meaning. The aim was to uncover interpretations of events through systemic frameworks rather than discover systems in existence. These efforts are not elaborated on here. However, systemic interpretivism, which is actively researched today, underpins approaches to debate that are discussed in the second half of Chapter 8.[7]

Both cybernetics and systemic interpretivism may tend toward forms of isolationism (discussed in Chapter 1). This occurs when knowledge is identified with natural or social science and life is placed in theory, so that theory is reflected in the conduct of those who subject themselves without reflection to its discipline. Cybernetics believes that all science of organisation must be aimed at developing knowledge of cybernetic laws. Systemic interpretivism believes that the scientific approach to social life cannot imitate the natural sciences and must rather engage in a quest to understand cultural reality. What does not fit these theories is regarded by their advocates as irrational.

---

[7] As will be shown in Part 3, the way we deal with the issue of debate is by making systemic interpretivism a springboard to jump into a discussion of debate which can allow for other ways of entering debate while also recognising the need to become aware of other arenas of discourse. In this way we position the potential isolationism of systemic interpretivism.

Consequently, all methodological rules for making sense of reality are understood and universalised through a single favoured theory (or denatured if they are imperialistically brought over from another theoretical position). This means that each one's metatheoretical position becomes reduced to a theoretical one. Its metatheoretical position becomes a narrative which is able to accommodate only one rationality. This indeed is one of the characteristics of theoretical isolationism and imperialism, and one of the reasons why we and others have suggested that they are isolationist in their orientation. Once these rationalities are invoked by theorists, the resulting studies rarely lead to fundamental rethinking of the theoretical basis of methodological choices, that is the choice of how to go about viewing reality in the first place (see also Gergen, 1992: 213).

A number of attempts have been made to reconcile methodological approaches. Elements of each school of thought have been combined. However, these ignored fundamental theoretical issues and were accounted for largely by eclecticism at both theoretical and methodological levels (defined as pragmatism in Chapter 1). The debates covered in the previous two chapters, in areas such as philosophy of science, social theory, organisation theory, and so on, about ways of treating the diversity of theoretical and methodological options, were largely unattended to by systems interventionists until recently.[8] We now jump tracks onto critical systemic modernism where the debates have received some attention.

4.4 CRITICAL SYSTEMIC MODERNISM

4.4.1 Introduction and Summary

Critical systemic modernism is a complementarist approach that draws extensively on Habermas's foundational critical metatheory introduced in Chapter 2 (see Flood and Jackson, 1991b). It pleads for more reflection on human interests and purposes being pursued in methodology practice. This encourages deliberation over the way methodologies are linked to (implied) rationalities which they seem to endorse. It stands for thinking through possible or even likely consequences of operating with that rationality. The theory of critical systemic modernism, following Habermas, supposes that modern society and organisations are characterised by two fundamental socio-cultural forms of action – labour and interaction. The production and reproduction of human lives occurs through the transformation of nature

---

[8] Also in Part 3, we have drawn on some of the arguments that have been proposed in these areas, and have tried to develop our own proposal – which focuses on a way of treating the process of choice making. In doing so, we have injected what we see as the strengths of systemic thinking into the discussion – yielding a way of thinking about the issues which can in turn be fed back into the debates in these areas.

with the aid of technical rules and procedures,[9] and through communication of interests and purposes in the context of practical thought and action. Dialogue, however, may be dominated by social constraints and power relations.

4.4.2 Discussion

As noted in Section 2.4, Habermas in his *Knowledge and Human Interests* suggests that three knowledges can be derived from three human interests. Labour enables human beings to aspire to goals to bring about human well-being. The success of labour depends on achieving technical mastery. Human beings therefore have a technical interest in prediction and control over natural and social processes. Interaction secures and expands possibilities for mutual understanding. This is a practical interest, because disagreement between groups can be a threat to the continuation of social processes. Equally, an analysis of the exercise of power helps us to understand past and present social arrangements. It may help to show that there are forces which prevent open and expansive discussion necessary for securing increased and enriched understanding and indeed for defining the proper domain of technique (technical mastery). Such discussion should ensure ideally that neither technique nor culture becomes governed by a momentum that can no longer be challenged. Human beings therefore have an emancipatory interest toward developing more discursive modes of relationship. The three knowledge-constitutive interests which were identified by Habermas as epistemological categories of concern are focal points for critical systemic modernists.

The complementarist methodological principles of critical systemic modernism are critically self-reflective. They are interest based (or purpose based) and divide into three: technical, practical, and emancipatory. According to critical systemic modernists, technical interests are served by and large by methodologies from cybernetics, and practical interests by and large by methodologies from systemic interpretivism. The third category is a relatively new creation that is concerned with ways in which emancipatory agendas relate to organisational and process design as well as decision making, by being specifically sensitive to issues of power (for a typology of power, see Chapter 6). Since critical systemic modernism is built on Habermas's critical metatheory, it is vulnerable to criticisms set against Habermas's work in Chapter 2. Briefly recounted, the main reproach is that Habermas does not fully explain how choices can be made between theories and how consensus may be approved.

---

[9] Whether an approach to ecological issues which sees our relationship with nature as one of stewardship rather than mastery is compatible with Habermas's argument is a subject of contention. Habermas (1982: 246–248) argues in respect to this issue that it is only through human involvement that we can relate to nature.

Methodological guidelines for critical systemic modernism were offered as a way of reflecting on intervention in organisational and societal affairs by Flood and Jackson (1991a) and labelled Total Systems Intervention, or TSI[10] for short. Elstob's (1992) review of TSI provides an excellent introduction to the aims of the original account. What TSI does, he says, is to argue that there will never be a super methodology that can address all types of issue. The best strategy, therefore, is skilfully and sensitively to select whatever methodologies seem most promising and appropriate for each set of issues faced.

> Once the true significance of this strategy is understood, it becomes clear that problem solving practitioners who adopt it must indeed see themselves as creative [critical] problem solvers, for the fundamental point is that on each occasion the practitioner will need iteratively to evolve a creative [critical] solution suited to the particularities of the situation. (Elstob, 1992: 62)

Elstob carries on to say that TSI does not, indeed cannot, provide easy formulas or standard methodologies to direct people. Interaction with the issue domain is open-ended and creative. This generates uncertainties and frustrations. People's role in the process is carefully defined. They feed in and share expertise and experience rather than making attempts to impose designs and/or decisions on others. TSI, Elstob concludes, is thus in line with current trends that accept that human organisation is too diverse to be handled and manipulated like physical objects.

The former trend in systems thinking, between the 1960s and the mid 1980s, was to develop models and methodologies for managing diversity in practical situations. Limited theorising was undertaken about the nature of this diversity. Progress can be charted as a heuristic search for models and methodologies to deal with issues found in any practical situation (located by the preferred theory of the researcher). This search led to an explosion in number of models and methodologies, each with its advocates and between them their adversaries.

Diversity in models and methodologies in principle is beneficial because it diversifies the process of decision making, improving chances people have to make choices that are meaningful to them. Diversity of models and methodologies in practice, however, gave rise to many undesirable outcomes such as non-constructive adversarial debate between committed advocates of seemingly competing approaches. Ironically, systems thinking, the science of holism, broke up into many theoretical and methodological fragments. TSI in response refocused systems thinking on managing the diversity of models and methodologies in a complementary way that in

---

[10] The original version that we label TSI (Flood and Jackson, 1991a) was built from critical systemic modernist principles. It is distinguished from Local Systemic Intervention (LSI, Flood, 1995a: still called TSI therein) which establishes methodological principles following a postmodern critique of TSI's initial modernist stance.

turn enhances management of the diversity of issues found in any practical situation.

This refocusing is evident in Flood and Jackson's (1991a: xi) launch to their book *Creative Problem Solving: Total Systems Intervention*:

> In the modern world we are faced with innumerable and multifaceted difficulties and issues which cannot be captured in the minds of a few experts and solved with the aid of some super-method. We are faced with "messes", sets of interacting problems, which range from the technical and organisational to the social and political, and embraces concerns about the environment, the framework of society, the role of corporations and the motivation of individuals.

In other words, no single model or methodology exists or can ever be invented capable of addressing the above logged diversity of issue domains. Systems thinking was encouraged therefore to get a firm handle on the following three research crunch points.

- To accept the diversity of issues confronting decision makers.
- To continue developing a rich variety of models and methodologies (the dominant research agenda prior to the mid 1980s).
- To address continually the question, Which model(s) and/or methodology(ies) should be used, when, and why?

The newly emerging research agenda as incorporated in TSI clearly embodied and attached value to earlier methodological work, but wanted to manage the diversity of models and methodologies being created.

TSI promises to enrich the way decision makers manage the diversity of models, methodologies and hence issues they face. TSI organises systems-based models and methodologies according to ideal type problem situations that Flood and Jackson consider them most relevant to. The key to successful use of TSI, Flood and Jackson argue, is to choose (an) appropriate model(s) and/or methodology(ies) for tackling issues as they are perceived, but always to recognise that other possible perceptions of the issues are possible. Flood and Jackson (1991a: xi) make clear that by employing any model or methodology "congruent with that partial representation, one is addressing only certain aspects of 'interacting problems'". Alternative perceptions of the issues therefore had to be kept under continual review since there could be a change in the character ascribed to the problem situation, and hence choice of model(s) and/or methodology(ies). Flood and Jackson (1991a: xi) also made transparent at the outset that choice meant choosing dominant *and* supportive model(s) and/or methodology(ies) at any one time, "to 'sweep in' both the main issue of concern as well as significant side issues". They wanted to encourage people to think about which model(s) and/or methodologies should be used in a dominant role and which in a supportive role so that dominance does not occur by default.

What is clear, in Flood and Jackson's opening account, is that they are aware of the need to recognise different perceptions about issues faced and to respond to these views. They placed much emphasis on this challenge for intervention. On the other hand, they did not stress the importance of possible different interpretations people might have about the ideal type problem situations to which models and methodologies may be thought to be most relevant. Nor did they stress the process of judgement to define the relevance of models or methodologies. Indeed, Flood and Jackson (1991a: xiii) say that "What is needed is an overview of systems methods which enables them to be related to the problem situation *each best serves*" (our italics). This is out of line with the theory of diversity management because it reduces choices people have, in this case conscious choices about relevance of models and methodologies. It impinges on the creation and management of diversity, it limits meaningfulness of choices and decisions people make, and centralises in TSI's theory, rather than localises in people's lives, the relevance of model and methodology choice in space and time.

Nevertheless, steps in the direction of diversity management are evident. For example, TSI stands against pragmatism (i.e. non-reflective eclecticism). TSI was concerned that pragmatists as non-reflective eclectics proceed to act without considering the implications of mixing and matching agendas. Pragmatists do not reflect over theory. As a result, a preconceived, prestructured appreciation of any issue domain is likely to prevail in pragmatists' thinking, setting up predetermined solutions (by default). On this score, TSI has improved the chances of people making meaningful choices and decisions for themselves. It makes more possible the local relevance of choices and decisions in space and time.

TSI's form of complementarism also stands against isolationism and imperialism in their various guises. In terms of the argument of diversity management, employment of unlike models, methodologies and theories in some reasoned manner is preferable to the choice of one model, methodology or theory, because it preserves diversity thus enhancing chances of effectively dealing with great complexity in organisational and societal affairs. In short, it preserves diversity in choice. Choice is therefore more likely to be meaningful to decision makers and to be temporally and spatially relevant. Again, TSI had improved the chances of people making meaningful choices and decisions for themselves.

Flood and Jackson also declared what human well-being and emancipation means in TSI. They state that the thrust of TSI "is emancipatory in that it seeks to achieve for all individuals, working through organisations and in society, the maximum development of their potential" (Flood and Jackson, 1991a: 49). This intention on the face of it concurs with goals for diversity management. However, the validity of an intention can only be judged against what is actually done or said. With TSI what is done and said is rooted in the Habermasian argument that we introduced in Chapter 2.

The critical systemic modernist solution to managing diversity of interests can be summarised as follows. It is suggested that all rationally pursued purposes represent human interests. The interests are seen as incompatible in that the vision of reality through the different purposes will present different worlds based on different orientations to the world. The world presenced through the interest in prediction and control is different from the world presenced by a practical or an emancipatory interest. But the apparent incompatibility can bring forth fruits, such as progress in knowledge and action, if agreements can be reached as to how and when the purposes should be pursued.

The Habermasian way assumes that people together will know what is the best thing to do. Admittedly, so the argument continues, there is a need to create the right conditions, the ideal speech situation, but, that aside, it is possible and desirable for people to reach consensus decisions. The world is seen by modernists of the Habermasian persuasion to hold opportunities and constraints that must be controlled and/or managed. Choice in TSI comes about through consensus decision making.[11]

Diversity management, in disagreement, argues that the Habermasian way misses what is rudimentary to diversity. It misses *fundamentally different* fixes people have on issues because they evolve disparate value and belief systems, and grow their own needs and interests. Thus, judgement over differences of opinion has to be faced up to. The pressing dilemma is, How can we operate a process of judgement and manage differences of opinion that are likely to be encountered without reducing the whole process to consensus seeking? A driving force is needed that increases the opportunities people have to make decisions rather than grounding decisions in consensus-seeking processes all the time. Central to managing this dilemma is an acceptance that people can live their lives without consensus agreements on every issue that matters. Social life can and indeed does proceed without consensus and is enriched because of that. Indeed, consensus seeking may run anathema to people's ability to make meaningful choices based on their appreciation of issues. It may fail to achieve for all people the maximum development of their judgemental potential. For us, achievement of maximum potential means people living their lives with maximum chances to make meaningful responsible choices over issues that they face. This also entails people deciding what emancipation means for themselves, and how they can practise it with other people, knowing that it may have many meanings in space and time.[12]

---

[11] It is also possible to interpret Habermas's writings as recognising the importance of personal risk-taking in the light of the inevitable fallibility of knowledge (see Habermas, 1982: 223). However, this aspect of the Habermasian argument was not stressed in TSI. Furthermore, the tensions between the technical administrative "system" and the "lifeworld" (as discussed in Chapter 9) were not capitalised on within TSI.
[12] As shown fully in Part 3, diversity management locates a number of meanings embedded in design, debate and might–right discourses. It then discusses these as a way of enriching thinking about issues in ways that allow people to make responsible judgement.

What we are saying is that, at a metatheoretical level, TSI made significant advances in complementarism through its critical systemic modernism, but a carefully considered critique of TSI's metatheory surfaces significant limitations.

So, the advent of critical systemic modernism and TSI was a reflection in the mid 1980s of a newly emerging research agenda in systems thinking. Indeed, it could be argued that critical systemic modernism and TSI were catalytic in these changes. Catalysis is a good metaphor in the way it suggests critical systemic modernism and TSI accelerated the process of change. It is a poor metaphor in the way it suggests that this effect occurred without the catalyst itself undergoing change. Critical reflection on the catalytic process has brought about a dramatic change to the underpinning theory of critical systemic modernism and the structure and process of TSI. What has indeed happened is that a new approach has emerged from the cocoon of TSI that tries to balance on a tightrope between critical systemic modernism and postmodernism. Its emergence is a direct result of a postmodern critique on whose tracks we locate it.

4.5 POSTMODERN CRITIQUE

4.5.1 Introduction and Summary

The way we engage with the postmodern critique comes out of the discussion about postmodernism given in Chapter 2. A postmodern critique of critical systemic modernism forms a further view of societal and organisational affairs. Things that matter to people are the focus of attention in this theory. The theory hands over judgement to those localities. This post-critical condition conceives complexity in terms of dilemmas, differences and tension, which are subject to what we call triple loop learning to aspire to enriched awareness. There are no absolute optimal actions in social contexts. Quality of choice making is a key concern. We develop a source of legitimation in the following standard: the chances people have to make widely informed and locally contingent choices in the process of managing dilemmas that characterise organisational and societal affairs through triple loop learning.

4.5.2 Discussion

A postmodern critique has identified strains in critical systemic modernism. A line of postmodern thought was introduced by Flood (1990) when he highlighted the relevance of the Interpretive Analytics of Foucault (thus named by Smart, 1983). Flood offered a critique of critical systemic modernism in a project called Liberating Systems Theory (Flood, 1990, 1991). The project ran Foucault's postmodernist work through Habermas's modernist research (that underpins critical systemic modernism). The argument put forward, we believe, can provide a springboard for an improved understanding of complementarism and from that more relevant guidelines for action.

Foucault developed a theory of Interpretive Analytics that demonstrated a commitment to critical analysis by revealing subjugated knowledges that have either been lost or suppressed. He identified "centralising powers . . . linked to the institution and functioning of organised scientific discourse" (Foucault, 1980: 84). His solution was to develop a mode of critique as oppositional thinking, an instrument for fighters and resistors to deny assumed-as-being commonplace truths – it is of a liberating quality. In this sense it supports a drive for diversity and indeed fights to create diversity against some of the institutional forces we identified earlier.

The introduction of this agenda for liberating systems thinking suggested that theoreticians and interventionists have to be aware of the way judgements are made in the process of developing knowledge. Knowledge judgements often represent the outcome of the operation of political forces in which forms of knowledge have been culturally suppressed. What becomes agreed as a best way of thinking may easily echo governing forms of thinking that have become dominant in society through the *force of tactic rather than the force of reason*. This means that appeals to consensus, even when hoping to ground this in the force of the better argument, may not constitute a defence of a judgement made.

The postmodern challenge drew out the irony that if the process of liberating knowledge-forms and forms of argument was to gain any momentum, tactical decisions might have to be made to counteract the force of dominant reasoning in society. Foucault (1984: 382–383), for instance, argued that polemic forms of argument rely on persuading other people to concede to one's viewpoint – and that these forms of argument in society are too dominant. Argument oriented to consensus thus was not a sufficient criterion to employ to make better judgements. The dilemma facing postmodernists is how they themselves may ground judgements, once they have relinquished the criterion of referential speech as well as supposedly standardised forms of argument. Flood's (1990: 48–50) references to possible tension between Foucault and Habermas on this score and to the dilemmas to which this tension may give rise, is one of the features which can be seen to mark out a new position.

Flood emphasised the importance in the status of knowledge used by interventionists which distanced itself from realist and/or consensus claims to validity. He stressed, for example, the need for interventionists to recognise their close involvement in the process of intervention (Flood, 1994). Some may argue that this is an obvious statement which merely points to the presence of the interventionist in helping to facilitate forms of change.

However, it is also possible to draw out a nonrealist interpretation of this statement, which indeed is consistent with the non-objectivist position espoused by Flood and Ulrich (1990) and by Flood and Romm (1995a). In this interpretation the involvement of the interventionist as part of the circumstances, and the interventionist's recognition of this involvement, cast new light on the status of his/her knowledge of what is going on. It means that interventionists become aware that their knowledge about ways of operating in the situation is in turn part of the situation. When knowledge judgements are made about means to appreciate a situation, this constitutes an assessment based on conception(s) of possible actions that may be pursued in that situation. Romm (1995) also emphasised the judgemental character of knowing in/of the situation and highlighted for attention the suggestion that knowledge already implies some form of intervention. In this way the responsibility of those involved in knowledge generation began to come to the fore.

The quiz that remains is how assessment may be defended. How do interventionists deal with other people's theories while continually (re)assessing their relevance to action? These questions were answered implicitly in an argument for the utility of the trilogy, How?, What?, and Why?, in terms of TSI principles (Flood, 1995a: 189). However, the status of the judgements made still raises issues such as the quality of their grounding. It is these issues that we are continuing to explore since the trilogy is central to triple loop learning. We believe that these explorations have to walk a tightrope across critical modernist and postmodernist tracks. Balance comes in sensitivity to dilemmas posed for those who wish to ground their actions in some sort of defensible position. Practitioners and theoreticians as tightrope walkers must be aware of the problem of appealing to supposedly factual or consensual foundations. They must further be aware that end results are barely credible if based on whimsical and/or prejudicial judgement.

As we have seen in this book, Habermas's critique wanted to help us take control of our historical destiny. This is done through discursive reflection on purposes in terms of which people's understanding is directed. The quest was to allow these purposes to be more consciously engaged. As we have also seen, though, the discursive process of engaging these purposes was challenged in various quarters by those who were wary of Habermas's appeals to "the force of the better argument". For example, Foucault stressed the impact of "the force of tactic".

Nevertheless, Foucault's and Habermas's positions can be related in a rather interesting way. Foucault's critique aims to release subjugated ideas of discourse and subjugated forms of argument. He thus aims to diversify by fragmenting dominant perspectives and thinking patterns as part of a salutary process of rebelling against knowledge dominance in society. Diversity is seen as a strength. Interpretive Analytics is aimed at releasing rationalities, thus helping to grow diversity. Habermas's critical theory accepts openness and conciliation and welcomes diversity; his argument, however, pulls toward resolving these tensions in the quest for consensus. On the one hand, through Foucault, we acknowledge and attempt to deal with forces working against diversity through a liberating rationale. On the other hand, through Habermas, we seek ways of managing theoretical and methodological diversity. Liberating Systems Theory attempts to develop a metatheory that reframes positions by featuring them within a diversity of locations pointing to their constructed character, showing that the way objects become constructed within any theory seems to shut out other options (Flood, 1990:49–50). Taking this stance, Liberating Systems Theory offers a proposal for "releasing all systems based knowledge and methodological principles" in a complementary system of theories and methodologies (Flood, 1990: 48–50). Flood (1990: 50) argued that the construction of an adequate epistemology which could allow for such complementarism was no easy task, and would always be characterised by tension. As indicated in earlier chapters, the complementarist position that we now advance follows in the steps of Liberating Systems Theory, but draws more attention to the processes of developing and using the "system of ideas", and to the quality of the judgements implicated in these processes. It also draws out and at the same time extends other strains of thought in what we refer to as diversity management.

Admittedly, the result of the Liberating Systems Theory project does not rise to other highly relevant postmodernist demands; such as the demand that choices must be kept in consciousness and must be embraced with personal responsibility with no recourse to facts or agreements. Nor does it stress the need for judgement in the face of dilemmas. By bringing forward these ideas from earlier in this book and working them into the argument of Liberating Systems Theory an improved understanding of complementarist methodological practice begins to take shape. In this form there is the basis of a metatheory for intervention, one that is rehearsed below.

The idea is to (liberate) release and review subjugated ideas about theory and action, then, (critique) manage the tensions between rationalities that they proffer by locating discourses that can be appealed to in order to define ways of pursuing interests and purposes. This idea can be contextualised within our argument on diversity management summarised in the conclusion of Chapter 1. The aim of "liberate and critique" is to promote diversity and argument. Choices that have to be made are then locally decidable, temporally and spatially ephemeral, yet widely informed.

Before proceeding to the next chapter, we wish to indicate our position regarding the place of cybernetics and systemic interpretivism in the complementarist framework which we see as tied to the emergence of diversity management. In this framework, it is emphasised that the reason why cybernetics and systemic interpretivism slip into forms of domination is *primarily linked to their supposed scientific grounding*, and to their presumption that their logic is sacrosanct. It is when they operate with this grounding that people (theorists and interventionists alike) seem to think that they have to operate in terms of the rationality espoused by the position. Hence, cybernetics reduces the capacity to question this form of rationality as does systemic interpretivism, although each in their own way may promise forms of freedom (elaborated on in Chapters 7 and 8 respectively).

The promise of freedom *ironically becomes subverted* to the extent that advocates espouse their preferred approach as a *necessary* way of thinking and acting. This is precisely why it is not possible, from a metatheoretical position, to legitimise operating with any given methodology in terms of a simple non-reflective acceptance of its logic. There are forms of freedom that these logics account for (e.g. freedom through design and debate, see Chapters 7 and 8 respectively), but these should be understood as discursive constructions in order to be redeemed as freedom. This is what our complementarist framework attempts to draw out. It focuses on the constructed character of knowledge in a specific quality of choice making. This applies also to the search for freedom in terms of what we call in Part 3 a might–right agenda, which may become linked to specific practices. The proposals here advanced, about the way that a new self-understanding of science and knowledge may allow possible forms of freedom more scope, is tied to our complementarist argument.

4.6 SUMMARY AND CONCLUSION

In our now established style, we conclude this chapter by summarising our findings in bullet points.

- General Systems Theory (GST) was the first (popularised) systems theory whose aim, using logico- and empiricist–positivist science, was to identify a system of laws and generalised theories to unify all sciences. Systems thinking was, therefore, pitched in the domain of metatheory right from the start.
- GST falls to many criticisms levelled against metatheoretical approaches in the previous two chapters. A Quine-type analysis sees GST as a web of concepts easily altered with new isomorphies to account for contradictory evidence. A Feyerabend-type critique identifies GST as another dogma.
- Cybernetics is a form of isolationism. It believes that all science of organisation must be aimed at developing knowledge of cybernetic laws. Cybernetic reasoning underpins the great majority of designs that are discussed in Chapter 7.
- Systemic interpretivism is a form of isolationism. It believes that the

scientific approach to social life cannot imitate the natural sciences and must rather engage in a quest to understand cultural reality. Systemic interpretivism underpins most of the approaches to debate that are discussed in the second half of Chapter 8.

- Both systemic interpretivism and cybernetics assume knowledge is identified with science and life is placed therefore in a totalising theory, each proposing its own one.
- Critical systemic modernism is a complementarist approach that has drawn extensively on Habermas's critical theory. It called for more reflection on purposes being pursued in methodology practice. Emancipatory practice became a main focus, as did issues of power (see Chapter 6 for a typology of power and Chapter 9 for approaches aimed at digging into issues of power in terms of the might–right problematique). The main problem is that it does not fully explain how choices can be made between models, methodologies and theories, and how consensus may be defined.
- Total Systems Intervention (TSI) operationalises methodological guidelines for taking critical systemic modernism into action. Its main problem is that it (at least) partially determines people's choice making, in particular in the selection of models and methodologies, and it defines for people what emancipation means. In contrast diversity management proffers and invites people to consider a variety of discourses on the meaning of emancipation (design, debate and might–right discourses as discussed in Part 3).
- A postmodern critique of critical systemic modernism gave rise to a new form of complementarism. It encourages deliberation over purposes ascribed to models and methodologies in time and space. It caters for tentative and localised judgements in the face of fundamental diversity. The theory of diversity management, following the postmodern critique, supposes that society and organisations are characterised by dilemmas, difference and tension.

In this chapter we have reviewed developments in systems thinking and positioned them within the debate on metatheory provided in the previous two chapters. There are many forms of systems thinking that belong in one way or another to the modernist camp. From this camp, critical systemic modernism stands out as the only attempt to grapple with the issue of complementarism. Critical systemic modernism has given birth to a complementarist approach to methodology practice called Total Systems Intervention (TSI). Critical reflection on this catalytic process has brought about a dramatic change to the underpinning theory of critical systemic modernism and to the structure and process of TSI, resulting in a new metatheory called diversity management and a new style of practice called triple loop learning. We conclude this part of the book in the next chapter by drawing the contours of diversity management before moving on to triple loop learning in Part 3.

Chapter 5

Contours of Diversity Management

5.1 INTRODUCTION

In Chapter 5 we crystallise out defining tips from our discussion on metatheory. Sketching a line of argument linking these tips draws the contours of diversity management. These contours are sketched out below.

5.2 DIVERSITY MANAGEMENT

In our role as cartographers we first establish the lie of the land with a quickmap from Chapter 1, that is repeated here verbatim. Diversity management is about managing the increasing diversity of issues that confront humankind[1] in contemporary organisational and societal affairs. Initially this meant people managing the increasing diversity of issues they confronted by increasing the diversity of types of model, methodology and theory available to address those affairs. Diversification, however, created a brand new issue to be managed – how to choose between the models, methodologies and theories. Consequently, the emphasis in diversity management switched to people managing the increasing diversity of models, methodologies and theories that continue to come to the fore, thus improving

---

[1] As we said in the Preface to the book, issues of humankind to us refer to physical, biological and social cares. That is not to say that the physical and biological worlds are there for human exploitation. For example, ecological issues may be issues to be cared about not solely in terms of human needs. No matter how these issues are seen, humankind must take some responsibility for their care.

management of the increasing diversity of issues confronted. Diversity therefore means that more choices are made available for people to manage organisational and societal affairs. Management means that these choices, which after all have to be made, are thought through intelligently and made responsibly. Intelligence and responsibility are the defining features of triple loop learning, which is mapped out in the next section. First we magnify contours of diversity management from the quickmap just given.

Diversity management understands well that no argument is dilemma free. For every argument put forward, it is possible to locate barby dilemmas in its solutions. This is also true of our complementarist assertions. However, we propose that a strength of our complementarist argument is that it actually increases awareness of the existence and barbyness of dilemmas so that they can be handled carefully, rather than be ignored, or blindly dodged, with cutting consequences. The principal dilemma facing diversity management is how to manage the diversity of theoretical voices that we hear.

Management of the diversity of theoretical voices for us begins with a mentality of toleration. Yet toleration must be supplemented by a meta-theory that accounts for choice making at the level of methodology practice. Toleration must allow for comparison between theories through some form of argument. At the same time it must be recognised that comparison itself requires defining criteria to effect comparison as a basis for and as part of choice making. When a methodological choice is made by interventionists, it is vital that they hold a definite theoretical image in mind that directly informs the action. For this reason, theoretical development, or theorising, is not in itself dangerous, as long as interventionists are aware of the constructed character of their theoretical images.

Recognition of the constructed character of theories installs in interventionists theoretical sensitivity so that they can take on board news that fails to accord with an initial theoretical image that normally influences them. This implies a reflexive quality of re-evaluating favoured images and hearing news and information from other perspectives. Informedness does not, however, imply that the character of the news is directly translatable between the languages of the theories. This is precisely why the theorists need to loop between alternative visions to take on board new information and to recognise it as different news. This loopiness does not mean that action is thereby stalled. Our discourses for three theoretical categories covered in Chapters 7, 8 and 9 are a testament to this claim. Invoked knowledge makes explicit details of any theoretical vision chosen for the purpose of intervention. Practitioners, therefore, are able to make choices intelligently and live with the consequences of chosen actions as a matter of personal responsibility.

Theorising is thus important, but how can theory actually lead to intelligent and responsible choice making? Jackson and Carter (1991: 110) suggest that once we accept the necessary impact of knowledge in and on the world, different knowledge claims should, ideally, "be resolved in the light of their implications for social praxis".[2] Other postmodernists too suggest that the hallmark of good theory is whether "it supports patterns of relationships we feel have positive rather than negative consequences for social life" (cf. Hassard, 1993: 134–135). Yet, once again we are left with a dilemma, questioning exactly how decisions are to be made in accordance with these laudable abstractions.

Yet more dilemmas pop up. For instance, how can choice-making of interventionists be vindicated after admitting that standards for choice making differ? For a champion of cybernetics standards are primarily linked to purposeful design and organisation. For a champion of systemic interpretivism standards are linked to the provision made for accommodation between people to be reached through a process of debate. And for a champion of critical systemic modernism some normative standard will be called upon to measure the quality of debate, assessing the extent to which dominant forces shape the debate. And if we accept this fluidity in criteria employed to make judgements, then how can interventionists, if at all, become involved in meaningful action? There is a need to establish a base for judgements, so that interventionists do not enter into an anything-goes romp. Diversity management must provide a base of guidelines for choice making.

Diversity management argues that critique and self-critique can lead to a quality of choice making that avoids relativism as well as absolutism. In diversity management, *choice is a post-critical moment when results of critique are harvested so that decisions can be made.* Purposes are selected that are judged worthy to pursue. Judgement cannot be absolutely vindicated. It is, however, likely to be better if there is explicit recognition that choices adopt decided purposes. Habermas makes relevant assertions here. He suggests that normative purposes are better insofar as their normative content is less "crypto". At least their content is opened up for discussion and partial assessment.

[2] Understanding that theorising affects and enters the conduct of social life has a long history in (meta)theory. Radnitsky (1974: 51), for example, argues that "it is characteristic of the human sciences that their theories have direct implications for the *praxis* of life". Images of people are built into our theorising, which thus becomes linked to endorsing forms of social existence. The interconnection between theory and praxis, though more starkly evident in social scientific theorising, can be extended to theorising about the physical world. Norgaard (1989) offers a classic example of theorising affecting the physical world. Agroecologists recognise that traditional agricultural systems are products of the beliefs of the culture – their theories. Micro-organisms through insects have evolved characteristics in response to the selective pressures of human intervention in plant management that has come about from dominant theories (Altieri, 1987). All of this means, for us, that judgement on a theoretical vision is related to judgement about which actions are defensible. Knowing is related to action commitments.

The word partial is deliberately added in the above assertion. It commissions the tension between a modernist and postmodernist position. Postmodernists wish to emphasise that all judgements are fragile. Arguments used to vindicate judgements are never foolproof. Judgements are easily ruled by dominant modes of reasoning in society and this, at least, has to be kept in mind by those willing to pursue a complementarist agenda. Choice making needs to be guided by a sensitivity to power that is (often invisibly) built into knowledge and action-based decisions.

So, where does all this reckoning lead us? Are we any nearer to helping theoreticians and interventionists managing choices that they face? We believe that awareness of the theoretical and methodological work done, undertaken in this part of the book, if treated with a sensitivity to some of the dilemmas raised, is the first step toward guidelines for better choice making and hence diversity management. It provides a framework within which theoreticians and interventionists can evaluate purposes that may be aligned to any theory, methodology or model. It helps those people to consider the relevance of different purposes and the way that they may be accorded priority by different people (or groups) at distinct places and distinct points in time. People's choices obviously will be a matter of judgement, but their defence rests on a broader framework that arranges purposes in relation to one another. This allows for some measure of debate between theoreticians, interventionists, and indeed any other people, about the relevance of possible choices that they can make.

What is important, in these debates, is that we do not substantiate judgements by reference to so-called external reality or to consensual agreements about reality as if these realities have authority. We follow Foucault and Lyotard in their suggestions that the authority of such realities should be replaced by patterns of thought that are able to admit their own premises. With diversity management theoretical underpinnings are called purposes, which then can become explicit moments of any research investigation or intervention.

Nevertheless, we expect that positivists, realists and modernists, of various kinds, are likely to argue that our approach borders too close to a relativist position, where theoretical and methodological judgements cannot be substantiated. Our reply is that we are devising theoretical and methodological tools that allow us to build castles made of sand. Our sand castles are theoretical images that call forth specific purposes for action. Our range of sand castles allows life to ensue in a variety of ways, as different methodological decisions are made. They can be used as guides for action, for now. All the evidence we have brought forward suggests that castles made of sand, slip into the sea, eventually.

Our counter-argument to positivists, realists and modernists is that meta-narratively grounded theorising of their type is too forceful in this respect.

Building concrete castles, as they do, is a dangerous activity. It does not guard against the dangers of monolithic thought, or put in terms of our metaphor, against the dangers of building concrete castles in which everybody will have to live, and live according to the laws of the castle. Tolerance of diversity surely is a more curative tonic, even though it means managing diversity of criteria by which to judge theoretical and methodological choices.

Discussion in this book allows us to reconsider the question of incommensurability between theories, methodologies and models, whose diversity and difference are endorsed in our complementarist framework. We accept incommensurability between options for presencing the world and relating to it. We suggest theoreticians and interventionists think in terms of theoretical and methodological (in)commensurability. The bracket within the term incommensurabilty points to tension in consciousness; between knowing that choices at the moment of action exclude other possibilities, but being able to submit a defence for decisions made. There are tensions involved in trying to maintain a position that neither "accepts differences between paradigms but slips into a paradigm mentality" (akin to isolationism), nor "denies differences between paradigms" (also akin to isolationism). The bracket within the term incommensurability suggests a way of managing, while not denying, or evading, this tension. The suggestion translates into action with triple loop learning, the contours of which are drawn in Chapter 11.

5.3 SUMMARY AND CONCLUSION

We conclude Chapter 5 with a quickmap of the contours of diversity management in the form of bullet points.

- Diversity management is about managing the increasing diversity of models, methodologies and theories, that continue to come to the fore, thus improving management of the increasing diversity of issues confronted.
- Diversity management understands well that no argument is free of dilemmas.
- Diversity management argues that critique and self-critique can lead to a quality of choice making that avoids relativism as well as absolutism.
- Diversity management recognises that castles made of sand, slip into the sea, eventually.

The discussion in Part 2 of *Diversity Management: Triple Loop Learning* unveils in our opinion an acceptable form of complementarism. We chiselled out our brand of complementarism working with a narrative on metatheory, philosophy, the history of knowledge, theory, methodology, and systems thinking. We endorse a metatheory that operates somewhere between critical systemic modernism and postmodernism. We are open about the dilemmas that inevitably have to be faced when operating in this way (or any other way!). We manage dilemmas rather than solve them. Diversity management redefines (insoluble) issues that keep popping out of the paradigm incommensurability thesis. We have argued for theoretical and methodological (in)commensurability. We put up a defence using choice making as a standard of accountability. Diversity management explains this and triple loop learning indicates what such accountability may mean in order that choice does not slip into repetitive re-endorsement of a singular brand of general theorising and/or methodology and/or model.

We have now captured from Part 2 the crucial methodological ideas of diversity management. Part 3 introduces triple loop learning as an over-arching metadiscourse that co-ordinates three discourses, respectively covering the trilogy, How?, What?, and Why?. Models, methodologies and other approaches that support the trilogy are the centre of learning for each discourse. The discourses are supported by case studies that cover a wide range of (insoluble) issues in organisational and societal affairs. Theoreticians who move on with us to Part 3 will see how ideas presented in Part 2 are applied, thus helping them to understand much better our (meta)theoretical ideas.

PART 3
Triple Loop Learning

Preface to Part 3

Part 3 introduces our methodological and model-based thinking about diversity management in the form of triple loop learning.[1] It puts triple loop learning into action, and draws into triple loop learning a headline issue that we posted in Part 1 and Part 2 – emancipatory practice. One of the most pressing concerns when it comes to intervention is the limited breadth of understanding about power that informs most decision making. Power expresses itself in many ways and confounds decision making that ignores it. Peeling off the blindfold, we develop in Chapter 6 a typology of power, and then explore through this interpretation possible ways of achieving effective emancipatory practice. Ensuing discussion about models and methodologies for action are thus sensitised to issues of power and emancipatory practice.

With this preparation complete, the three loops of triple loop learning are then tracked in Chapters 7, 8, and 9, respectively. Loop 1 puts design issues at the centre of learning, inviting people to explore the broad question How?, or, Are we doing things right? Loop 2 puts debate issues at the centre of learning, inviting people to explore the broad question What?, or, Are we doing the right things? Loop 3 puts might–right issues at the centre of learning, inviting people to explore the broad question Why?, or, Is rightness buttressed by mightiness and/or mightiness buttressed by rightness? Our own contribution to might–right management follows in Chapter 10. However, triple loop learning requires juggling all three loops, that is, triple looping. Chapter 11 discusses triple looping. Abstracts of each chapter follow.

Chapter 6 Typology of Power

Chapter 6 puts the spotlight on emancipatory practice, developing a typology of power through which emancipatory practice is explored. This sensitises

[1] *Triple loop learning* has been used in literature on the processes of learning (e.g. Swieringa and Wierdsma 1992). We conceptualise the term quite differently to show how principles and discourses are somewhat incommensurable as well as how people can deal with this. We also relate this to wider debates, making our view of organisation broader than ones normally addressed.

following discussions on models and methodologies for action to issues of power and emancipatory practice. It paves the way for a more decisive discussion about models and methodologies for triple loop learning.

Chapter 7 Loop 1. Design Management: How?

Chapter 7 begins our three chapter presentation of models and methodologies for action that support triple loop learning. Chapter 7 concentrates on How? people can aspire toward efficient and effective design. It makes How? its centre of learning. Also investigated is the kind of emancipatory practice that such designs can offer people.

Chapter 8 Loop 2. Debate Management: What?

Chapter 8 covers models and methodologies that help people debate the question What? designs and/or decisions they should choose. It makes What? its centre of learning. Also investigated is the kind of emancipatory practice that can arise from debate.

Chapter 9 Loop 3. Might–right Management: Why?

Chapter 9 covers approaches that reflect on the rightness and mightiness of designs and decisions as outputs from Loops 1 and 2 respectively by asking Why? Why this design and/or that decision? It makes Why? its centre of learning. Also investigated is the kind of emancipatory practice that can arise from might–right reflection.

Chapter 10 Loop 3 Continued. Enhancing Emancipatory Practice

Chapter 10 explores our own option for might–right management that amounts to redirection of models and methodologies in terms of purposes not normally associated with them. We call this kind of option the oblique operation of purposes. Oblique intervention enhances emancipatory practice.

Chapter 11 Contours of Triple Loop Learning

Chapter 11 explains triple looping by bringing together into a triple loop the three questions from the three loops, respectively, How?, What?, and Why? It introduces a reflexive consciousness as interventionists continually loop between these three questions. The looping helps interventionists to develop a meta-discourse yielding meta-learning and diversity management.

The path to emancipatory practice through triple loop learning begins in Chapter 6 to which we now turn our attention.

Chapter 6

Typology of Power

6.1 INTRODUCTION

Approaches to intervention have matured considerably in recent years. A persistent and in our view fair criticism, however, is that these approaches have not dealt adequately with power and its abuses. As part of our counter-measure, we establish in this chapter a platform for wide-ranging discussion on this topic. We form a typology of power that reflects types of emancipatory practice that can be employed through triple loop learning. The typology fulfils another role by introducing the three loops of triple loop learning and hence the following three chapters.

The typology organises three *arenas of discourse* around three issue areas: structuralism, intersubjective decision making, and might–right management. Structuralism deals with power issues encircling organisational design and process design when inefficiency or ineffectiveness in design are thought to prevail. Intersubjective decision making deals with power issues encircling processes of debate, relevant insofar as there is no clear-cut view on strategies to pursue or other ways forward such as choice of design. Might–right management deals with disempowering social practices that can lead to: a lack of relevance of designs to (many of or some of) those who have to live with experienced consequences of them; or a lack of influence in debating processes leaving decisions ill considered for (many of or some of) those who have to live with experienced consequences of them. The arenas of discourse isolated by the typology provide not only different conceptions of power, but also suggest possible practical responses to abuses of power.[1]

[1] The suggestion here to concentrate on separate arenas of discourse that involve different visions of the world (as noted in Part 2) draws on Kuhn's (1970) conception of paradigms. However, the intention of this book is to achieve considered choice making in the face of diversity – in this case, the diversity of ways of seeing power.

Chapter 6 begins by positioning our typology of power in the literature of such typologies. This brings our work into focus. Then each of the three arenas of discourse reflecting types of intervention are explored. The order of presentation is: structuralism, intersubjective decision making, and might–right management. We then conclude.

6.2 TYPOLOGIES OF POWER

To surface and bring into focus our typology of power we first explore the literature of such typologies. Two typologies were found particularly useful and so shape the text, while some other important work in this area is dealt with briefly in footnotes. The two main typologies we draw upon are summarised from original accounts of their artisans, Oliga (1996) and Clegg (1989).

Oliga suggests a division between what he calls "objectivist", "subjectivist", and "relational" perspectives. With objectivism he refers to theories that focus on power as *capacities located in social structures*. These tend to be either synergistic (e.g. Parsonian collective – see Section 6.3.2) or conflictual (e.g. Marxian conflictual – see Section 6.3.3) theoretical orientations. With subjectivism he discusses theories that focus on power *possessed by agents*. With relational approaches he places theories that conceive power as *a property of interaction among social forces*.[2]

Oliga recognises that his typology bears some likeness to Clegg's (1989) trifold "circuits of power". These circuits, as Clegg defines them, refer to distinct conduits through which power may pass in society. Clegg relates these passageways to theoretical arguments in the literature on power. He sees his "circuits of power" as grounded in "the grammar of power as a concept" (Clegg, 1989: 239). Clegg's first circuit, the "dispositional" circuit, focuses on the structure of social rules and the way they incorporate the capacity to mobilise bias.[3] It draws on structuralist argumentation, seeing power rooted in objective

[2] Comparable categorisations have also been recognised by other commentators. See, for example, Knights and Vurdubakis's (1994: 170) reference to functionalist (including Marxist-oriented functionalism), voluntarist and relational approaches. Consider too, how Morgan's (1980: 608) four paradigms can translate into a three-fold categorisation, because he sees functionalist and radical structuralist approaches as being objectively oriented. These orientations are distinguished from interpretive ones focusing on agents' meaning making, and from "radical humanist" agendas which concentrate on readdressing human relationships. Morgan (1980: 612) believes these categorisations may be relevant to encourage what he calls a spirit of critical inquiry which cautions against excessive commitment to any particular point of view. This tallies to a large extent with the proposals of Gouldner (1973: 489–495), who in locating functionalist, interpretive and critical theoretical types of argumentation, calls for a (self-)reflexive relationship to all of them. Clegg's (1989: 37) discussion of circuits of power, discussed below, represents an attempt to relate alternative theoretical orientations to a framework which may allow us to avoid using any one conception of power.

[3] Here Clegg (1989: 76) refers to the celebrated work of Bachrach and Baratz (e.g. 1962: 95) to point to the way in which the "rules of the game" may allow for *non-decision making* to take place so that items which may be relevant to the concerns of some classes in society are left off the agenda of social discussion.

capacity (Clegg, 1989: 209–210) and resembles Oliga's objectivism. Clegg's (1989: 214) next circuit, the "episodic" circuit, views agency(ies) as paramount. It matches Oliga's subjectivism. This includes pluralist conceptions of episodic power and may allow for the exploration of pluralist or elitist power exercised in specific contexts.[4] The third circuit, the "facilitative" circuit, identifies possibilities for transformative action through empowerment (Clegg, 1989: 227). The facilitative category is presented as a broad category for collecting *all* references to productive power[5] – although Clegg (1989: 236) concentrates here on the facilitative possibility of resisting relationships of domination by generating alternative *modes of relationship*. With this focus the facilitative category can be seen to match up with Oliga's relational approach.

We suggest that it is possible to spread the notion of facilitative power across the three arenas of discourse, drawing out *different facilitative possibilities* as they arise in these arenas. We present our rationale for this in Sections 6.3, 6.4 and 6.5. The kinds of facilitation offered in our two other arenas of discourse (which correspond more or less with Clegg's dispositional and episodic circuits) are differentiated by their focus: structuralism offers a (facilitative) notion of power to *co-ordinate by design*; and intersubjective decision making highlights the (facilitative) power of the *intersubjective process to aid decision making*. In effect we have translated Clegg's circuits into arenas of discourse that all allow for intervention toward improved use of power so as to minimise its abuses, a core concern of this book.

We have a practical interest in intervention as well as an interest in theoretical reasoning. In the structuralist arena the practical question becomes, How can design aspire to optimum relevance in the minds of those who have to live with the consequences of design? In the intersubjective decision-making arena the practical question becomes, What do decision-making processes involve that may influence how well-considered decisions turn out to be in the minds of those who will live with the consequences of them? In the might–right management arena the practical question becomes, Why should we believe and trust that power relations can shift to aspire to new forms of social relationship.[6,7]

Each of the three arenas of discourse are now explored. The order of

---

[4] See also Lukes (1974: 11) on the notion of "pluralism" as being sufficiently open to incorporate elements of "nonplurality". Dahl's (1961) argument is cited as such a position.
[5] Which allows Clegg (1989: 15) to place Parsons in this category too.
[6] This may also involve assessing why entrenched modes of relations become sustained. It is not to be confused, however, with Bhaskar's (1993: 392; 1994: 218) type of questioning, which invokes the display of structural absences in the system which are to be remedied. The analytic focus in Bhaskar's (1994: 221) conception of "transformative capacity" is a route to real relations that require transformation. This fits uneasily with the "medley" of philosophers to whom he refers (Bhaskar, 1994: 215), including Derrida, Habermas, and Foucault, all nonrealists who are wary of making realist-oriented distinctions between "truth" and "illusion", for they believe that this in itself may threaten the creation of new forms of social relationship.
[7] Flood's (1993b) conception of freedoms made possible through design, debate and disemprisonment and his conception of alternative priorities written into How?, What?, and Why? questions (Flood, 1995a) link up with the argument here.

presentation is: structuralism, intersubjective decision making, and might–right management.[8]

6.3 STRUCTURALISM

6.3.1 Opening Remark

We have chosen to introduce our thoughts on structuralism through two lines of discourse; Parsonian and Marxian, in that order. These arguments are used to open up debate about forms of design that feature in Chapter 7.

6.3.2 Parsonian Discourse

Parsons' structural–functional position is premised on the idea that power is primarily a collective resource. It promotes a synergistic view of power as a collective property of "the system". We referred to this when introducing Oliga's classification in Section 6.2. Power to attain goals is seen as a normal part of the functioning of all systems – including social ones. This analysis applies at the level of society as a social system as well as all other "systems" in society. So, for social systems to be stable they need a stable base of (legitimate) power, vested in part of "the system" geared toward attaining collective goals. A goal attainment subsystem is institutionalised to serve the collective. Parsons (1973: 271) admits, however, that "the whole problem of the institutionalisation of authority so as to insure adequate acceptance where necessary and protect against its abuses is difficult".[9] He admits that there may be a tendency for those strategically placed to exploit the weaker (Parsons, 1973: 271). Despite this Parsons argues that measures can be taken to control and counteract such tendencies. Parsons (1957, 1963) thus concentrates on power as "power to" serve collective goals.

6.3.3 Marxist-oriented Discourse

The view of power sometimes called the Marxist conflict view[10] concentrates on identifying instances of "power over" (rather than "power to"). It converges debate on the way in which vested interests may be served by

---

[8] Our argument concentrates on emancipatory possibilities in society. However, it should be noted that these possibilities also imply new ways of addressing eco-friendly relationships with nature, through, for example, developing designs geared to respect nature, establishing alternative decision-making priorities; and redefining our being through our involvement with nature.

[9] Parsons argues that power, as he defines it, cannot be abused because by definition it is the capacity to serve collective goals. This does not mean, however, that abuses of authority are hereby excluded from his view. What it means is that he defines them under a different label. Nevertheless, the complaint of authors such as Gouldner (1973), Giddens (1977), and Wrong (1995) is that Parsonians may be overoptimistic about the propensity for collective goal attainment via the capacity of power.

[10] So named by, for example, Oliga (1996); Wrong (1995); Zhu (1995).

systematic entrenchment of dependencies in class systems. It is suggested that the mechanisms of the capitalist system, in particular, are geared to meeting the needs of some people at the expense of others (see, for example, Bachrach and Baratz, 1962; Ojo, 1983; Bhaskar, 1994). The "power over" argument has been extended to deal with many structures and their biases other than class structure. For such theorists, it is important to generate alternative structures that will be more conducive to serving collective goals/interests. Within Marxist argument, discussion of possibilities for co-ordination at both societal and smaller-scale organisational levels is still going on (see, for instance, Sayer and Walker, 1992).

6.3.4 Implications for Practice

Intervention suggested by structuralist discourse is about setting up designs that facilitate the way in which collective goals can be served. In essence, structuralism proposes design solutions to potential or actual abuses of power. Structure can be designed sensitively to allow for co-ordination of efforts to aspire to collective goals irrespective of the scale of operation. Structuralist discourse sensitises us to abuses that can occur when design issues are not delicately addressed and managed. The graph in Figure 6.1 depicts intervention possibilities and provides a stimulant to a practically oriented discourse about design.

Figure 6.1 abets debate about better designs, i.e. design relevant to co-ordination of efforts. On the graph, better design is represented by move-ment from the point of "structure" on the X axis, upwards toward "most relevance" on the Y axis, so as to maximise "a". The point marked "A" is a point which marks an ideal. Our suggestion is to study optional designs with the aim of pushing "a" upwards, towards realising the ideal of a most relevant design for the circumstances.[11] Failing this, "no structure" and "superstructure" begin to stifle choice making of participants and hence reduce freedom. In "no structure", there is control by inefficiency and its demands (Beer, 1973; Flood, 1993b: 9–10). In "superstructure", rules and procedures of the system become the controlling force (Beer, 1973; Hofstede, 1994: 135).[12]

"No structure" and "superstructure" are shown on the X axis as abuses of power (here labelled "power over"). The further left we move on the graph the less relevant are designs because of lack of structure, as indicated by the

[11] Circumstances means the situation as seen in terms of a chosen focus of attention. This allows people to get involved in defining the issues. Suitability of design therefore is subject to circumstances. There is no right design independent of interventionists. If circumstances change such that there is a different mix of people, the decision on suitability of design may change too.

[12] We do not use *superstructure* in the Marxist sense to express a distinction between society's economic basis and its superstructural features (polity, legal system etc.); but rather to high-light the difference between what we call *no structure* (lack of structure) and *superstructure* (excessive structure) in design solutions.

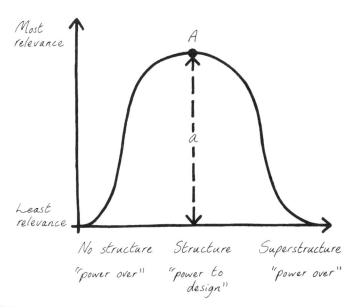

Figure 6.1

graph itself which falls away from the ideal. The left extreme on the X axis resonates with situations where people have to cope with consequences of insufficient structural arrangements (that is, of rules co-ordinating the pattern of conduct). People become frustrated by *ad hoc* rulings that are created to deal with issues on contingent bases as a matter of course. In management speak this is a form of crisis management, one where concerned participants find the lack of reliability frustrating or even threatening. At the right extreme, by contrast, there is an excessive focus on rules, to the extent that organisational activities become regimented responses to rule following. The further right we move on the graph the less relevant are designs because of too much structure, as indicated by the graph itself which again falls away from the ideal. Here, power capacities invested in "the rules", or the appeal to so-called rightness of a style of co-ordination, become (ab)used to define organisational responses that are expected (of others).

Neither of these extremes, however, has absolute meaning independent of the context of their use. That is why we keep making reference to "circumstances". So, for example, what some people experience as a frustrating lack of rules, others may find refreshing. Similarly, what some may regard as a suitably pitched design for organisational co-ordination, others may encounter as superstructure. This points to the significance of the *experience* of structure and in this sense transcends structuralist positions as expounded by some structuralist authors mentioned above (including authors stressing the importance of more adhocratic or informal designs). This is because the focus of many structuralist arguments is largely "getting the structure right". This can result in a structuralist mentality on the part of professional theorists as well as lay theorists. A structuralist mentality can exclude ways of addressing the design issue, for example, through *debate about the experience* of structure. To concentrate on experience of structure may indeed require a shift in perspective as we noted earlier. Our argument encourages theoreticians and interventionists to be sufficiently open to acknowledge this. The discussion in the next section on intersubjective decision making carries this point forward and opens up debate about debate, the theme of Chapter 8.

6.4 INTERSUBJECTIVE DECISION MAKING

6.4.1 Discourse

The intersubjective decision-making arena of discourse concentrates on ways that people make decisions in conjunction with other people (or agents).[13] Theorists of this persuasion do not believe that the way events work out in everyday life is due to capacities written into social rules, or resource distribution, or official definitions of authority, or any other feature of design. They prefer to highlight the central role of agency in both defining and using rules and resources and authority (including the way in which other agents respond to such use).

The intersubjective view provides an alternative to structuralist discourse. Many critics of the intersubjective view complain that it cannot address the issue of how and why power is exercised because it concentrates too much on episodes of interaction (issues picked up in the next section). The counter-contention is that it can address the problematics of power; however, it does so in different terms.

Power is seen as something to be used in the course of interaction, but its exercise is conditional on the way the user and others involved in the interaction define events. Theorists argue that this theoretical conception resonates well with people's experience of power in everyday life. The opportunity for people to influence decision making occurs in the process of interaction. Here, meanings are exchanged and perceptions defined and redefined (Czarniawska-Joerges, 1993: 56). Power to influence depends on other agents' responses. However, neither observers nor agents know in advance how much power others possess (Dandridge, 1985: 145–146; Knorr-Cetina, 1988: 46–47; Romm, 1994a: 333–334).

The amount of power possessed can never be defined outside the way things are worked out in the process of interaction. People may, for

[13] This dynamic is difficult at times to disentangle from might–right dynamics. This becomes especially apparent when actually attempting to disentangle practical cases (see Chapter 9).

instance, decide to draw (predictably or unpredictably) on third parties as means of influencing decisions. They may struggle to shift the definitions which accord other people authority. They may decide to review their own resource base by redefining the value of commodities that they, together with other people, possess or can muster up (such as capacities for labour, (dis)loyalty, or voting power).

Checkland and Scholes (1990: 51) argue that there are many "commodities of power" that observers and participants experience. What is interesting with this point of view is that as their operation is given more exposure, so their relevance and force may be altered. By making more public the way in which meaning is constructed, rules interpreted, and decisions made, power may come to operate in different ways. Some proponents suggest that power may become both spread and enhanced through these social processes. Power as a facility for decision making can become (re)generated in social interaction, through explicit attendance to practices of consultation and participation.

6.4.2 Implications for Practice

The intersubjective decision-making arena of discourse lends itself to new intervention possibilities. Some of these are rendered explicit (e.g. Checkland, 1981; Checkland and Scholes, 1990; Ackoff, 1981, 1993; Lundberg, 1985). The idea, broadly speaking, is that decision making in social life should, as a matter of principle, encourage a variety of viewpoints. This variety can be brought to bear when defining options for action. The facility of decision making can be enhanced by nurturing an environment conducive for exchange and development of viewpoints. Achieving this, as seen below, is a tightrope walk for professional theorists and interventionists alike.

Figure 6.2 advises that action can be taken to aspire to better decisions, i.e. well-considered ones. Well-considered decisions attain enrichment of perspective through the facilitative power of debate. This can be conceptualised as a push up from the point of "decision making" on the X axis, toward "most considered" so as to maximise "b". The point "B" marks an ideal; an ideal of most considered decisions informed by a process of debate.

Both "no decisions" and "superdecisions" stifle choice making and hence suppress freedom. With "no decisions", the extreme left on the X axis, the debating process is presented to participants as if no point of decision is possible. For example, it may be argued that all viewpoints are equally relevant and so there is no basis for choice making. Here, in effect, no decisions are taken and existing power (perhaps power built into structures) prevails by default and implements its attendant biases. The further left we move on the graph, the more decisions are experienced as ill considered by many who have to live with their consequences.

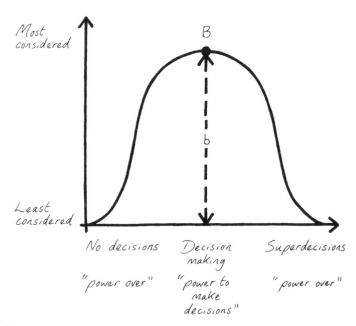

Figure 6.2

With "superdecisions" on the extreme right of the graph, ossified mean-ings may fix the framework within which all decisions are made. Decision making is thus facile. Decision making is directed by predefined obvious-ness. This point, or tendency, on the X axis, can also be operative when, for example, it is assumed that decisions have to bear the mark of full consensus of all concerned parties. In this case, "superdecisions" may become directed by this requirement and accountability is then bent toward fulfilling defined arrangements, or at least seeming to fulfil them. Here, super-decisions created via an appeal to the value of consensus may come to forbid discretionary elements on the part of participants, leading to mis-trust of their exercise of choice.

Like the graph on design management, dangers located in the inter-subjective decision-making arena of discourse, represented by the extremes on the X axis, are not definable outside of context. It is only in context that assessments can be made about the character of possible abuses. The utility of the graph is the way that it sensitises people to possible dangers and indeed opportunities which they need to be aware of.

It is important to recognise that assessments in this arena may themselves be caught up in a cycle of thinking in which options for action are insuffi-ciently informed by wider considerations. For example, an issue with inter-subjective decision making, which is difficult to manage within its own discourse, is how to challenge the rightness of decisions taken. Challenge seems possible only by recourse to given processes of intersubjectivity, during which, using Checkland's (1981: 219) terminology, "accommodations" are pursued. But there are concerns to be raised here. For example, "Once a consensus or compromise [accommodation] upon rightness has been arrived at . . . there is no methodological requirement for further challenge" (Midgley, 1992: 166). The next section considers how such challenges may require an alternative discursive agenda. They are discussed under the banner of might–right management, opening up a discussion that is taken forward in Chapter 9.

6.5 MIGHT–RIGHT MANAGEMENT

6.5.1 Discourse

The distinguishing character of this arena of discourse is the degree to which authors (or rather arguments[14]) are concerned about disempowering relationships that become entrenched in social practices. This may indeed occur when people insist on seeking "design solutions" or "decision accommodations" to tackle pressing organisational or societal issues. However, failure to consider power as entrenched in forms of social relationship may mean, *inter alia*, that people:

- fail to activate areas of conflict over issues that people seem to have consented to (see, for instance, Lukes, 1974: 32);
- fail to allow for continued moral deliberation over issues which appear resolved (see, for instance, Gutmann and Thompson, 1995: 108; Habermas, 1989: 205–208);
- fail to alert participants to the way in which debates may become rigged by the way arguments are (mis)used (see, for instance, Forester, 1987: 273);
- fail to consider ways in which conversation may become stacked by the excessive reliance on the force of valid argument as a means of generating fair practice (see, for instance, Lyotard, 1990: 340; Jackson and Carter, 1991: 125);
- fail to consider and practise counter manoeuvres to address forcefulness of administrative apparatuses which discipline and routinise patterns of relationship (see, for instance, Foucault, 1986: 239–242).

[14] It is important to remember that what are being categorised in the typology are arguments and these may coalesce more or less with the writings of individual authors. It is useful to have categories so that one can address the writings of authors and consider the way in which their arguments tend in a specific direction (with consequent implications for practice). This is not to say that authors cannot shift in time their stance in a way which would allow us to recategorise their tendencies. Nor is it to say that theorists are unable to move reflexively between options in their thinking. Indeed it is such reflexivity that is endorsed by diversity management.

Space to explore some of these issues is opened, in Part 2, by debates within and between critical modernism and postmodernism. This space is widened here with implications of power for practice.

6.5.2 Implications for Practice

The focus in this arena of discourse is on power relations brought about by the way the game of knowledge production is played in society. Interventionists may become involved in most serious intrusions into the way knowledge–power relations are directed (see, for instance, Foucault, 1984: 378–379). The grandness of efforts aimed at shifting plays of power in society, and the way in which interventionists should become involved in theorising alternative possibilities, constitutes a subject of contention here.[15] Another subject of contention in this arena is whether an appeal to the force of the better argument Habermasian-style itself constitutes a form of force; and whether Habermas's reluctance to embrace fundamental dissensus in social life should be seen as threatening in some way. A brief comment on some intervention possibilities in this broad arena of discourse is a taster of our elaboration in Chapter 9.

Five ways to keep alive this arena of discourse are outlined below.

• Activating the potential for moral deliberation in society by becoming involved in rethinking how fair(er) judgements in social life may be fostered. This includes initiating and vitalising people's education programmes (Freire, 1985; McKay and Romm, 1992); unfurling arguments for a moral citizenry (Habermas, 1993; Gutmann and Thompson, 1995); and/or intervention with the intention of raising and discussing "ought" questions (Ulrich, 1983, 1994; Forester, 1989; Babüroglu and Ravn, 1992).

• Offering theoretical accounts of the way in which processes of knowledge construction in social life may serve to entrench patterns of social domination, and suggesting ways in which people may realise mutual respect by rethinking relationships between themselves (Romm and Romm, 1987; Shotter, 1993; Gergen, 1994). This may include involvement in cases that point, perhaps only embryonically, to such potentialities (Gergen, 1994).

• Aiding the vulnerable in society to become more self-reliant while creating a base for empowering action (Fals-Borda, 1991; Rahman, 1991). Ideally these initiatives do not aim simply to serve one fraction of people to the detriment of others, unless this form of action itself has gone through considered moral deliberation (see Maghimbi's, 1990a, 1990b, discussion of peasant co-operatives in Tanzania; and Vanderplaat's, 1995, discussion of "empowerment-oriented social programmes"). The intention, in Cohen

---

[15] See, for instance, Benhabib (1990: 121–122); Hartsock (1990: 164–165); Parker (1993: 209); Gergen (1994: 66).

and Arato's terms (1994: 532), is to establish initiatives where involvement with "the system" is not solely about extracting benefits, but is in large part about refreshing modes of relationship.

• Exploring the way in which intelligent protest may be used to resist the demands of "a system" geared to discipline and intransigence in its control function. Protest initiatives are then a critique of the way of life embodied in the pervasion of such administrative rationality in society (see, for instance, Clegg, 1989: 231–239; Cohen and Arato, 1994: 564–604).[16]

• Practising what Flood and Romm (1995b) call "oblique" intervention that addresses the (officially) powerful while at the same time undercutting coercive practices, from an angle which strategically redirects designing and debating models and methodologies (see also Schön, 1989; Payne, 1992; Donnellon and Kolb, 1994).

It is possible to isolate two extreme difficulties faced in the way the game of knowledge production is played in society by bringing together issues raised above. The consolidation is reflected in Figure 6.3.

The first difficulty, the left extreme on the X axis, is that the *might* of "power to mobilise" may become seen as the only way to gain empowerment. This then means that force, as *strategy without attendant moral deliberation*, may come to rule. This is manifested, indeed, when so-called liberatory endeavours operate without thought about how more attractive power relationships can be generated.[17] Some theorists associate Foucault's position with this abuse (e.g. Nola, 1994: 39). It seems, at times, not able to distinguish "better" from "worse" systems of knowledge–power creation. Denzin (1991: 41) makes a similar comment regarding Lyotard's micropolitics of subversion. He notes with concern that appeal only to personal conscience, and the denial of the relevance of grand narratives to think through issues of justification, "always leaves open the potential of the very reign of terror he . . . so vehemently opposes".

The other danger, the right extreme on the X axis, is sometimes associated by critics with Habermas's argument. It is the danger of unduly endorsing or valorising a set of validation procedures presented as the correct means to generate both truth and rightness in society. The concern is that the force of "better arguments" may come to exclude those less enskilled to enter the exchange; may come to exclude people from utilising other modes

---

[16] This is not to say that other domains of discourse offer no thoughts on protest. The point is that in structuralist discourse protest is seen as properly aimed at a critique of structures with the purpose of instituting an alternative. In the intersubjective decision-making arena, protest aims to invigorate co-operative decision making. The researcher may help to make these possibilities visible and hence foster them.

[17] The terminology "more attractive" comes from Knights and Vurdubakis (1994: 189) who note this as an issue that should be recognised. They try to show how a sympathetic reading of Foucault readdresses the issue by considering the possibility of endorsing particular struggles.

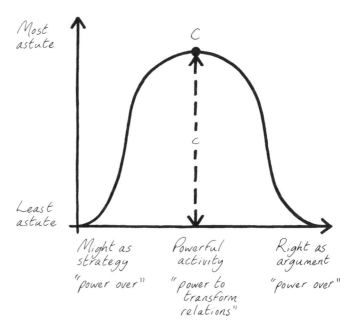

Figure 6.3

of exchange; may come to exclude those who prefer to introduce different criteria of "good" argument into the conversation, etc.

Astuteness in Figure 6.3 refers to a consciousness needed to maximise transformative potential in this arena of discourse. Intervention possibilities are chosen judiciously, taking into account the danger of reversion into a might mentality, and conversely a reversion into a mentality relying on good argument, without awareness of its fragility. Efforts of theoreticians and interventionists ideally aim to keep alive the arena so that new modes of social relationship can be explored.

As with the discussion of Figures 6.1 and 6.2, a word of caution is also in order. Care has to be taken not to become bounded by a belief that the engagements plotted in Figure 6.3 offer the only possible way of addressing issues faced in all circumstances. The danger of such a perspective is that it inclines the viewer consistently to probe behind specific rulings or accommodations which seem to have been, or which may become, consented to in society. Obsessive probing leads to self-generated mistrust of affairs and suspicion of manipulation. Yet the grounding for such mistrust may be circularly related to an initial exclusivity of perspective. This is not to say that the attention given within this arena of discourse to the might–right problematic *is* exclusivist.

6.6 SUMMARY AND CONCLUSION

To conclude this chapter we provide in our established style a summary in bullet point form.

- Intervention suggested by structuralist discourse is about setting up designs that facilitate the way in which collective goals can be served. Structuralism proposes design solutions to potential or actual abuses of power. Structuralist discourse sensitises us to abuses that can occur when design issues are not delicately addressed and managed.
- Intervention suggested by intersubjective decision-making discourse concentrates on ways that people make decisions in conjunction with other people (or agents). Theorists of this persuasion do not believe that the way events work out in everyday life is due to capacities written into social rules, or resource distribution, or official definitions of authority, or any other feature of design. They prefer to highlight the central role of agency in both defining and using rules and resources and authority.
- Intervention suggested by might-right discourse addresses power relations brought about by the way the game of knowledge production is played in society. The grandness of efforts aimed at shifting plays of power in society, and the way in which interventionists should become involved in theorising alternative possibilities, constitutes a subject of contention here. Another subject of contention in this arena is whether an appeal to the force of the better argument itself constitutes a form of force; and whether reluctance to embrace fundamental dissensus in social life should be seen as threatening in some way.

In this chapter we have introduced a typology of power. It forms three *arenas of discourse* around three types of intervention: structuralism, intersubjective decision making, and might–right management. The arenas of discourse isolated by the typology provide not only different conceptions of power, but also suggest possible practical responses to abuses of power. Treading a path between and around the various issues requires some careful consideration. This we have undertaken in the following three chapters, each one expanding discussion about an arena of discourse in the order given by our typology. These arenas of discourse are the three loops of triple loop learning.

Chapter 7

Loop 1. Design Management: How?

7.1 INTRODUCTION

Chapter 7 begins our three-part (chapter) presentation of models and methodologies for action that support triple loop learning. Chapter 7 concentrates on How? people can aspire toward efficient and effective design. It makes How? its centre of learning. Also investigated is the kind of emancipatory practice that such designs can offer people. We create in this chapter images of design through theoretical development and by supplying some empirical resonance of the images in organisational contexts. The chapter covers two aspects of design; the first is organisational design and the second is process design. We front this material with a discussion about design.

7.2 ABOUT DESIGN

In the previous chapter we introduced a form of graph with which it is possible to evaluate interventions in terms of power/freedom and relevance. For this chapter on organisational design and process design those evaluations translate as follows. With power/freedom through design we mean chances people have to make widely informed and locally contingent choices, given degrees of structure and the nature and relevance of that structure. By relevance we mean how "comfortable" people feel with designs in the circumstances. Circumstances means the whole (local) situation which in the case of Loop 1 implies everyone and everything that is assessed as having proximity to the design.[1] Suitability of design therefore is subject to those circumstances. There is no right design independent of the interventionists' assessments of the situation. If circumstances change such that there is a different mix of people, the decision on suitability of design may change too. For example, Lawrence and Lorsch (1967: 209), concerned about organisational design, talk of the "goodness of fit" of structure and orientation with "the predisposition of members", i.e., their state of mind(s). Design accordingly cannot be independent of debate and many of the findings in the next chapter (about debate) support the process of determining suitable design. The point with this chapter is that we want to encourage and inform debate about design.

To encourage and inform debate about design we bring forward from the previous chapter the graph (see Figure 7.1) contextualised to evaluate designs. The aim in the next two sections is to explore theories about designs in the form of rules of design and their possible relevance to people subject to the rules. Each design has rules that define the degree and nature of structure and operation (Scott, 1992). Rules describe how processes are to proceed and how functions are organised to support processes. "Rules are mechanisms that say how actions from different positions are to be fitted

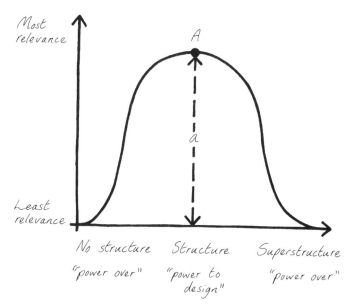

Figure 7.1

[1] As argued in Part 2, local does not exclude awareness of wider issues that help to inform local understanding. This chapter indeed raises awareness through design-relevant discourse. The next two chapters raise awareness through debate-relevant and might–right-relevant discourse.

together; they say what must be done first, and which positions do certain tasks" (Ahrne, 1994: 105). Rules help to achieve reliable results and make planning possible. We want to interpret and assess a range of rules in terms of efficiency and effectiveness, but in the context of power/freedom; although of course no final conclusions can be made here.

"Much research [has been] done to explain different forms [of structure] and find out which are most efficient and/or democratic" (Ahrne, 1994: 20). Our interpretation is a contribution to this debate from a diversity management perspective, helping people to be widely informed. A part of our contribution is to operationalise, by suggesting guidelines, some types of design that remain otherwise abstract in the literature. In essence, we want to spell out the details of a representative set of designs and assess them against the standard proposed in this book.

A simple explanation of the graph in Figure 7.1 in these terms follows. "No structure" leaves people imprisoned by inefficiency. Inefficiency takes away choice. Time has to be spent dealing with the crises of inefficiency restricting opportunities for meaningful choice making and implementation. "Superstructure" on the other hand leaves people imprisoned by efficiency where rules are so tight that there is no scope for meaningful choice. Superstructure in effect makes decisions for people and therefore "resolves" issues. Balanced between no structure and superstructure, "structure" is needed that prioritises freedom for people to make choices. The graph states that design evaluation is about finding degrees and nature of structure, between superstructure and no structure, that people in the circumstances judge maximises freedom and choice and relevance to their needs. (Consult the previous chapter for further theoretical support to our graph.)

As mentioned above, by design we mean two things: organisational design and process design. Organisational design means rules about effectiveness of functions and their organisation. By effectiveness we mean to achieve chosen tasks of functions. Operating within any organisational design are processes. Process design means rules about efficiency of flows and control over flows. By efficiency we mean to work without any unnecessary waste of time or resources. Based on the graph shown in Figure 7.1, the methodology for evaluation of design followed in this chapter is a system to criticise efficiency and effectiveness of designs against the standard proposed in this book. We first turn our attention to organisational design.

7.3 ORGANISATIONAL DESIGN

7.3.1 Introduction

When talking about design models we say that design is a focus on a number of core design issues. The main design issues are hierarchy,[2] role and task definition, division of labour, rule creation, interdependence of roles and tasks, communication, monitoring, co-ordination, control, and flexibility. Our evaluation of design is therefore undertaken broadly in these terms but put into the context of power/freedom and relevance.

A representative selection of designs proposed in the literature is evaluated below with the graph acting as a catalyst for discussion. The designs chosen in order of presentation are bureaucracy, circular organisation, organic organisation, viable system organisation, community organisation and postmodern organisation. Each design is explored in terms of theoretical structure and empirical resonance in cases discussed. A review of the evaluations is given at the end of the chapter. Ultimately we construct a discourse on relevance of designs which is a stimulant for further discussion by users of triple loop learning.

Analysis is built on the premise that we need distinctions between designs and should not homogenise designs through critique and interpretation. It is not our intention to demonstrate that one or more designs are right or wrong. Nor do we wish to suggest that all forms of organisation are possible everywhere. These positions stand against the spirit of diversity management. Rather, the critique and interpretation are part of our attempt to help the reader to be widely informed in local decision making that diversity management advocates.

7.3.2 Bureaucracy: Traditional Hierarchy

Weber (1947) established an ideal type view of bureaucracy as follows.[3] A bureaucratic structure is hierarchically arranged yielding clear division between activities (see Figure 7.2 for three examples). The arrangement represents lines of authority. Authority is both rational and legal. Each person in the hierarchy is subject to a higher authority. This division establishes roles and tasks. Activities follow clearly defined yet general rules that replace the need for continual giving of instructions. The rules include controls and sanctions.

---

[2] There are two aspects of hierarchy that we wish to draw particular attention to: vertical and horizontal. Vertical tends to deal with lines of authority and at which· point on the hierarchy decisions should be made. Horizontal tends to deal with job grouping and task formation.

[3] Weber (1973: 78) argued that "where the bureaucratisation of administration has been completely carried through ... the individual bureaucrat cannot squirm out of the apparatus in which he [sic] is harnessed. ... In the great majority of cases he is only a single cog in an ever moving mechanism ... The official is entrusted with specialised tasks and normally the mechanism cannot be put in motion or arrested by him, but only from the very top." It is for this reason that bureaucracy is associated with vertical hierarchy. Weber (1973: 77) had an ambivalent relationship to the process of bureaucratic rationalisation which he saw as characterising "modern culture". Clearly he saw it as constraining people's meaning-making enterprises and he lamented its rendition of people into cogs in a machine; but he also suggested (Weber, 1973: 77) that it "offers ... the optimum possibility for carrying through the principle of specialising administrative functions according to ... objective considerations" (that is, it allows for the "objective" discharge of business according to calculable rules).

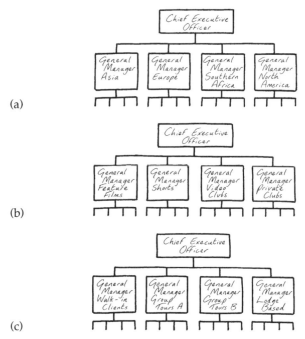

Figure 7.2

Criteria are designed with which to categorise general rules to reflect specific problems as they arise. Employees are trained and therefore skilled, salaried experts. Officials are appointed by a superior or win the job through impersonal competition. Only the most senior positions are elected thus representing the electorate and building-in some flexibility. Performance is monitored.

Weber's intent was to consider the notion of efficiency through bureaucracy but in practice bureaucratisation seems to arise from other processes (Gouldner, 1954: 206). For example, mock-, representative- and punishment-centred bureaucracy have rules imposed from different sources with observed effects.[4] Social processes lead to different degrees of bureaucratisation (Gouldner, 1954: 28). The way that differentially distributed power affects the growth of bureaucratic organisations (or indeed any set of rules of any organisational form) is discussed by Gouldner (1954: 27).

---

[4] Defining characteristics of each form of bureaucracy follow. *Mock*: rules are neither enforced by management nor obeyed by workers; usually entails little conflict between the two groups; joint violation and evasion of rules is buttressed by the informal sentiments of the participants. *Representative*: rules are both enforced by management and obeyed by workers; generates a few tensions, but little overt conflict; joint support for rules buttressed by informal sentiments, mutual participation, initiation, and education of workers and management. *Punishment-centred*: rules either enforced by workers or management, and evaded by the other; entails relatively great tension and conflict; enforced by punishment and supported by the informal sentiments of either workers or management (Gouldner, 1954: 216–217).

Case Study

In 1989 a strategic decision was made by the department of Management Systems and Sciences (MSS) at the University of Hull, UK, to launch a unique (critical) systems-based MBA course at a number of sites internationally. The purpose was complex, but briefly the main aim was to generate additional income that would support an expanding research activity in MSS while securing a strong position for MSS in the University as a main source of additional revenue. The project was spearheaded by Bob Flood. In 1995 the business grossed over £6 million. MSS enjoyed about £1 million of that. Departmental money is invested in ten full-time researchers (mainly in the Centre for Systems Studies), research students, additional lecturers who share the teaching load and a local administrative team who bear the burden of departmental administration relieving academics who therefore have more time for research.

The business was established on informal rules with only financial and quality control arrangements spelled out along the following lines. To arrange business locally, private commercial agencies were set up in nine countries outside of the UK, each taking a share of the gross. All seminars are offered in the country in which the student resides. Lecturers concerned are paid for this voluntary additional work. Air travel, hotel accommodation and living expenses are covered. A quality control system audits performance of agencies, lecturers and university administration. All these procedures were established by MSS and the agencies. University procedures for academic control were implemented.

In 1990 the business grossed about £1.5 million. By 1992 this had risen to £3 million. 1994 saw the gross income at around £5.5 million. As stated above this has now risen to over £6 million. By any standards this is a rapid growth although growth has tailed off for reasons explained below. The adhocratic (see Section 7.3.4) nature of the business alongside the rapid growth led to a number of core issues. Resolution of these issues has come in the form of centralisation and bureaucratisation. The form of hierarchy now in place reflects Gouldner's (1954) punishment-centred bureaucracy. This case study explains some of the reasons for this shift and discusses the consequences of the shift for the business and for those involved in the business.

We accept that this case reports the way that Bob Flood experienced events and that there may be other interpretations of events. Nevertheless, the case provides a discussion with which the reader may engage, thus stimulating discourse on the matter of relevance of rules to those involved and affected by them.

The initial adhocratic[5] structure operated according to a relatively small

[5] Adhocracy is a term used for a form of organic organisation, which is discussed in Section 7.3.4.

number of crucial rules about finances and quality as already mentioned. Co-ordination, intelligence gathering and policy setting was undertaken less formally as and when strengths and weaknesses were identified in the operations, or opportunities and threats were perceived in the operational environment. There was no formal meeting structure. Discussions were held by fax/phone or when Bob visited the location in question. Issues were debated over a meal or in a bar and future arrangements agreed upon and implemented straight away. The operation was very flexible and dynamic. There was a strong entrepreneurial spirit in MSS with new initiatives being proposed at every departmental meeting. The business ran and expanded reasonably smoothly with only a few hiccups; a consequence of the complex nature of the operation (dealt with quite well by the flexible design of the adhocracy) rather than a lack of rules and procedures. There was an informal understanding between Bob and the agencies that led those proximal to the cause of any problem to deal with it. Sometimes this understanding broke down and there were squabbles about who was responsible for the problem and who should clear it up, suggesting that a few rules and procedures directed at such incidents might have been appropriate.

Those involved directly in the adhocracy were highly motivated. The informal structure gave space in which decisions could be made quickly by those closely involved in them and allowed for necessary flexibility in a highly competitive market. Confusion sometimes occurred, however, when entrepreneurial activities were launched from other departments at the University of Hull, widening the adhocratic activities. These tended to be much smaller operations piggy-backing the large-scale business operating from MSS. However, the lack of co-ordination between initiatives led to a growth in the number of agencies at each site. This gave rise to confusion in the minds of potential clients, about the quality of an operation from Hull University that created (sometimes aggressively) competing agencies in single locations. Some agencies attempted to sabotage the operations of others, for example.

Central administration of the University of Hull permitted activities to carry on in this way. There was some tension between MSS and central administration since the new operations rarely conformed to university rules and procedures. For example, the Academic Registrar's office was geared up to deal with applications and entries at the start of the new academic year only. The operation from MSS involved start ups in the different locations any time a viable uptake number was achieved. There was a clear lack of understanding on both sides that was partially resolved by installing new procedures better co-ordinating Central Administration and MSS. Nevertheless, all negotiations and arrangements for the activity remained in the hands of MSS and the local agencies, including things such as credit control over the agencies resulting in rapid collection of debts (preventing accounts extending beyond 30 days).

In 1993 there was a turnover in many of the senior positions in Central Administration. This included the Vice Chancellor, the Registrar and Secretary, and the Academic Registrar. A contrasting brand of administration was installed. New policies saw increasing centralisation and colonisation of power over the operations by Central Administration. A revamped university-wide meeting structure was established and increasingly new rules were created and enforced. A series of committees was set up to oversee operations such as MSS's. A battery of audits was undertaken as directed by Central Administration to discover how the operation worked and how it was (assumed to be) "failing". This was the tone of the interest shown and investigation carried out.

Many new rules were implemented that have removed the possibility for direct dialogue between MSS and the agencies. These are keeping people like Bob away from the agencies (a sort of grounding of departmental staff) and hand over all strategic and policy responsibility to a small group of people at the centre of Central Administration. The aim was twofold: to coordinate better and harmonise activities, and for the university to vet possible agencies thus increasing their control over them. These rules seemed increasingly necessary by Central Administration as the size of the operation grew and adhocratic conflicts arose. The standing of MSS also posed a perceived threat to Central Administration because of its potency given the resources that it controlled.

Establishment of centralising rules massively slowed down operational processes. New initiatives in the first two or three years following the launch of operations took about three to six months to pass through necessary committees before being accepted at Senate. This slipped to nine months and longer. When Central Administration made its main bid for control it imposed a moratorium on all new activities, meaning initiatives were frozen for over 18 months. In addition credit has grown massively with over £0.5 million owed to the University in mid 1995. This led to despair in MSS and significantly damaged the standing of the business in a highly competitive and changing market place. Central Administration considered this cost to be acceptable given wider issues such as the University's reputation overseas.

The new arrangement can be likened to elements of Weber's (1947) ideal-type view of bureaucracy. The organisational structure has become increasingly hierarchical. A clearer distinction is made between Central Administration at the top and the departments lower down, leading to division of roles and tasks, for example, through colonisation of control by Central Administration. Lines of authority have become clearer and stricter. Activities have been proceduralised.

This new bureaucratic arrangement can be meaningfully contextualised through Gouldner's (1954) punishment-centred bureaucracy. Rules now are enforced by Central Administration and evaded as far as possible by departments such as MSS. Central Administration enforce them because of growing concern about control over the operations and consequences for the University such as its damaged reputation and impact on overseas recruitment if the operations went wrong. Departments like MSS avoid the rules because they feel they rigidify operations, taking away flexibility and killing the entrepreneurial spirit. Not surprisingly this has led to great tension and conflict between Central Administration and departments like MSS. The rules are increasingly enforced by punishment with memos being circulated, for example, that warn of grievance procedures that will be implemented if the rules are not adhered to. The rules are supported by the informal sentiments of Central Administration as a whole.

The impact of these new design arrangements in terms of their relevance to MSS can possibly be measured by the level of new entrepreneurial activity. As mentioned above, in the early days of the business new initiatives were being launched at every departmental meeting. It is now 18 months since the last initiative was launched. A conscious decision has been made to concentrate on existing business and, in the language of strategic management, "to milk the cash cow" while alternative means of support are pursued for research activities. The growth curve of the business reflects more closely the changing nature of the internal organisational design rather than a "natural life-cycle". The perceived lack of freedom and choice in MSS has led to a sense of irrelevance in the arrangements and to giving up on this particular operation.[6]

Discourse About Relevance

In this discourse we provide an extended discussion that sets out many general points of debate about relevance of design as well as crucial ones specific to bureaucracy. The general points will be referred to in subsequent discourse about alternative forms of design although not elaborated on at that point.

One of the benefits of structure in terms of extensive systems of rules advocated by bureaucratic structures is that (in principle) they make operations clear cut. They are all-encompassing, leaving no room for ambiguity. This should then enhance reliability since the operations are not frivolous. Memos and statements actually help organisational members since everyone knows where they stand. This was clearly an intention behind Central Administration's bureaucratisation of the MBA operation discussed in the case above.

---

[6] There is a double irony here from MSS's viewpoint. First, that the rules put in place undermined the health of the business. Second, that the rules removed from the process of management of the business those who are employed by the University to be so-called experts about management and business.

Rules also reduce favours that people may receive when rules are not clear cut and do not cover proceedings and functions in total. The bureaucratisation of the MBA activities certainly surfaced this issue. Although nothing sinister went on, there were undoubted favours shown to those who provided support in MSS's resistance to bureaucratisation. In more extreme cases rules can make corruption explicit as seen in the case of a large tourism company discussed in *Systems Practice* by Flood and Zambuni (1990; a case detailed in Chapter 10).

Rule-bound organisations in principle enable customers (internal and external) to know what they will receive by way of products, services and/or information. However, clear and all-encompassing rules can reduce flexibility and therefore hinder efforts to conclude negotiations with customers about what they want, especially when they prefer something new. Rules facilitate co-ordination but tend to make organisation less flexible (Perrow, 1986: 20–26). There is a danger that people may experience bureaucracy as superstructure rather than structure.

Bureaucracy is sometimes criticised as serving only the purpose of those who set up the organisation. A counter-argument demonstrates that it *is* possible for people to participate in rule changes and even organisational purpose. The process though is very slow as the hierarchy comes in to play. People feel distant and uninvolved. Distance and slowness kill innovation, creativity and, ultimately, effectiveness. Arguably this is how key players in MSS in the case above experienced the process of bureaucratisation. Things were experienced in Merton's (1964) terms as bureaupathic.

One difficulty encountered when operating rules is that it is easy to forget the spirit of the rule, or even purpose of the organisation, in an obsession to ensure that the rules are implemented without exception. A rule on equality, for example, might in some circumstances create inequality if implemented literally without exception. Sticking with universities, rules that define duration of examinations (say, exactly three hours) mean that all people have an equal amount of time, but this does assume that equally capable people can make equal progress in that time. Certain factors mean that in some cases this is not true. For example, some overseas students studying in the UK speak English as a second language and could not possibly meet their potential in a fixed-time examination in the same way that a home student is able to. Again, rules may lead to a sense of superstructure. This issue can be accentuated by bureaucrats who find pleasurable precise and careful implementation of systems of rules.

When a system of rules is (too) complex the organisation can get easily bogged down – as people become preoccupied with getting them to work, spending a large proportion of time in monitoring activity. Because so much time is spent defining and monitoring rule-following, this opens the way in politicised environments for tactical exploitation on the part of those who wish to use the system to pursue their own agendas. They take advantage of the complexity – which offers them a smoke screen behind which to operate tactically (to their own advantage). Rules therefore are not guaranteed to be reliable after all. Large numbers of rules often require or introduce a policing mentality that can distract efforts away from the declared organisational purpose.

Being subject to a higher authority encourages decision making and responsibility to flow up the hierarchy. Only those at the top feel responsible for decisions made. Senior management have to carry the entire burden of responsibility and thus become governors and police. Decisions are made far away from the point of action without availability of necessary information. Those who have to implement decisions at the point of action see them as obscure rather than relevant (certainly how MSS experienced bureaucratisation in the preceding case). Implementers do not take ownership over decisions made in this way thus accentuating the need for further policing (often undertaken by establishment of yet more rules requiring yet more policing – what we might call creeping superstructure). Furthermore, the flow upwards in a pyramidal structure leads to information overload at the top making it difficult for senior managers to sort it out and relate it to issues they are tackling. In some cases this can cause organisational paralysis. The top of the pyramid becomes like a black hole – it receives calls, memos and requests for discussion, but these all disappear into the black hole, which remains silent except for the instructions it initiates on its own accord.

Bureaucracy is to some extent mechanistic. It does not recognise organic interaction of subsystems and therefore loses opportunities for efficiency by forcing verticalness. It misses opportunities offered by horizontal functioning, for example, that permits and therefore makes effective communication across levels in the organisation.

A superstructural incident of bureaucracy is that it creates the organisational person who is a slave to the rules (Whyte, 1972). The hierarchy often has accountability in one direction only – upwards. It sometimes tries to make people responsible downward without giving authority, raising fear and suspicion among the workforce. It does, however, provide a clear career structure, although this has a tendency to encourage departmental mindedness rather than organisational mindedness. These factors, among others, can lead to conflict but also mean that conflict resolution technology does not exist.

Weber's aim was to define an ideal type bureaucratic structure as a form of human organisation. Despite much criticism the bureaucratic form has remained extremely resilient for around a century and may in some way show a technical superiority over other forms. It offers a clear form of co-ordination and control, especially needed by very large organisations. It offers standardisation and continuity. But it has a tendency toward superstructure because excessive rules reduce freedom of choice, minimising relevance to organisational members who are subject to those rules. Authority and specialisation suppress freedom (Ahrne, 1994: 96). Many of the positive ideas of bureaucracy in practice have been found to get in the way of efficiency and effectiveness. Relying on a system of rules for co-ordinating performances may mean that people's involvement in redefining appropriate performance is hampered. Furthermore, as explained above, it may open more space for unfairness, especially if very complex, that it is ideally meant to minimise as people find ways of utilising loopholes to serve own interests.

The circular organisation is one attempt to keep alive the promises of efficiency and effectiveness through hierarchy, while eradicating some of the tendencies of bureaucracy toward superstructure.

7.3.3 Circular Organisation: Democratic Hierarchy

A description of the circular organisation was published by Ackoff (1981) and is subsequently explained in the context of democratic organisation (Ackoff, 1994). The circular organisation is in fact a democratic hierarchy. It is a form of organisation that is meant to cater for more active contribution of people in co-defining their involvement in the organisation. It has "three essential characteristics: (1) the absence of an ultimate authority; (2) the ability of each member to participate directly or through representation in all decisions that affect him or her directly; and (3) the ability of members, individually or collectively, to make and implement decisions that affect no-one other than the decision-maker or decision-makers" (Ackoff, 1994: 117).[7]

The main structural characteristic of a circular organisation is the board, i.e. a body of people from a local area in the organisation (see Figure 7.3). Every person in a position of authority is a compulsory member of their own board. Each board, except the ones at the top and bottom of the hierarchy, has "the following [voluntary] minimal membership: the manager whose board it is, that manager's immediate subordinates, and that manager's immediate superior" (Ackoff, 1994: 118). Any board may, as seen fit, add members from within or beyond the organisation as long as it improves representation of the principle stakeholders. The number of representatives should not exceed the number of subordinates, thus maintaining a majority with the latter.

Boards at the lowest level of the hierarchical organisation should include all their subordinates. "All employees should have an opportunity to serve on their immediate superior's board" (Ackoff, 1994: 121). If the number of

---

[7] It is difficult to accept Ackoff's third point since complexity in social situations makes it impossible to determine total consequences of decisions. It is impossible to contain consequences of decisions.

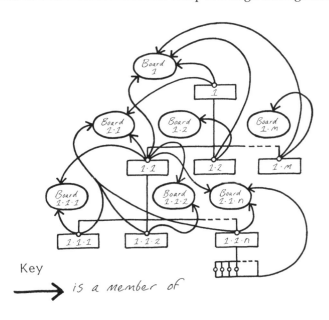

Key

→ is a member of

Figure 7.3

subordinates is too large for all to serve on one board, they should be divided into semi-autonomous work groups. Each group selects a leader who reports to the lowest level manager. The leader has a board comprising themselves, the lowest level manager and all members of the group.

There are six responsibilities of each board: (1) to plan for the unit whose board it is; (2) to make policy for the unit whose board it is; (3) to co-ordinate plans and policies of the immediately lower level; (4) to integrate plans and policies – its own and those immediately below it – with those made at higher levels; (5) to improve the quality of work life of the subordinates of the board; and (6) to enhance and evaluate the performance of the manager whose board it is. Each board designs their own operating procedures.

Case Study

The case on circular organisation is taken from Lartin-Drake and Curran (1996) and Lartin-Drake *et al* (1996); both papers can be found in *Systems Practice* (Volume 9). The authors work in Penn State's Herschey Medical Center, Pennsylvania. They have experienced significant change in health care and have witnessed the transformation of hospitals. Within this scheme of things they and their colleagues decided to place extra focus on improving patient care. A second goal was to create an institution that would provide a high quality of work life for all. Barriers they identified included a lack of co-ordinating mechanisms between nurses and physi-

cians detrimental to patient care, a high degree of fragmentation, devalua-
tion of the contributions of ancillary staff, and problems created by a
bureaucracy experienced as unwieldy.

The interventionists reached an impasse. They struggled to come up with
an agreed plan to meet their goals. Russell Ackoff was invited to talk to them
about his circular organisation. The interventionists became more widely
informed by his presentation. After debate about design a well-considered
decision was made to implement a form of circular organisation. The circular
organisation was appealing because the interventionists saw it com-
plementing the existing hierarchy. They thought the primary benefits
would be an increase in productivity, speedy decision making, and
improved employee satisfaction.

Lartin-Drake and her co-workers decided that boards should be designed
around populations of patients rather than managers and departments in
order to co-ordinate patient care. This would help to deal with the complexity of internal and external stakeholders. It would tackle perceived fragmentation of care. The planners began the process of inventing a version of
the circular organisation to take into account key aspects of vertical integration and horizontal co-ordination (see footnote 2), with consensus-based
decision making where appropriate.

A version of the circular organisation was implemented that has differences with the account given above. Horizontal co-ordination was considered to be of greater importance than vertical integration because of the
need to improve interdepartmental collaboration (job grouping and task
formation). The focus therefore became patient populations rather than
departments. A three-tiered board system was constructed to cover three
(planning) pilot units: Surgical Unit, Medical Unit, and Pediatric Unit. The
boards were expected to address issues of unit-wide relevance, such as
shared resources and policies. The unit boards also were expected to co-
ordinate the work of three or four service-specific boards working under
the unit boards. Service boards were designed to co-ordinate the care of
patients in each service. Larger services developed their own board. Smaller
ones grouped together to form general service boards such as Children's Surgical Services. A steering committee was also set up to provide the pilot project with a broad, institutional view, to remove barriers, and to assist with
implementation of planned changes. Stakeholders on the service boards
included support (i.e. clerical), clinical (e.g. nurses), administrative (e.g. from
Finance) and ancillary staff (e.g. pharmacists), as well as patient representation.

Board members were made responsible to their colleagues and super-
visor for sharing all information, such as sharing with their board discussions about issues of concern from their constituent groups. This system of
representation provides members of all boards with direct contact with
members of other departments at a variety of levels. Compromises were

made to overcome anticipated unwieldiness with three levels of every group represented on each board. For example, each board chose its own degree of vertical integration (loading down responsibility to the lowest level at which it could be handled). Now let us turn to our discourse about relevance.

Discourse About Relevance

We continue the discourse about relevance of designs started in the previous section. The aim here is to introduce new insights that arise through the circular organisation. Further insights are offered in each of the following sections and the discourse they offer.

The circular organisation enhances people's chances of participating and making a rapid and meaningful contribution. Hierarchy is legitimated through participation (cf. Heckscher, 1994: 35). The circular organisation breaks with strict verticalness by introducing a circular element (although the extent of this has to be determined locally as in our case study). In doing this it introduces more responsibility throughout the organisation. It introduces responsibility by spreading participation, whereas bureaucracy spreads responsibility only in terms of an individual's competency. The circular organisation increases flexibility to respond to changing circumstances, although much still depends on the nature and extent of the governing rules. If they are cumbersome then the democratic process may be stifled.

The circular arrangement therefore overcomes some of the concerns levelled at traditional hierarchy (and creeping superstructure). It does this by adapting the existing dominant structure which allows a greater degree of participation, on issues that within a bureaucracy would have been bounded by position or official function, without causing organisational trauma.[8] As Lartin-Drake and co-workers state in our case study, the circular organisation can be seen to complement traditional hierarchy rather than radically overhaul it. Organisational trauma can occur when radical change is made. The possible downside to this is that the circular organisation does not break totally from traditional hierarchy and may (as a sort of default) experience some of the issues discussed in the preceding section (avoidance of

---

[8] Ackoff and co-workers (1974, 1978, 1981; Ackoff *et al*, 1984) recognise the importance of debate in the process of design. It is, however, not clear from his writings thus far whether he believes that the circular design proposed is to be regarded as a prerequisite for debate itself or whether this question is left in abeyance, to be decided by participants *in situ*. It is also not clear whether debate about design could justifiably lead to other design suggestions being seen (at times) as more relevant. When discussing the importance of debate as a process of participation, Ackoff and co-workers recommend a process labelled Interactive Planning (incorporating Idealised Design) which at a methodological level parallels Soft Systems Methodology (Checkland, 1981; Checkland and Scholes, 1990). We have chosen to review the last of the two in Chapter 8 because the originators relate their work to action research which forms the core discussion in Chapters 8 and 9. One account of Interactive Planning, including a brief description of it, is presented in Chapter 10.

superstructure is not guaranteed). It could even be suggested that the circular organisation is a rather conservative response to worries about traditional hierarchy.

Despite these worries about hierarchy, our interventionists report positively about the circular organisation. For example, they gained from the assurance it offers that ideas and proposed solutions will not die based on one person's (or group's) authorisation to refuse their (potential) significance. They gained from enhanced effectiveness achieved through incorporation of the viewpoints of many stakeholders. They gained from better communication. They found the circular organisation elegant in design, although its implementation proved challenging. Overall, they found the circular organisation offered a relevant angle on the issues to be dealt with. Another angle on organisational design, one that has dominated the literature for many years, is the organic organisation.

7.3.4 Organic Organisation

Burns and Stalker (1961) identified two radically different management styles: mechanistic (along the lines of traditional hierarchy) and organic.[9] They observed organic adaptive and evolutionary styles most often when the organisation faced rapid technological change and market change. Stable circumstances favoured forms of operation characterised by standardised procedures and standardised outputs.

Roots of the organic view are extensive. Barnard (1938) dealt with the nature of organisations as systems; in fact co-operative systems. Efficiency and effectiveness of systems can only be achieved through interaction between people managed by formal and informal structures. The role of executives is central. Executives must establish a sound structure for the organisation and make people aware of it and, indeed, bring them into a co-operative relationship with it. Organisational purpose is formulated and instilled at all levels.

Selznick (1948) developed this traditional systems approach looking at subsystems essential for survival and effectiveness of organisations as systems. The discussion was strongly organic with organisations being adaptive systems primarily oriented to survival. Organisations had needs to be met if survival is to be achieved and so it is essential that parts co-operate.

Parsons and Smelser's (1956) research identified four essential organisational subsystems. Subsystems are needed: to maintain a relationship with the environment (an adaptation system); to mobilise resources to meet defined goals (a goal attainment system); to co-ordinate activities (an integration system); and to motivate members of the organisation to aspire to adaptation, goal attainment and co-ordination (a latency system). The

[9] Recent literature that has influenced many executives includes the organic view argued for by Peters and Waterman (1982) in their famous *In Search of Excellence*.

systems view was developed as a general theory by Bertalanffy (1955) and others as discussed in Section 4.2.

Contingency theory (e.g. Woodward, 1958; Burns and Stalker, 1961; Lawrence and Lorsch, 1967; and Perrow, 1986) which is dominant in organisation theory today is based on theoretical breakthroughs made by traditional systems thinking. The argument accepts organisations as sets of interacting subsystems open to an environment, but denies the notion of one best way to structure activities in all circumstances. Contextual factors influence structure since they pose constraints. The core idea of contingency theory is that certain forms of organisation are more effective than others in given circumstances.

Tying all these views together we can define the basic notion of an organic organisation. An organisation is a system that comprises subsystems. It is open to its environment and must therefore adapt and change in order to survive and to aspire to organisational goals. Some advocates of the organic model see the system influencing its environment (e.g. networking). The organic view promotes a need for broad commitment to organisational goals from employees. Division of labour is informal and flexible. The organisation is team based, adaptable and less rule bound than bureaucracy. Communication is based on horizontal task-related needs, not a vertical hierarchy. Situational authority is more important than formal authority and so influence (power) depends much more on the contribution a person can make to managing issues rather than formal authority (Khandwalla, 1977). Duties and responsibilities are therefore shaped by situational demand. Interactions tend to ignore departmental boundaries and channels of communication do not follow any so-called organisational chart. The organisation comprises small face-to-face groups of mature people attuned to the big picture through meetings, briefings, teleconferencing, etc. There is sapiential floating authority (as and when expertise is needed) with a person or group responsible for articulating and maintaining focus and vision. The organisation is a collective effort (Banner and Gagné, 1995: 189–191). The less rule-bound, more informal, organic organisation not surprisingly was named adhocracy by Mintzberg (1979).

Recent developments in organic thought include flattening the organisation. Flat organisations encourage decentralisation and an increased scope of operational authority at lower levels. Managers are put back to work instead of doing "management jobs" only offered to them because organisations need a structure to reward them for excellent operational performance. The aim is to tighten up, to eliminate slack and to reduce layers of hierarchy. Cutting out hierarchy, however, poses new challenges in maintaining organisational integrity. Networking is one solution promoted widely in the literature (e.g. Banner and Gagné, 1995: 183–186).

Networking replaces hierarchy and bureaucracy – the horizontal link replaces the vertical one (see Figure 7.4). The replacement is vertical dis-aggregation of business functions or compartments (such as finance, marketing and product design; Miles and Snow, 1986). Business functions are treated as independent organisations that are networked using egalitarian methods (Naisbitt, 1982). Methods include internal and external brokering where there is subcontracting for services, or facilitation among specialisations with equal standing. Brokering provides co-ordination, supervision and control of projects and contracts. Responsiveness to needs of customers and other stakeholders substitutes for many administrative mechanisms so that the organisation is bounded by market forces rather than formalised structures and plans. Networking also entails full disclosure through information systems, for example, Local Area Networks that link independent organisations enabling instant checking and eradication of duplication. Networks can be thought of as federations without hierarchy (Heckscher, 1994: 34) or a web of negotiated relations.

Along with flatter organisations and extensive networking, a recent development within the organic tradition is compartmentation (Fairtlough, 1994). Compartmentation is a key concept in biology, since all life is organised in cells. Molecules diffuse freely throughout a biological cell, and the same applies to information within an organisational compartment. Complete openness aims to build trust among a compartment's members, starting a virtuous circle of openness and trust. Likewise, if the compartment's members are fully involved in setting the compartment's goals, a virtuous circle of empowerment and commitment may develop, meshing with the circle of openness and trust.

Complete openness is not possible beyond a certain scale because the information to be shared becomes too extensive to handle. Thus, if virtuous circles are to develop, the compartment must have no more than a few hundred people. The aim is to build an assemblage of skills and knowledge within a compartment of this size, providing the potential to do extraordinary things. This may be achieved when there are more-or-less common purposes, fair and rotated distribution of tasks, a shared language and set of concepts, and a clear boundary to the compartment.

Compartments are restricted in scale, which means they cannot tackle certain large tasks. For large tasks compartments can build themselves into networks and the whole network is then capable of much bigger undertakings. This self-organised co-operation between compartments needs well-developed boundary-spanning skills.

Large organisations can transform themselves into networks of creative compartments in a five-stage process: (1) development of communication, interpersonal processes and goal definition skills; (2) compartmentation of tasks; (3) establishment of networking and critique; (4) change of legal status, with compartments becoming subsidiaries of the parent organ-

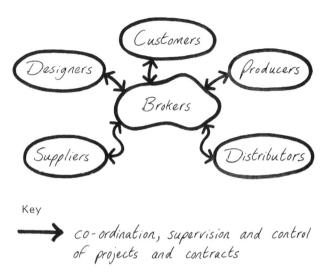

Key

→ co-ordination, supervision and control
of projects and contracts

Figure 7.4

isation; and (5) local choice of leadership (Fairtlough, 1994: 188–190). Large organisations can alternatively form temporary creative compartments, each with great autonomy, as Japanese firms do for major projects (Nonaka and Takeuchi, 1995). The case study that follows concentrates on compartmentation and networking (other organic forms such as adhocracy feature in earlier case studies).

Case Study

In 1980, a biotechnology company, Celltech Group plc, was founded in the UK with the co-operation of the UK Medical Research Council, who had made many of the basic discoveries on which the new technology depended. Since then, Celltech has developed a range of innovative biopharmaceutical products and now has a quotation on the London Stock Exchange, with a market capitalisation of over £300 million. Staff numbers are now over 400, being mostly scientifically qualified people. Celltech is a network of a few creative compartments. The company has remained independent, in spite of being a possible takeover target for pharmaceutical firms.

The founder CEO of Celltech was Gerard Fairtlough. He reckoned that a new company such as Celltech would need a new organisational form. Creative compartmentation was thus born. Fairtlough's management team set out to share all information with everyone in the firm, including doubts and difficulties. Everyone's voice would be heard on any issue. Early on, with fewer than 50 people, the mechanics of information sharing were easy; except that staff who had come from organisations where secrecy was the norm found openness hard to handle. They were afraid of being penalised for mistakes. Once openness and trust began to reinforce each other, people stopped withholding information as a power play and entered into the spirit of Celltech as a creative compartment.

The integrity of Celltech as a creative compartment is exemplified in the following anecdote. In 1989 Celltech's largest shareholder got into financial difficulties. This kind of situation would often trigger a takeover bid. The Board of Directors, however, kept this information secret from the outside world for about three weeks. Everyone in the company was given the information in confidence even though it would have been hot news for any financial journalist. The secret was kept because of the high level of trust among the 400 people in the company.

In its early years, Celltech's technological innovation (creativity) depended on its project management system (Fairtlough, 1989). Anyone could champion a potential project. A team of experienced scientists and business people gave support to the self-appointed champions in developing their ideas into candidate projects. To become a candidate, a candidate recruit had to pass through a decision gate. The gate was a review undertaken by the management group. Some weeks later the champion returned a better defined candidate project to the next decision gate. If it passed this review it became a fully resourced project with a budget of £250,000 or more. Although management controlled this system of decision gates, proposed decisions were justified to everyone in the firm enabling employees to challenge them before implementation. Celltech's scientific creativity depended heavily on this unconstrained communication.

Celltech competes in drug discovery with major pharmaceutical companies. To do so needs resources beyond those of a small compartmental arrangement. Resources tapped into include academia, other small-scale firms, and, on a selected basis, pharmaceutical majors. Organising these collaborations required strong networking and boundary-spanning capabilities. Communication across compartmental boundaries is inevitably less open than within a compartment itself. However, creative compartments are skilled in goal setting and communication and for these reasons are well adapted to networking. Celltech, for example, was able to build co-operative relations with key academic groups and with other businesses that in some cases have endured for a decade or more. One example is the development of anti-cancer products based on engineered antibodies. This required transatlantic co-operation between Celltech, a pharmaceutical major, and five academic groups. The creativity and productivity of this networked group underpinned the success of the development.

Discourse About Relevance

With adhocracies there is a danger that the setting of goals becomes opaque and distant because of informality. People do not really know what is going on. This can increase internal battles and reduce understanding and dialogue (Heckscher, 1994: 33–34). There is not enough structure and so people may experience diminished choice-making possibilities.

For other reasons adhocracies may not be as relevant as bureaucracies. In stable environments adhocracies are more subject to loss of focus or excessive costs. A counter-view is that team-based work leads to flexible problem solving (Heckscher and Donnellon, 1994: 9). The case in Section 7.3.2 gives some support to the counterview, but only for the circumstances of that case (i.e. in that case people like Bob experienced the arrangements as a structure that at least satisfied freedom and choice to a large extent and was relevant to MSS's needs). Furthermore, adhocracies see traditional organisational boundaries as artificial and flexible. This tractability has advantages, for example improving responsiveness to customers (internal or external). It enhances adaptability that may be necessary when the operational environment is turbulent.

Organic organisation suggests federation. Federations may cater for individual freedom, but with federations how do organisational members develop overall strategy? Who sets the rules? Who makes choices and how is relevance attained? This ambiguity increases chances of internal squabbles (a flavour of this is evident in the case in Section 7.3.2). Also, the organic form lacks a method of reflection that is necessary for people if they are to evaluate whether in their view the organisation works and what their relation is to the whole. And organic organisation seems to do little to increase dialogue among parts of the organisation or create a system of collective experimentation (Heckscher, 1994: 29). Networking, however, makes some structural provision for dealing with these (ongoing) issues.

Compartmentation is exemplified in our case study. It encourages technical specialisation and distinctive competencies within and between compartments. There is an interdependence between compartments. There is a low level of supervision which creates space for people to participate in decision making about their own duties and tasks, the way work is organised and carried out, making all these more relevant for those who carry them out. Participation is based on results, since results are made public, encouraging accountability which secures trust. In this way participation is made responsible.

However, if a combination of compartmentation and networking is as effective as the case study above suggests, then why have so few organisations followed the example of Celltech? Clegg (1989) suggests that it is difficult to initiate new organisational forms because organisations imitate each other, so that once a pattern gets established it is hard for a rival pattern to get a serious trial. Furthermore, because the prevailing pattern suits those in official power very well, they are likely to strive to perpetuate it.

Organisational design is intertwined nowadays with the management of information technology and the location of judgement in managerial decision making (Konsynski and Sviokla, 1994: 102–104). Standardisation reduces the need for continuous flows of information reducing the problem of co-ordination. It allows for wider spans of control but, as mentioned above, may be less desirable if an environment is heterogeneous since flexibility is reduced. Also, when information needs are low then there is less need for a hierarchy. If information needs are high then a hierarchy can get overloaded and so flat organisations may be more appropriate (Scott, 1992; Woodward, 1965). The amount of structure necessary to resolve such issues, so that structure is relevant to the needs of people operating within it, can only be determined by those people participating in debate about relevance (the theme of the next chapter).

As information science has grown so too has the need to adapt and develop theories that respond to those changes. One such development is the viable system organisation. This form of organisation may be regarded as a new form of organic enterprise – which places much emphasis on "intelligence" (information needs and information flows).

7.3.5 Viable System Organisation

One cybernetic approach to organisational design "with intelligence" is the Viable System Model (VSM; Beer, 1981, 1985, 1989; Espejo and Harnden, 1989; Espejo and Schwaninger, 1993; *Systems Practice*, Volume 2, Issue 3). The model brings together five key management functions and organises them according to a carefully worked-out series of information flows and communications.

The functions are: operations, co-ordination, control, intelligence, and policy. The types of flow and communication are: lines of command and control, audit channels, vital information about issues faced in the operations, and vital information about opportunities and threats in the organisation's environment (see Figure 7.5). The information flowing around the communication channels in the model is information about how the different parts of the organisation, and the organisation as a whole, are performing in relation to their respective goals.

Broadly speaking the model separates out the main operations and specifies the relationship between the operations and the four management functions that serve them. The operations comprise a number of divisions (a, b and c in Figure 7.5) with their operational managers. Operations with their own management are the primary activity of the organisation. Each division is

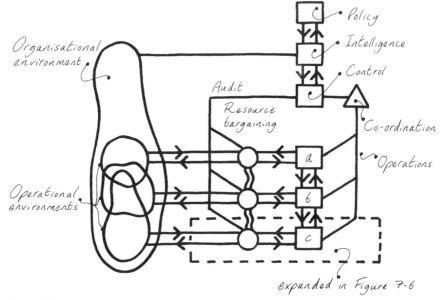

Figure 7.5

considered to be a viable entity in its own right. Viability here means that the division holds some guarantee of continuity. The divisions are serviced through four management functions. These are, from above: co-ordination, control, intelligence, and policy.

"Co-ordination" is directed toward an efficient and stable use of resources achieved in a harmonious fashion, i.e. it also attempts to manage conflict. It receives vital information about short-term problems faced in operations. "Control" is an audit and control function that is geared to maintaining relatively stable equilibrium between the interdependent parts. It does this in various ways. Control deals with vital information about problems in operations that co-ordination is not able to cope with. Control manages resource bargaining. Control also audits the divisions in a regular and routine manner. These include operational, quality, and financial audits such as budget reviews. Control action is taken when audits show up operational issues that have not or cannot be dealt with through co-ordination.

The "intelligence" and development function captures information about the total environment of the division. This comprises the internal and external environments. Intelligence is gathered, about the strengths and weaknesses of the internal processes and the opportunities and threats in the external environment. Vital information about strengths, weaknesses, opportunities, and threats are disseminated in the organisation to those who benefit from it. "Policy" deals with strategic decisions and issues of management style. It receives all relevant information about strengths, weaknesses, opportunities, and threats, and on the basis of this information reviews and modifies policy.

The viable system interacts strongly with an *environment*. Information flows from the operations to the operational environments and from intelligence to the system environment are amplifiers. The aim is to influence (control) events in the environment by increasing the diversity of the system's flows into the environment.

Each function *filters variety*. It deals with most of the variety of information flows and communication coming in but passes information on when procedures unique to the function are unable to deal with issues arising from information received. This attenuation prevents data overload occurring in any management function and allows for local autonomy. The five functions together deal comprehensively with all management information. The great variety of (issues pertaining to) information which the organisation faces is systematically absorbed, not only by management functions as already seen, but also by recursive levels.

Recursion means that the whole can be found in the parts. That is, a whole viable system can be found in the parts of a viable system-in-focus, which is itself a part of another viable system (see Figure 7.6). This offers a novel way in which a mission can spill down a business or organisation. A corporate mission is determined by policy ideally using a participatory method that leads to the development of some sort of corporate identity. Submissions are determined locally within the identity of the whole. At higher resolution recursive levels the mission is interpreted and implemented. Using a recursive design helps to avoid the negative effects of coercive structures. Recursion implements through management *function* whereas traditional hierarchy implements by management *authority*.

Recursion, for example, promotes *autonomy*. The parts have as much independence as is possible given the constraints that exist when co-ordinating and controlling to maintain a whole. The viable system organisation allows for *participation* (in terms of functions to be fulfilled). For example, channels for resource bargaining exist between implementation and control. *Vertical loading* is encouraged. This means loading down responsibility to the "lowest level" at which it can be managed. *Task formation* is encouraged to reverse mechanical reductionist tendencies and to produce whole jobs. People then have responsibility over their work. They can determine the needs of their customers and work out for themselves how this can be best achieved. *Job grouping* is encouraged to bring together efforts that are logically related. This would bring together groups of jobs in the manufacturing process, and sales efforts, for example, by geographical location or client type.

Achievement in most organisations is measured in terms of money by

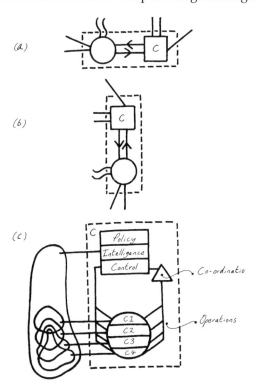

Figure 7.6

those in control; the criteria of success being the extent to which profits are maximised and costs minimised.[10] A traditional approach to *measurement* therefore tends to call upon short-term measures. An example is cost accounting in the form of cost and sales prices and the direction and route of cash flows. The aim is to minimise cost and maximise profit,[11] but ignores long-term control instruments like latent capabilities. An important set of measures that go with the VSM helps to indicate the achievements of the business or organisation. The advocated indices are:

- productivity = actuality/capability
- latency = capability/potentiality
- performance = latency × productivity

[10] It may be more helpful and indeed productive to handle profit as a constraint rather than a goal. In our interventions we introduce and explore this idea. A more meaningful goal can then be negotiated, which most often realises a much richer understanding of the organisation's primary purpose, which in turn improves chances that the profit constraint is met or surpassed. For example, it may be far more productive to think about a pub or bar as serving needs for social satisfaction rather than profit making. Look after social needs in the pub or bar and the profits most likely will look after themselves. This angle on profits accommodates for people who prefer to choose an adequate level of profit rather than demanding an obsession with profit maximisation.

Potentiality is what could be achieved by developing resources and removing constraints. Capability is the possible achievement using existing resources within existing constraints. Actuality is the current achievement with existing resources and constraints. Two ratios can be derived from these; latency and productivity. Performance is then the product of latency and productivity. Let us now focus on one of the many applications of the VSM.

Case Study

A particularly pertinent viable system organisation case study is written up in *Systems Practice* by Walker (1990). The write-up below is abstracted from Walker's article. He recounts an attempt to design an effective organisational structure within the style of co-operative work practices, i.e. maintaining collective responsibility and self-management. The dilemma faced by the co-operative Walker worked with was, on the one hand, the co-operative had experienced rapid growth and needed a system of organisation, yet, on the other hand, "co-operative principles ruled out almost all the usual solutions to organisational problems" (Walker, 1990: 442). Co-operative principles advocate collective responsibility and self-management, not the imposition of a boss who tells people what to do. The Viable System Model seemed to offer a relevant answer "to what was becoming an increasingly pressing problem" (Walker, 1990: 442).

Strategic decision making was undertaken at a weekly meeting of all members (prior to the introduction of a viable system organisation). Given the relatively large number of people the meeting was unwieldy and decision making ineffective. There was a lack of optimisation, future planning, and central co-ordination. The basic operational work ran reasonably well, however, and the work got done. This, Walker argues, was a result of members being free to sort out problems; indeed, they felt it was their responsibility to sort out problems because no one else would.

A decision was made to regroup into small workable units following a series of debates that entailed a viable system diagnosis (employing the VSM in diagnosis mode). Small-group viability was dependent on thorough discussion between all members on all issues. This yields a real-time and complete model of the enterprise. Walker reckoned that the limit of membership for a small group to be effective is between seven and eleven. The small groupings stuck to the departmental structure despite plans to group

[11] In the case study below the redesign of a co-operative using the Viable System Model is considered. Notably, the case concludes on a positive note, and a part of that note is that profits were considered *adequate*. This means, adequate to the members of the co-operative as a whole since such views are realised through collective reasoning. This raises again the issue and importance of debate over all issues relating to design. We look forward to exploring the relevance of debate to matters of design in the next chapter.

departments together. The problem now was how to cohere the small groups into one integrated whole.

In terms of the VSM, setting up small groups introduced a new level of recursion. Reorganisation was needed. "The intermediate level of recursion had to be properly designed as viable, autonomous groups, and then the four . . . [service functions] . . ., which cohere and co-ordinate the small work groups had to be properly articulated" (Walker, 1990: 443). Operational stability through co-ordination was enhanced, Walker argues, by the politics of co-operatives, in which everyone has some commitment to the common good, all wages are the same, and all profits are equally split. This philosophy was consolidated into coherent procedures utilising a good information network as recommended by the VSM. This enabled, for example, goods to be moved backward and forward in a stable manner and smoothed out day-to-day operations.

Control, or internal optimisation, was enhanced by the appointment of a Finance Officer and a Personnel Officer. The Finance Officer has been tasked to set budgets, deal with resource bargaining, and provide financial information. The Personnel Officer deals with recruitment, morale, and attempts to improve efficiency by placing people where they are most needed. Other control-type functions are dealt with by "the Hub" (which is discussed later), for example tasking individuals to identify more efficient ways of working together.

The intelligence function was satisfied by establishing a Futures Group. The Futures Group initially formulated a business plan, considered future accommodation, and looked at possible diversification. This function is carried out by three members of the co-operative who meet weekly and present monthly reports to the co-operative via the Hub.

The (self-named) Hub deals with policy. It gathers views and makes decisions accordingly. Large policy issues are dealt with at Quarterly General Meetings of the entire membership. If the Hub works effectively then these meetings are found to be unnecessary.

Indices were established on a trial basis for one division of the new organisation. The overall aim was to demonstrate that each part of the co-operative was doing its job properly hence overcoming possible mistrust. The experiment was successful showing that indices could be quickly worked out at the end of each day providing a real-time record of important factors, and providing daily feedback that helped in the improvement of, for example, productivity (enhancing output using existing resources).[12]

The organisational redesign was not without its problems but enjoyed substantial success. Walker (1990: 449) comments on the success of the pro-

[12] An option and indeed, for some, a co-operative's main purpose is to enhance lifestyle rather than productivity by limiting output pressure on individuals, where individuals recognise that this means taking home less wages.

ject. "I view the application generally as a success. The co-op continues to grow, customers are happy, profits are adequate, and most members find it a good place to work. . . . The Viable System Model enabled us to present a complete and thorough package and, thus, played a crucial role in the development of the co-op." These reflections lead us nicely to discourse about relevance of viable system organisation.

Discourse About Relevance

One criticism levelled at viable system organisation particularly troubling in any debate about emancipatory practice is that it underplays the purposeful role of individuals. In other words, it seems to propose superstructure. The counter-argument is that, to the contrary, a viable system organisation can increase personal freedom and choice. The model requires only as much control over individual freedom as is necessary to maintain cohesiveness in a viable system. The deal is, accept the need for cohesion and enjoy the benefits of cohesion's protection of individual freedom. Control and freedom, it is argued, are not antithetical (Flood and Jackson, 1991a: 112). Much depends on how the relationship between the two is established through debate. (It is relevant in this regard to refer to our graph of design management, and to consider how proposals for design are informed by considering what it means to strive to accomplish structure without superstructure. In this debate, we would suggest that other design options such as those discussed in this chapter would also have to be taken into consideration.)

The appeal by VSM proponents to necessary functions may, indeed, already be considered by some to constitute an (unnecessary) imposition on actors. Furthermore it may be argued that a VSM-type concentration on functions performed may fail to show up undercurrents of resistance, difference and tension that may operate informally. Again we make reference to the need for debate.

A related concern asks, who in a viable system organisation is responsible for determining the purpose of the organisation? Application of the VSM which stuck to its principles would ensure that all participants have a say in the purpose. Policy must represent all people. Then and only then might limitations in the name of cohesion be acceptable (Flood and Jackson, 1991a: 112). Jackson suggests that the model places as much emphasis on surviving within and developing a set of relations as it does upon goal setting and seeking (Jackson, 1991: 119). As noted above, however, it concentrates on these developments through its particular design proposals, which we believe should be placed in the context of debate about design more generally.

Another line of critique is that a viable system organisation is easily corrupted. The effective organisation can be used most effectively to pursue certain interests at the expense of all others. A fair response is that the same sort of argument holds for any design. Corruption is a misuse, in this case, of the VSM and a violation of the principles of viable system organisation.

With a viable system arrangement issues are managed as closely as possible to the point that they occur. There is relative autonomy granted to the parts. Motivation and commitment are increased at lower levels (Jackson, 1991: 118). It encourages self-organisation and frees management to concentrate on systemic functions rather than local control. In many respects the viable system model seeks structure that is relevant to participants – by proposing a design based on a notion of management functions.

The viable system arrangement has four main management support functions. Co-ordination harmonises conflict. Control maintains stability. Intelligence enhances adaptability. Policy balances overall needs between internal and external factors and embodies people's purposes. In these different ways, it is argued, the management functions help to increase local freedom. A postmodern critique, however, argues that the quest for harmony and stability tends to assimilate people, which is oppressive and denies the need for vital differences and tensions in organisation. These are points to which we will return after discussion on community organisation.

7.3.6 Community Organisation

Community-type organisations utilise peer networks structured by the relation to a shared set of values rather than an organic organisation's structuring around broad commitment to goals. They have a strong and unified culture. Shared values lead to control through shared purpose. There is a high level of trust and co-operation. Community organisation often needs a corporate guru as a sort of spiritual head. Structure is found in patterns of behaviour in terms of people's relationship to social rules and practices rather than formal technical rules.

Case Study

A classic account of a community organisation can be found in *Systems Practice* presented by Davies (1988). The story below is abstracted from Davies's article. The organisation is a small retailing firm that has outlets in the southwest of England and in Sweden. The org isation sells goods and wares. It employs about 30 people many of whom are part time and/or temporary. The managing director had previously been a Methodist minister with a strong reputation. Much of his time as a minister was spent in developing countries such as India. On leaving the Church he bought a village shop in Somerset, England. From the shop he sold furnishings and objets d'art purchased from developing countries. His purpose was to support developing countries economically rather than through aid by providing retail outlets for goods they produced. To help the process he set up and trained mediators in developing countries where his goods were purchased. This was his vision, one that enthused those working with him.

The managing director was able to direct those around him by expressing his beliefs. He was a visionary and a charismatic leader. He ruled by preaching his vision and by drawing upon his charismatic personality. Personnel with whom he had contact declared total commitment to his vision. A chain of stores was established through which he hoped to spread his vision.

The managing director was in effect a designer, an artist and an entrepreneur. This coterie of talents, Davies (1988: 19) points out, worked well while the business was small and local. As it developed and grew he had to become a financier and an administrator. He was not keen on these roles nor did he have the expertise to meet the demands that they set. Indeed, he felt that his talents as a designer, artist and entrepreneur were wasted in his administrative duties.

The organisation's finances slipped into an unhealthy state. There was no coherent and adaptive pricing policy. Each of the outlets was run by a manageress appointed by the managing director (and committed to his vision). The outlets were run as retail centres, not profit centres. The managing director made clear that it was immoral to take a profit as such from developing countries. Pricing and costing policies and the analysis of profit were directed from central headquarters. In his obsession with mediating developing countries' economic development the managing director neglected management of his own organisation's economic development.

Many of the manageresses were part time and so had little opportunity to visit the headquarters. The managing director occasionally but increasingly rarely visited them because of ever growing demands on his time. The manageresses were frustrated with a large amount of paperwork and the (recent) formal interaction only with headquarters and other shops. The whole management operation had developed into crisis management. Morale had become low but a commitment to the vision kept things going.

In the case, Davies describes her problem-solving efforts and reports some successes. After the case she draws out a number of insights highly relevant to our discussion. She explored the organisational culture and concluded that a useful image of it was an ideology-managing system. The ideology virtually replaced formal design.[13] The organisational structure was found in patterns of behaviour in terms of people's relationship to social rules and practices rather than formal technical rules. The ideology and its focus on non-profit making, however, made profit management a difficult issue, to the extent that it was not managed. There were other

[13] Design principles *can* accommodate ideology, as long as it can be seen as a design solution and treated scientifically as a form of design for living together.

problems too. Managerial tasks were not being delegated. Individuals felt isolated despite their common ideological beliefs. The corporate culture dominated everything. Davies suggested that hierarchy and communication could be brought into action to resolve some of these issues, suggesting this could be managed through subcultures that localised issues and ways of managing them (although she did not elaborate on this innovation).

Discourse About Relevance

The community organisation gives a common focus to all and a sense of specialness, as distinguished from other cultures. The case above provides a classic example of such "an ideology-managing system". With community organisation, however, it is very difficult to exert effective evaluation and discipline because there is little technical discipline. There is a danger that in some ways people will experience insufficient structure for them to implement effectively the chosen ideology.

The case above illustrates well the impact of an absence of technical or managerial discipline. The ideology was dominant and left no space for even basic rules of operation. Strategic flexibility was restricted by a set of corporate values. Informal relations held things together whereas formal roles emerged from the informal system. The shared vision just about kept things together but, as Davies (1988: 18) points out, the organisation was on the brink of financial disaster. There was too much dependence on the leader (cf. Heckscher, 1994: 30–32). Despite the highly relevant ideology that the employees shared with the leader, the lack of rules made lack of operational decisions, and hence the trading activity, increasingly irrelevant to them. The details of the case suggest that the organisation would be plotted on our graph in Figure 7.1 near to "no structure".

The notion of a common ideology as a guiding value is in principle all right but must not be taken for granted. The ideology must be revisited. Failure to do this runs the risk of ideology becoming dogma and dogma restricts choice making. Furthermore, although not obvious in the case above, community organisation can also nurture a sense of in-group superiority. And a last point, poor performers can be carried for long periods to maintain a family atmosphere. That stated, let us now turn to the tricky notion of postmodern organisation.

7.3.7 Postmodern Organisation

We stated in the Preface to Part 2 that there is currently a tensionful debate in the philosophy of the social sciences between modernism and postmodernism. Chapter 2 considers some implications of this for metatheory, philosophy and the history of knowledge. Throughout the book this debate implicitly shapes the argument of diversity management. Now it comes to the surface again as we consider what a postmodern organisation might look like in terms of organisational design.

The task is not an easy one. The fundamental issue is that postmodernism is difficult to pin down. Postmodernism is not supposed to be about clarity of definition. Postmodernism is about irony and playfulness. Produce a definition of a postmodern organisation with rules that define the degrees and nature of structure and operation by all means, but postmodernists will play with it through irony. What a slippery fish! How can we ever know what a postmodern organisation might look like?

An impressive sense of postmodern organisation emerges from Hannigan's (1995) Trend Report on the postmodern city. His objective is to assess whether the postmodern city is a significantly different form of urbanisation. Our objective is to sense from his work (his metaphor) what postmodern organisation might be like.

The postmodern city is characterised by a loosening of ties to any specific space so that units of any sort are capable of being inserted anywhere and everywhere. Units include malls and theme parks or anything else. Units often provide themed environments, sorts of historical and cultural simulations. Units are obsessed with implementation of surveillance and security. Ultimately there is fragmentation since the coming together or development of the postmodern city does not occur in any organic or evolutionary fashion. There is geographical and sociological fragmentation. Units are artificially inserted without regard to neighbours or integrity of the whole (Hannigan, 1995: 160–161).

Architecture and urban design therefore shape up as follows (Hannigan, 1995: 165). Space is independent and autonomous leading to fragmentation of the metropolis. Things are geographically decentralised. Design celebrates vernacular traditions; it is eclectic and irregular, decorative and playful; advocating many experiences. Design is both consultative and market oriented. Things are messy in this way rather than clear (Jencks, 1977).

The postmodern urban lifestyle is characterised as follows. Social involvement is incidental. The importance of the family is replaced by consumerism. Home activities are replaced by dining out and shopping. Social composition is no longer of a class but is diverse (Hannigan, 1995: 180). The tourist experience of postmodern cities can be likened to a set of games with multiple texts and no single authentic experience (Lash and Urry, 1994: 275–276).

Now we will construct an image of postmodern organisation from this metaphor of the postmodern city.

The defining factor of postmodern design is fragmentation. Postmodern organisation will therefore be fragmented with units that it comprises being different, independent and autonomous within a confederation where the following rule exists – wherever actions affect a plurality of agents, those agents should encourage the (tensionful) play of actions. The organisation may well be geographically decentralised. There are no clear boundaries. The organisation will celebrate localised vernacular traditions. Units will not be inhabited by a class of workers since the social composition will be diverse. Units in combination are eclectic rather than functional, playful rather than purposeful, and messy rather than clear. "Management" style is consultative. Rules are set locally. There is experimentation with participatory democracy. The aim is to surface rather than submerge social differences. This requires an institutional means for fostering politicised cultural discussion, and making forums and media available for experiment and play (Young, 1990: 152). Decision making aims to prevent assimilation, maintaining and even creating difference. Organisational life is playful and decorative with many themes and no authentic experience of "what it is like to work in this organisation". If there is any sense of culture it is consumerism, a focus on the "purchase" of goods and services through market-oriented mechanisms.

Case Study

In the case study illustrating viable system organisation we discussed Walker's (1990) account of the redesign of a co-operative. In this brief (fictional) case we revisit both viable system organisation and the co-operative by running through them ideas of postmodern organisation. In this way we intend to present postmodern options and their possible consequences for the co-operative.

Viable system organisation is fundamentally about balancing the need for self-organisation with the need for control to protect individual freedom thus enabling self-organisation and attaining viability. This offered an appealing route forward for co-operative members who read their situation as lack of relevance of (the lack of) existing structure given the needs of a growing co-operative. Traditional alternatives, however, were abhorrent, given the ideological stance of the co-operative and the commitment to a more "co-operative" structure.

Superficially the co-operative solution can be likened to postmodern organisation. Problems are dealt with as closely as possible to the point at which they occur, which suggests localised decision making. Recursion encourages viable systems to take on their own identity, which suggests difference. Policy must represent all people, which suggests participatory democracy. But there is a common difference on each account. The difference is that with viable system organisation we are asked to address these features within the framework of cohesion, identity and harmony. With postmodernism the call is for rules of sorts to prise out cultural difference rather than stitching things cohesively together through identity, and for rules that create and manage tension rather than manufacture harmony.

Perhaps it is here that we can draw a most useful distinction between viable system organisation and postmodern organisation. Viable system organisation is technical. It is about design and procedures to follow to maintain viability and aspire to harmony. Postmodern organisation centres on mentality. It is about cultural differences that should be created, that will lead to tension which has to be managed in celebratory fashion.

In what ways, then, might postmodern organisation have influenced redesign of the co-operative? In our view the essential influences would be in the way we interpret the ideology "the common good" and subsequently the way we seek to implement that ideology. The notion of the common good, for example, would be a much looser concept with postmodernism. The common good becomes a general will where the general will is to protect differences, which is for the common good. The supposed common good would need to be revisited, therefore, with great frequency.

The co-operative has gone some way toward establishing institutional means for implementation of the ideology but falls short of the postmodern ideal of fostering politicised cultural discussion. Accountability needs to shift from showing a commitment to the common good to sharing a commitment not to sabotage other people's intentions, thus protecting differences. This in itself would entail debate about what is meant by sabotage. No structure (as a tendency in our graph presented as Figure 7.1) in the postmodern scheme would be avoided through trust and tolerance, while creating and accepting tension as part of co-operative life. With this discussion in mind, our ongoing discourse about relevance of designs is further developed.

Discourse About Relevance

Postmodernism's experimentation with cultural renewal can be considered a good thing. It promises refreshing new purposes and ways of perceiving order, emphasises innovation, and values difference and change. In other ways, however, cultural renewal, that denies the relevance of forms of structure discussed above, introduces high risk since fragmentation can become divisive and negatively conflictual. Resistance, tactic and strategy threaten the celebratory mood. Perhaps the postmodern response would be to raise *ad hoc* attacks as and where risk becomes too threatening.

Young (1990) has constructed an argument that attempts to build something positive out of fragmentation. The idea is to build in forces that work against unity hence creating difference. This is done for a new brand of common good (as mentioned in the case above), through a general will, where the general will is to protect differences, which is for the common good. Unity, or universality, actually justifies hierarchical decision-making structures that the postmodernists want to avoid (Young, 1990: 97). Unity privileges some at the expense of others (Young, 1990: 116). Postmodernism sees the setting of rules as culturally oppressive.[14] What is needed is some institutional means for discussion which replaces the need for excessive rule setting that, in the postmodernists' view, symbolises superstructure (as we have defined it).

Postmodernism has invoked this image of what is needed which benefits discussions such as ours, but has not operationalised the image realising possible forms of action. Some tentative ideas on this score are offered in the case study above. The issue of operationalisation of postmodern organisation will benefit from further debate.

The postmodern image counters fears of loss of identity by illustrating some differences that already exist. In fact, organisations are full of differences. It argues that there are benefits of encouraging differences. For example, benefits come through opportunities available to an organisation in terms of insights and possible responses to issues faced.

The trouble is that the sort of arrangement that postmodern organisation seems to be advocating can be slow to respond. It seems to recommend a lengthy process of conflict resolution that may mean there are missed opportunities. Ironically it could be damaging for all involved (Ahrne, 1994: 107). Tensions still arise between organisational rules such as a democratic constitution, with people's rights to choose, and needs such as quick decision making and rapid action.

Ultimately, it has to be asked, can the "postmodern form of organisation" effectively generate decisions that maintain some sense or semblance of order, or is this a modernist mentality infiltrating the postmodern image? If taken literally, it is difficult to accept the postmodern view that everything is totally contrived, lacks transcendent experience and exists in continual flux. What evidence is there that this disillusionment of some intellectuals is reflected across a broad spectrum of society?[15]

7.3.8 Concluding Comment

A major debate at the moment is between the contingency way of handling design or whether there is an evolutionary process at work moving toward the post-bureaucratic organisation (Heckscher, 1994: 15). Our position is neither. We believe that a critical approach is required. Critical does not mean contingency. Contingency says certain designs are suited to certain

---

[14] It sees, for example, dangers with the Total Quality Management idea of monological culture; as if organisations are really like that; as if organisations are or can be unified, solid, coherent and integrated.
[15] Postmodernists might respond here evidencing their intellectual debate with examples of everyday sabotage of totalising systems such as hierarchical decision-making procedures.

circumstances. We say, even if there appear to be trends along the lines of contingency theory, there is no absolute guarantee that any design will be experienced as most relevant in any given time and place.

Each organisational design is a theme around which an organisation can compose its own variation(s) (cf. Ackoff, 1994: 118). Consequently, organisations tend to be hybrids (Khandwalla, 1977: 239). Mintzberg (1979) identified what he saw as five pure types of organisation: simple structure, machine structure, professional bureaucracy, divisionalised form, and adhocracy. He noted that in reality most organisations are hybrids of these. Design, however, is not really like a blueprint. Designs are constructed and continuously readjusted.

Critics here would point out that the hybrid idea simply jumps from contingency to eclecticism. It is not critical at all, it is pragmatic and eclectic. We agree that one (in our view impoverished) interpretation of hybridisation is the pragmatic eclectic one. A critical view (that underpins triple loop learning) states that hybridisation may be carried out in conjunction with explicit reasoning about the purpose and principles in play. Choice must be made about the form of the hybrid, the (main) purpose that is to be pursued, and the principles therefore that have to be followed. Choice is not once-and-for-all-time, however. Choice in the critical scheme of things will be revisited and may change. Purposes and principles that operate in a kind of support role to the current choice may at some later stage become *the* choice.

The important thing then is to introduce knowledge about designs into organisational debate. It is wise to remember, however, that it is easier to change charts and blueprints than to change what people are really doing (Ahrne, 1994: 104). Any set of rules may be rational or expedient only for one set of actors (Gouldner, 1954: 18). And there may be many sets of concerns of actors within any organisation. This is where the importance of debate surfaces. Debate is an important part of the process whereby people's decision making becomes increasingly well informed in terms of other people's concerns.

Before moving on to debate there is an immediate issue to deal with. In addressing issues of organisational design it might also be necessary to consider the impact on efficiency of operational processes, and further, the relevance of those processes to organisational design. The next section explores process design with case studies from private organisational enterprises (where our practical experience so far lies).

7.4 PROCESS DESIGN

7.4.1 Introduction

When talking about process design we say that design is a focus on flows and controls over flows. The main design issue is the efficiency of the processes. Our evaluation of process design is therefore undertaken broadly in terms of efficiency but put into the context of power/freedom and relevance. Two approaches that address efficiency of processes are Quality Management and Business Process Reengineering. These are evaluated below with the graph in Figure 7.1 being used as a catalyst for discussion. The two approaches to process design are explored in terms of theoretical reasoning and empirical reports about the reasoning in action. Ultimately we construct a discourse on relevance of process designs that provides a springboard for further discussion by users of diversity management.

As with the previous section on organisational design, it is not our intention to demonstrate either approach to process design (or indeed any other approach) is right or wrong. That would not fit within the spirit of diversity management. Rather, the critique and interpretation is part of our attempt to help the reader be widely informed in local decision making that diversity management advocates.

7.4.2 Quality Management

There are two main principles that drive Quality Management (QM).[16] First, efficiency of processes can be achieved by continuously redesigning them in line with customers'[17] agreed requirements. Second, the key to good management is to ensure that customers are satisfied by continuously meeting the agreed requirements through efficient processes. Implementation of QM involves a culture change among organisational members so that they become customer focused. The new culture encourages staff to look for causes of variability in processes that cause the output of processes to fail to provide consistently customers with products or services that have been agreed upon.

Underpinning QM is a belief in many cases that processes organisation-wide are convoluted and confusing and therefore prevent customers' needs from being satisfied. There seems to be no logical or rational reason that explains why processes are carried out in the way they are. Indeed, on analysis processes appear somewhat illogical and irrational, only replicating the way things "have always been done"; these being forged into place through repetition and occasionally added to through random elaboration. Development of a metaphor introduced by advocates of Business Process Reengineering helps to illustrate the point (consult Figure 7.7).

[16] Although there are many different expressions of the quality idea; from ISO 9000 to Kaizen. A thorough discussion is found in Flood (1993a).
[17] Customer in Quality Management means any person or group internal or external to the organisation who is provided with a product, service or information. This reasoning redefines the idea of organisation and has led to important changes in research. For example, there is a growing literature on supplier development (reviewed in Flood and Isaac, 1993) where suppliers are embraced as part of the organisation. The idea can be extended to include stakeholders in the wider general public, permitting issues such as physical, biological, and social concerns to enter the debate about, What is quality?

A dairy farmer manages a herd of cows. Every morning at 8.00 am the farmer walks from the farmhouse to the cowshed and opens its door. The cows slowly work their way, as always, to the gate of the field in which they spend their day. On entering the field, the cows move gently around eating grass, filling up after the night in the cowshed. They meander about seemingly without direction. As noon approaches the temperature rises. This, coupled with the hard morning's work munching grass, makes the cows thirsty, so they meander toward the drinking pool. At various points on the side of the pool the cows stop to take in water. After about half an hour of this they stroll circularly to an area of shrubs where they like to rest and sleep. They try several locations and positions until comfortable. After sleeping for several hours the cows are keen to start munching grass again. They set off in a roundabout way to another part of the field where afternoon grass is particularly tasty and amble around that region until the farmer comes at 5.00 pm to allow them back into the cowshed, for milking and resting up for the night.

The next day the farmer opens up the cowshed at 8.00 am and the cows enter the field. They replicate the previous day's activities. They munch grass as they enter the field. They get thirsty and drink. They get tired and sleep. They amble their way to the gate for 5.00 pm. The following day the same happens all over again. And then the following day. In fact, every day the cows' behaviour is the same. The repetitive process finally becomes marked out on the cowfield. The cows actually follow the same routes day after day. These routes can easily be seen as brown mudpaths on the otherwise green field. The routes, however, show no obvious logic or rationale – they simply meander all over the place.

Those concerned with inefficiency of processes may argue that the cowfield is a good metaphor for the way processes are carried out in most organisations today. The processes are carried out in the way they are because they were done that way yesterday, and the day before, and the day before that, and . . . . Organisational processes are like brown cowpaths in a green cowfield. The processes amble and meander all over the organisation.

The metaphor (which we will return to in the next section on Business Process Reengineering) introduces the need for an organisation-wide QM approach. QM wants to improve upon perceived undesirable inefficiency to help organisations meet agreed customers' requirements. The way forward is to set up a number of Quality Action Teams (QATs – comprising cows, often termed cats[18]). There would be a QAT dealing with early morning

---

[18] A distinction can be drawn here between cows and cats that raises an important point. Cows tend to be herded and led. Cats are individuals and like very much to do their own thing – but it is hoped that their talents can be harnessed in QM. QM respects that people may wish to become involved in (re)defining their contribution in the context of defining the services they may provide. This in turn implies that they themselves may wish to define their contribution as open to continued revisitation (as part of the process of liaising with customers).

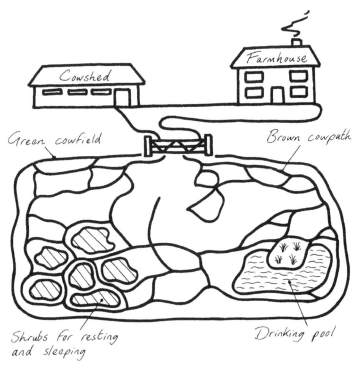

Figure 7.7

munching. Another would deal with the drinking process and another with the noon resting. A fourth team would deal with late afternoon munching. Each team looks for inefficiencies and improves the process design. Efficient munching, drinking and sleeping routines might be worked out and implemented (see Figure 7.8). Efficiency may be raised overall by say 8%. Let us temporarily exchange this metaphor for a real-world case study.

Case Study

Our case reports on the early stages of a QM intervention that Bob was involved in. The Managing Director of Diagnostic Biotechnology (Pte) Ltd (DB) in Singapore, Mr Lim Jiu Kok, invited Bob in May 1990 to consult in the company.[19] DB researches into and produces diagnostic kits and offers laboratory services using the latest biotechnology. As the company's name suggests, its business is diagnostics using biotechnology.

Sessions involving 40 out of about 120 staff started with a frank and open discussion about the main issues faced by DB. All present had strong feel-

[19] An extended version of this case can be found in Flood (1993a).

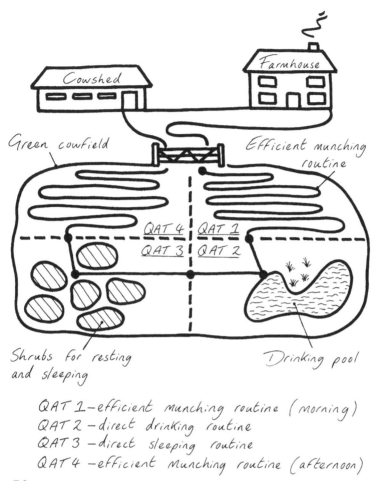

QAT 1–efficient munching routine (morning)
QAT 2 –direct drinking routine
QAT 3 –direct sleeping routine
QAT 4 –efficient munching routine (afternoon)

Figure 7.8

ings for which issues were most relevant. In summary, people expressed concern about the following issues.

- A lack of mission.
- No sense of pride, commitment, confidence, role or identity of individuals.[20]

[20] It should be noted that the experience of "identity" with one's work may be influenced by both cultural context and individual preference. In this context (DB in Singapore) it appeared that pride achievable by identifying with work tasks was regarded as important by many. This is not to say that all people felt exactly the same way about the degree of such desired identification. It should also be noted that the notion of pride or pleasure in work that is here invoked runs somewhat contrary to the idea of working only to fulfil the demands of a wage contract. In order to make provision for the diversity of choice making of people, we prefer them to decide the intensity of their involvements (identification) with specific work tasks. Donzelot offers an interesting historical account of variations in the notion of work that have been

- That the company is young and so are many of the staff, giving rise to a lack of overall experience.
- Control, communication and organisation are weak.
- DB is a success story but, Is it competitive?
- "The future seems to hit us before we have had a chance to prepare for it."

There were two dominant concerns underlying these issues. First, that the company had undergone substantial expansion in 1989 but had not put in place relevant communication, co-ordination and control procedures (there were cybernetic failings). Second, that the company was young and had yet to develop a corporate culture. The first concern was convincingly captured by ideas of viability, while the second fell in place with ideas of quality. Participants also concluded that viability and quality in this case implied each other. Both had to be tackled if processes were to become more efficient.

QM was introduced to the participants. It was explained as a systemic approach to intervention, acknowledging that it assumes issues stem from a lack of quality caused by inefficient processes. The ideas and methods of QM were found to be highly relevant to DB's difficulties (as outlined above).[21]

There was one main worry at this stage. Traditionally quality is implemented top-down using the organisational hierarchical tree. This can be problematic because it implements quality according to a formal power structure that can negate many of the benefits that QM has to offer. The concepts of traditional hierarchy and QM run against each other. We therefore began to conceive of the organisation in different ways to develop a more useful appreciation of organisational design and organisational behaviour. Mr Lim had already been working on a highly participatory auditing and decision-making approach within DB. He had created a series of committees to act as "think-tanks" about the organisation. Think-tanks involved people from all levels and all functions of the organisation. Each committee (equivalent to a QAT) was tasked to focus its attention on a particular area of the organisation. The committees were: Manpower Planning,

---

provided for in different discourses. He notes that the idea of "joy through work" is valorised in a range of discourses, including Nazism (where government discourse defined work as making-free), socialism (with its ideal of non-alienated work in socialist society) and some brands of traditionalism, for example, via the appeal to traditions of craftsmanship (sic). Of course, it can be used (abused) by those who wish to secure the commitments of workers to, as Donzelot (1991: 259) puts it, "assume responsibility themselves for the risks and benefits of the enterprise instead of practising the irresponsibility encouraged by the wage system" (in so-called capitalist systems). But then again, the conception of this as abuse or not cannot be determined outside of the way that people (ongoingly) define the relevance of (and need for) specific drives for quality. What we have pointed to in this section is a description of processes of QM as a means for developing efficiency of processes.

[21] We should bear in mind that in this case (context) some standardisation of the quality of the products had to be achieved in line with the biotechnical requirements of customers. This, however, is not necessarily a requirement of all QM.

Corporate Strategy, Customer Services, Control Systems, Research and Development, and Technical. Each member of one committee would also participate in one other committee. Thus each committee was capable of looking in a focused way at processes within its area of responsibility, and at the same time would develop its understanding of the organisation as a whole. Bob's task was to ensure that Mr Lim's innovative arrangement covered all aspects of process and so he worked with these committees, helping them to be clear about their outlook with an ongoing process redesign. The arrangement of the committees is shown in Figure 7.9.

QM was implemented in the following way. First of all a company quality mission was set by all 40 participants. This took a whole morning, but the value of the exercise was to begin to create a company image that all participants felt they could relate to and had ownership of. Many staff commented that this was the first time that they had grasped a meaningful understanding of DB as a whole. Following this, committees were reformed with specialist and non-specialist participants in each group. Committees were then asked to define their mission within the spirit of the company mission, enabling the new identity to filter throughout the company. A viable system perspective was extremely useful here because it encouraged identity, through the mission, to spill down recursive levels.

The committees then identified their customers (both internal and external), customers' requirements (as far as possible at this stage), and were asked to identify weaknesses of processes in satisfying those requirements. With this information each committee defined a number of projects that aimed to improve customer service. Some means of measuring the effectiveness of each project was requested. On completion of project definition committees were brought back together to present and share their findings. Main themes of projects were analysed and discussed. Implementation proceeded from hereon.

Discourse About Relevance

In what ways did the first stages of intervention in DB tackle the issue of relevance to the participants of process redesign? A perceived major achievement felt by participants was overcoming the lack of identity in DB by formulating a company mission. Working out the mission not only gave direction to DB, but had the added value of generating employee commitment through mass participation in its construction. Setting committee missions allowed people to define ways that they wished to contribute within the organisation. This did help to develop pride, as did the sense of continuous process improvement. Control, communication and other processes were targeted by many of the defined projects which, therefore, promised to improve efficiency of processes thus supporting preparations

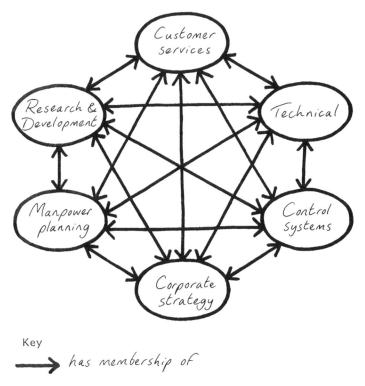

Key

→ has membership of

Figure 7.9

for the future. For this reason the QM approach was experienced by many participants as highly relevant.

The sessions were generally accepted as a breakthrough for the company by the participants, although there were notable exceptions. For example:

- a senior member of staff did not participate (and left the company)
- the company had to keep functioning over the duration of the workshop and so only limited contact could be made with "shop floor" staff
- the amount of time available was hardly enough to "routinise" the new procedures and quality culture
- the managing director had a powerful character and hold over the company which, despite his revolutionary management style, would probably continue largely to shape DB.

QM in this case arguably had a role to play. There are other general issues that need to be considered which the case did not surface. These are discussed below.

QM is often associated with documentation. If done well, documentation can provide a thorough record of processes that promotes knowledge transfer, adds clarity to people's roles and duties, and improves chances of tracing causes of error. The downside is that adaptability, flexibility and responsiveness of an organisation may be reduced. There are echoes here of worries about traditional hierarchy. Some critics say this is not surprising because documentation simply puts in place a paper bureaucracy. The process of managing QM, we suggest, requires a consideration of the kinds of issues that we raised in our discussion of structures for design above. This is because the flows of the processes of QM are set within such structures and are thus subject to similar considerations.

Considerations revolve around issues such as the following. To what extent can bureaucratisation (*in situ*) be seen to guard against excessively prejudiced interpretations of standards? By defining documented procedures for their measurement and by ensuring that personnel are trained for their measurement? A related question asks whether bureaucratisation helps to guard against arbitrary differential treatment of different customers; or whether it is felt that, say, the participation implied by (more) circular organisation may appropriately perform the function of rendering standard setting accountable in terms of customers' requirements (as negotiated *in situ*); or whether, say, it is felt that the information feedback mechanisms put in place by the viable system structure is a more appropriate way to ensure quality of performance, and so on. The discussions in Section 7.3 provide some indication of the way that issues of quality are likely to be refracted in different structural settings. Of course, it may also be felt (by some) that there is no need to institute defined modes of QM – in which case postmodern organisation would probably be pertinent, as discussed below.

The postmodern concern is that approaches like QM tend to assimilate people into monocultures – where a monolithic commitment to ways of implementing quality seems to be encouraged as a cultural norm. This is disliked because, as we have already explained, postmodernism values cultural differentiation and cultural renewal. QM in this sense is oppressive. Reconstructing QM from a (more) postmodern-oriented angle would lead to key changes. People would not be expected to identify with a defined role or contribution. They would rather be invited to treat tentative and temporary performances as an opportunity for moments of skill deployment. QM would become a process of people co-experimenting. Provision for this form of design (in this case process design) relies on trust, toleration, and generous celebration by customers of unfamiliar behaviour. Customers' requirements (internal and external) could become attuned to celebrating surprising behaviour in which both they and their servers are able to invent themselves anew by transgressing familiar patterns. Brokers for such a postmodern-oriented way of doing QM may be able to find or create a niche in the market, or in people's consciousness, for performances geared in this direction.

7.4.3 Business Process Reengineering

Business Process Reengineering (BPR) is a recent phenomenon on the management scene. Some protagonists say that BPR replaces QM. Diversity management disagrees with this, arguing that each way of managing processes offers ideas on design that people may experience as relevant.

The seminal popularised text is Hammer and Champy's (1993) *Reengineering the Corporation: A Manifesto for Business Revolution*. There are four main principles that guide BPR. First, BPR is proactive. Second, changing processes means radical improvement rather than continuous improvement. Third, there is a need to manage processes rather than functions on a company-wide basis (i.e. to defunctionalise the organisation). Finally, operational strategies drive business strategies (i.e. the processes are leveraged into the market place).

BPR aims to leverage processes into the market place following radical change. This achieves an operational lead. It focuses on what organisations can do beyond what must be done. BPR adds this extra competitive dimension to QM. QM only focuses on what organisations must do to give customers what they want, to attain a lead in customer satisfaction.

BPR wants efficiency in processes. Most processes meander through the organisation, worn into place like a cowpath in a field as our metaphor in the last section imaged. The routes are followed day after day and eventually take on a historical importance along with the functional organisation, but are inefficient. The QM approach is to set up Quality Action Teams that strive for continuous improvement in the areas they hold responsibility for. BPR approaches the problem of inefficiency in a radically different way. It is not content with 8% improvement in efficiency – it wants 80%!

The focal point of BPR is to improve processes radically. It thus sees the processes of the cowfield as a motif on a china plate. This old functional scheme is then smashed as if breaking the china. BPR puts the china back together again in the form of about five to eight core business processes made lean and nimble. The core processes with perceived increased value are leveraged into the market place.

Operational strategies are used to drive business strategies. Core business processes are set up to achieve operational strategies. The core processes are broad in coverage, streamlining the whole business from suppliers through to consumers. Process management is very wide, cutting across all organisational activities.

Often associated with reengineering projects are downsizing and outsourcing. To achieve 80% improvement in efficiency often means some things have to go. Downsizing literally means reducing the size of the organisation. This may mean redundancies although job losses can be managed through natural attrition or efforts can be made to secure jobs for people in another organisation. But let us remember that whichever way jobs go, jobs go. Outsourcing is where non-essential activities go. One way of doing this is to help current staff set up their own independent companies using existing assets and resources. Independence is qualified since the deal is that the existing company has first call on the new company for products and services it needs (and normally will schedule payments for assets and resources made available).

Case Study

Our case study, which we describe very briefly, is taken from Warren Topp's (1995) account of BPR in Southern Life Association, Cape Town, South Africa. It is discussed more fully in the discourse about relevance. Warren was a member of the core reengineering team. Southern is the fourth largest life assurer in South Africa with branches nation-wide.

The Cape Town branch investigated the possibility of a reengineering project in July 1993. A pilot project was launched in Annuities. Pilot schemes are common when reengineering, allowing core personnel to gain some experience before reengineering processes on a larger scale. Vision and values were established. A key value was staff involvement and participation leading to a shared future structure. Five broad principles for reengineering were developed.

- Map the current business processes.
- Undertake walk-throughs and critical reflection on these asking why a process should be carried out in the way it currently is.
- Redesign the business processes in the light of new technology and the learning gained during the above two steps.
- Redesign teams and structure.
- Implement new technology and structure.

Mapping the existing business processes was undertaken with the participation and learning of as many members of the Annuities team as possible. Once mapped they were checked for accuracy by participants. Small immediate improvements were instituted. A declared policy was no forced redundancies. Further work drew heavily upon image technology,[22] especially useful for paper-driven companies such as those in life assurance,

---

[22] Image technology allows an image of a document to be stored electronically on a computer. The image is created by scanning the paper through a scanning device. The image is indexed and stored electronically allowing efficiency in handling. It can be viewed by more than one person at a time. It can be used to trigger work electronically. It reduces the need for paper.

allowing massive gains in efficiency to be attained. Many of the issues we wish to draw out have been raised through Warren Topp's case study and are discussed in the following discourse about relevance.

Discourse About Relevance

Of fundamental concern is the problem of downsizing and outsourcing. It is hard to believe that those who are victims of such decisions will see the relevance of the reengineered design. BPR proponents are to some extent aware of this issue. The solution advocated, however, falls short of what we believe is necessary. It amounts to a kind of employment agency facility whereby those who it is deemed have to be released are helped by the organisation to find new employment. Then there is a counselling service provided for those who remain, who are likely to be in a state of shock. The combined feelings of shock in the remaining staff lead to organisational trauma that has to be managed.

The question here is ultimately about, who decides that reengineering is needed?, and, who is involved in the reengineering effort? Taking Topp's case we have to assume that the decision to reengineer was made at a senior management level although the process of reengineering was carried out in a participatory manner. This participation gave people the chance to explore the relevance of reengineering and to contribute recommendations for change. There were no fears of job losses since Southern made a declaration of no redundancies, preventing an atmosphere of fear dominating the change process.

There were according to Topp four main issue areas faced when implementing BPR: values, vision, the reengineering problem, and the problem of power in reengineering.

Reengineering took place against a company-wide process of *value development*. Every employee in the company attended a two-day workshop where they participated in crafting the values they believed the organisation should aspire to. Representatives from all areas of the company were then democratically elected to harness the results of the workshop toward outlining acceptable company values.

Tensions arose when it came to *vision setting*. Groups of stakeholders held very different interests. Topp is not explicit about the way tensions were resolved (if at all). For us, this issue invokes the need for debate and we refer you to the next chapter.

The *reengineering problem* refers to issues that surfaced when attempting to proceed with radical change. Topp expressed his concerns well through a series of questions. How do planners involved in reengineering ensure that they are honest and working toward a transparent and legitimate purpose? How do we ensure that reengineering is not just a change of the management guard achieved through restructuring and manipulation of staff? What is the real purpose of reengineering? Is it to reduce costs, reduce staff, reduce middle management, change the culture, provide ownership to staff, empower employees, improve quality, or contribute to societal development? Do the affected, in the form of those not involved in the redesign, have a chance really to challenge the process and its design? In fact, these are questions that anyone involved in reengineering should ask if wanting to aspire to the ideal (about choice) set in this book for diversity management. It again points to the need for debate.

Topp was understandably concerned about boundary judgements being made when mapping processes. This he declared must entail a think-through of assumptions and judgements being made. Therefore reengineering should strive to reveal the boundary judgements being made. These can be highlighted through critical reflection – which includes taking into account some of the expressed (and possible) concerns of those most seriously affected by the designs. It is the designer's responsibility to attempt to ensure the transparency of assumptions (as far as possible) and to show that s/he is able to take on board "bad news" that may be presented from other standpoints.

This ultimately leads on to Topp's fourth concern, that of the problem of power in reengineering. Most reengineering projects centralise power in a small group of people known as the reengineering team. The people involved here represent only a small portion of an organisation, yet have vested in them the power to change radically process design, which in turn may radically change people's working and indeed external lives. Again, there is a need for transparency. Topp's astuteness over the wider might–right issues led him to employ a critically reflective approach discussed in Chapter 9 (see Ulrich, 1983).[23] This allowed for a more sensitive implementation of BPR. It reminds us that not all contentious issues concerning design can be referred to debating processes. Some issues have to be referred to discourse about might–right management and astuteness.

In a section called "Reflections" Topp offered a number of conclusions about the Southern experience that we believe are relevant to all BPR projects. First, that questions about reengineering structures and business processes are never fully answered. As the context of a project changes over time the questions have to be re-examined. Second, in order to make transparent our own assumptions about relevance of processes we have to surface them first for ourselves. Third, that the reengineering team must not assume the role of expert otherwise their (biased) assumptions will unfairly hold sway and limit the influence over and relevance of any

---

[23] We recognise that Ulrich is more concerned with developing a mature citizenry. We suggest that Topp acting as manager may also display sensitivity as citizen. As manager and fair citizen he could become attuned to wider social issues.

redesign. Fourth, that it is easy to forget wider social needs in the drive for efficiency.

7.4.4 Concluding Comment

The two main sections of this chapter cover two aspects of design: the first is organisational design and the second is process design. Images of design are created through theoretical development and by supplying some empirical resonance of the images in specific organisational contexts. A finding of this inquiry in the sections on QM and BPR is the need to consider at the same time issues relating to organisational processes and organisational design. Processes flow through structures. Structures shape flows. Let us now turn to our summary and conclusion.

7.5 SUMMARY AND CONCLUSION

The chapter now concludes in our established style that summarises the main ideas in bullet points.

- In this chapter we evaluate organisational design and process design in terms of power and freedom as well as, respectively, efficiency and effectiveness. Evaluation takes on the following meaning. With power and freedom through design we mean chances people have to make widely informed and locally contingent choices, given degrees of structure and the nature and relevance of that structure. By relevance we mean how "comfortable" people feel with designs in the circumstances. Circumstances means the situation as seen and assessed in terms of a chosen focus of attention.
- The main organisational design issue is effectiveness of design in terms of hierarchy, role and task definition, division of labour, rule setting, interdependence of roles and tasks, communication, monitoring, co-ordination, control, and flexibility. The main process design issue is efficiency of processes in terms of flows and control over the flows.
- Ways of considering effectiveness of organisational design within the spirit of diversity management include bureaucracy, circular organisation, organic organisation, viable system organisation, community organisation and postmodern organisation.
- Bureaucracy introduces traditional hierarchy into organisations, with clearly established roles and tasks that follow a system of rules. The aim is to achieve efficiency by making operations clear cut, to enhance reliability, to reduce favours, and to enable customers (internal and external) to know what they will receive. The main criticisms are that bureaucracy

serves only the purposes of those who set it up, change is very slow, rules can be implemented literally without (necessary) exceptions, complex rules are open to tactical exploitation and are not so reliable after all, and decision making and responsibility tend to flow up the hierarchy leading to ill-informed decision making. Despite these concerns bureaucracy has remained resilient for around a century and may show a technical superiority over other forms. The lingering worry, however, is that it has a tendency toward superstructure.

- Circular organisation is designed to complement traditional hierarchy and achieve democratic organisation. The main structural characteristic is a series of boards set up at each hierarchical level that enhances people's chances of participating and making a rapid and meaningful contribution. It also makes people responsible. The main criticism is that circular organisation does not break with traditional hierarchy and may experience some related problems.

- Organic organisation has an extensive history of development. Several forms of organic systems approaches have been proposed. The informal nature of organic organisation led to the term adhocracy being coined. Following on, contingency theory identified contextual factors that influence structure, concluding there is no one best way. Recent developments include flattening the organisation, networking, and creative compartments. Informality allows for flexibility, adaptability and responsiveness. Limited rules, however, permit ambiguity and confusion, and make it difficult to reflect on successes of the organisation. Networking and compartmentation tackle these concerns with minimal introduction of rules.

- Viable system organisation brings together five key management functions and organises them according to a carefully worked out series of information flows and communications. It separates out the main operations from the management functions that serve them. It introduces a systemic form of hierarchy called recursion. It offers freedom through viability, taking away only as much freedom as is necessary to maintain viability of the whole. The main criticism is that an appeal to functions places an unnecessary imposition on actors.

- Community organisation utilises peer networks structured by the relation to a shared set of values. This leads to control through shared purpose. The main concern is poor organisation because of a lack of structure in terms of technical and managerial support.

- Postmodern organisation is a confederation operating through the rule that wherever actions affect a plurality of agents, those agents should participate in feeding actions. Postmodern organisation promotes fragmentation which it points out already exists, and celebrates localised vernacular traditions. Decision making aims to prevent assimilation. It experiments with cultural renewal which may be a good thing. A main concern is that denial of the relevance of forms of structure introduces high risk since fragmentation can become too divisive and negative.

- Ways of tackling efficiency of organisational processes within the spirit of diversity management include QM and BPR.
- QM proposes a continuous approach to incremental improvement in organisational processes where product and process become predictable and/or reliable. It tends to create monocultures where people's actions are geared to becoming predictable and/or reliable. A main concern is that incremental improvement is never radical enough. Another concern is that monoculturing is oppressive.
- BPR proposes a radical approach to improving process efficiency by destroying the old operation and replacing it with an ultra-efficient, highly simplified series of processes built around a few core business processes. A main problem is the large number of job losses usually associated with reengineering. Another concern is that radical changes and job losses tend to be decided by projects that centralise power within small groups of people.
- A finding of this chapter is the need to consider at the same time issues relating to organisational processes and organisational design. Processes flow through structures. Structures shape flows.

In the concluding summary point we pin up the idea that a core need is to think about at the same time issues relating to organisational processes and organisational design. A strong relationship between design issues and debate issues also features in our theoretical and empirical reasoning. Design issues cannot be approached outside of debate about design. Yet some issues of design raise might–right issues. Such design issues cannot easily be approached directly through design. And debate as we discuss it in the next chapter does not offer the most direct way of avoiding, say, the might of an appeal to claimed necessities in order to buttress preferred conceptions. It does not easily avoid the right of appeal to forms of science and/or forms of presumed agreement to buttress such conceptions. Diversity management must therefore explore two more loops each with a different centre of learning; debate practice and might–right practice. These needs are accordingly fulfilled in the next two chapters, starting with debate practice.

Loop 2. Debate Management: What?

8.1 INTRODUCTION

Chapter 8 covers models and methodologies that help people to debate the question, What? designs and/or decisions they should choose. It makes What? its centre of learning. Also investigated is the kind of emancipatory practice that can arise from debate. Chapter 8 makes as its central concern possibilities for learning and understanding through forms of debate. It asks, How well considered are decisions resulting from those forms? The chapter works through six types of debate: Action Learning, (and the following two types of Action Research[1]) Participatory Action Research, Action Science, (and the following two so-called systems approaches) Strategic Assumption Surfacing and Testing, and Soft Systems Methodology, finishing with Postmodern debate. We prepare an ingress to these practices with a discussion about (the process of) debate.

8.2 ABOUT DEBATE

In Chapter 6 we introduce a form of graph that promotes evaluation of practical and research efforts specifically aimed at issues of power and freedom. For this chapter on debate and decision making, evaluation takes on the following meaning. With power/freedom through debate we mean

---

[1] The family of Action Research approaches is much larger than we have space to cover. We have, however, divided the family between Chapters 8 and 9; those in Chapter 9, we argue, contribute more to might–right practice.

chances people have to make widely informed and locally contingent choices, given degrees of participation in the process of debate, and the nature and relevance of decisions made in that process. By relevance we mean how well considered people feel are decisions made through the process of debate in the circumstances. As made transparent in Chapter 7, circumstances to us is a holistic concept which admits the need to choose an area of focus. We contextualise decision making to the local (proximal) decision makers in terms of some judgement about who is significantly involved and affected.

Debate is about episodes of communication. Human episodes of communication are highly dynamic where ideas and opinions are exchanged between individuals and groups, and are interpreted by participants in the exchange. The content and interpretation of exchanges remain intangible, "for this depends on the usually tacit assumptions that both parties bring to the marvellous and obscure process of sharing each other's understanding of some situation and even of changing their own and each other's underlying assumptions in the process" (Vickers, 1987: vii).[2] Debate, the argument goes, provides the opportunity for people to influence decision making through the process of interaction, or communication, by, for example, allowing them to challenge assumptions that might otherwise shape decisions.

The process of challenging and influencing assumptions casts a different light from designing on the activity of issue management. Methodologists such as Russell Ackoff phrase "influencing assumptions" in words like "problem dissolving", where assumptions held are falsified in the debate process, or become shared among the debaters; in such cases, assumptions, like barriers, are lowered and intervention may proceed more smoothly in a well-considered fashion.[3]

This process was likened by Flood (1993a: 133–135) to making escapes from trap-like preconceptions (cf. Vickers, 1970). Vickers' lobster-pot metaphor is a brilliant way of illustrating mind freedom. He pictures mind-traps as if they were human-traps working like lobster pots, and says in 1970 in his book *Freedom in a Rocking Boat*,

> Man-traps are dangerous only in relation to the limitations on what men [sic!] can see and value and do. The nature of the trap is a function of the nature of the trapped. To describe either is to imply the other. I start with the trap, because it is more consciously familiar. We the trapped tend to take our own

---

[2] As is explored below, the notion of sharedness does not imply that people try to inhabit a common world of overlapping meanings or that they direct conversation in terms of the idea that others will "understand" them free of interpretive input.

[3] Of course, the process of debate can become distorted by forms of power relations, meaning that assumptions, or felt interests, clash. The process of debate does not proceed as desired by methodologists of the debate persuasion. The possible impact of structure and design on the process of debate was discussed in the previous chapter. The might–right element of this discussion is detailed in the next chapter.

state of mind for granted – which is partly why we are trapped. With the shape of the trap in our minds, we shall be better able to see the relevance of our limitations and to question those assumptions about ourselves which are most inept to the activity and the experience of being human now.

Vickers' mind-trap idea can be extended to illustrate three things. First, that whichever mind-trap we are in, in principle there is a means of escape assuming that ideas (and ways of generating ideas) are not frozen, mirroring social inequalities (see Chapter 9). Second, that it does not matter how Houdini-like (Houdini – the great escapologist) we are, escaping from one mind-trap leads us straight into another. We never escape from our minds. And third, we are freer in the sense that we have a memory of all the mind-traps that once trapped us, and our means of escape from them, which have enriched our minds and our ability to make decisions with greater scope. We can pan through our history of great escapes to our advantage. We are freer. But we must never forget that we are still trapped creatures, trapped in our current thoughts. Each bit of freedom we secure, in the process described above, releases the grip of the traps, but our minds are still trapped.

The most adequate means by which we are able to work out how to escape from mind-traps, Vickers argued, is through debate. Each participant holds part of the combination for each other participant's current mind-trap. Participation in debate enables people to see more clearly the horizons of those involved. Ideally, these horizons will be brought together in one rich map that brings out new possibilities for all. This might, in practice, include working out the value of new technology, understanding friction that has evolved between finance and marketing employees, recognising that auditors are not necessarily spies, appreciating the rationale of a radical community leader, fathoming out that police officers can be genuine community officers, or learning that sending aid to undernourished people does not guarantee anything for their children's future. In general, debate offers real possibilities for participants to learn and understand.

To encourage and inform debate about debate, our graph form introduced in Chapter 6, and contextualised in Chapter 7 to evaluate designs, is now recontextualised to evaluate the process of debate (see Figure 8.1). We want to assess the process of debate against the standard proposed in this book.

Figure 8.1 can be explained as follows. "No decisions" arise when, for example, the view is held that there are no standards that make possible meaningful comparison of ideas or opinions. There is no basis for judgement and choice, so anything goes (in principle). In practice, no decision making leaves people feeling imprisoned by no action, or indeed the continuance of existing actions where existing power relations in effect determine decisions. Decisions are experienced as ill considered and the process of fruitless discussion a waste of time.

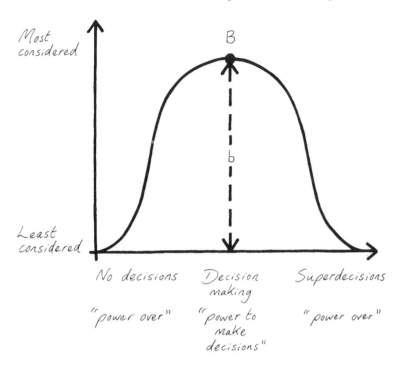

Figure 8.1

"Superdecisions" based on unchallenged assumptions lead to predefined solutions. Invisibility of assumptions lead to obvious or forced decisions, reflecting dominant wisdom and/or a desire for consensus (where the dominant decision is forced).

No decisions or superdecisions are examples of "power over", where existing power relationships shape decisions and people do not (immediately) possess "power to" influence decision making. Balanced between no decision and superdecisions is "power to" influence decision making, the ideal through which we wish to raise in people's thoughts possible abuses of the process of debate.

An important feature of the process of debate, that in part determines where on our graph in Figure 8.1 any process will map, is how meaningful the experience of participation is to people involved and/or affected by the decision. The point is made by summarising two categories expanded in following sections: the professional expert and the action research models. The professional expert makes a study and recommends a course of action to decision makers; leaving little room for meaningful participation thus mapping toward the superdecision region of our graph. An action researcher, we might conclude, is still a principal change agent but will, to degrees, negotiate with other people involved and affected by the decision; hence relocating the mapping in the direction of our ideal, away from superdecisions.

Despite such observations we will not recommend any approach as the best one. This would universalise rather than localise choice making on the issue of methodology choice. Researchers such as ourselves can never know for certain whether circumstances will prevail where the local decision makers prefer to leave responsibility in the hands of professional experts or action researchers. Either might be considered a viable choice to make in the circumstances. It is only for us to surface issues surrounding the process of debate, so choices made are well considered and locally relevant. Ultimately, we construct a discourse on consideredness of forms of debate which is a stimulant for further discussion by triple loop learners. Our construction begins with an appraisal of Action Learning.

8.3 ACTION LEARNING

Reg Revans's Action Learning (AL) dates back to 1945 (Revans, 1982). While not always associated with the family of Action Research (AR) approaches, it does make an interesting introduction by providing some methodological ideas embraced by AR. Revans makes his appeal as follows: "If one is facing conditions previously unknown . . . there are no rules. All that our managers could do to help each other [in the circumstances] was to debate" (Revans, 1982). From this we learn that AL and indeed AR have at their core the need to engender meaningful debate.

In AL the intention of debate is to disclose one's thinking to colleagues in group settings. This leads to

- learning about one's job/industry (giving rise to a learning community)
- learning about oneself in the job/industry (managers learning more about why certain decisions are or should be made).

Revans (1982) argues that those who hold responsibility do two things. They ask the following.

- What to do? (that we liken to our discussion about debate in this chapter).
- How to do it? (that we liken to our discussion about design in the preceding chapter).

What to do? engenders a sort of debate stimulated by these further questions.

- What am I (or my firm) really trying to do?
- What is stopping me (or my firm) from doing it?
- What can I (or my firm) contrive to do about it?

How to do it? raises debate about design and decision making guided by these further questions.

- Who knows what the line of action is that we are trying to implement?
- Who cares about getting this line of action implemented?
- Who can actually contribute anything toward getting it implemented?

AL is managerial mind supporting. It is argued by Revans that getting started requires commitment, sponsorship from a high level, a major issue to tackle, a manager designated to attack the issue, and a client (a senior person who owns the issue on behalf of the organisation).

In their interventionist's guide to AL, McGill and Beaty (1992) introduce AL as a continuous process of learning and reflection. People learn from each other by working on real issues and by reflecting on their experiences. The learning process is described as Experience, Understanding, Planning and Action (EUPA).

EUPA is a reflection and action cycle, an experiential learning cycle that helps people to learn about themselves and the organisation. Group work supports reflection and the challenging of assumptions. The process brings to consciousness awareness, feelings and reflections, that can usefully inform action. Action therefore is better informed.

A special feature (or recognition) of AL is that effective action is linked to the development of the person as well as the organisation – it strengthens both the individual and the organisation. Furthermore, AL recognises the importance of contextualisation, being interested in "the world out there" as it is related to the individual group member who is designated to attack the issue.

Boddy (1981) observes that group meetings provide an opportunity for group members to seek the help of other members in tackling their designated issue. Other members may raise questions or make suggestions. This widens the area within which a search for solutions and ideas occurs. The strategic objective of AL according to Bunning (1991) is to demonstrate a mode of functioning that maximises learning during the process of action in the everyday world and which can become more widely practised in organisational life.

In effect, then, AL is about meaningful debate over specified issues by a group to help an individual designated to tackle a given issue, while developing both the individual and the organisation in the same process. Action Research picks up on the ideas of AL, but goes further, as we shall find out in the next section.

Case Study

The case we have chosen briefly to review is presented by Boddy (1981). The company concerned is a subsidiary of Bowaters. It manufactures wooden doors and cubicles. The programme had three stages of thinking/action: a traditional course, an awareness-raising course, and an AL programme.

Initially, senior managers discussed with a training consultant ways of tackling a perceived lack of rapport between supervisors and management. Management's thoughts about possible action concluded with plans for a traditional formal supervisory course. This knowledge dissemination it was hoped would raise competencies in areas such as quality, work study, and industrial relations. Further investigation uncovered key information, the most interesting of which was that the supervisors had these competencies. The difficulty therefore was more likely to be attitude, possibly being unwillingness to employ these competencies, and so the plan to offer formal courses was dropped.

A residential awareness-raising course was planned instead. This was carried out over five days. The course included presentations from company speakers on issues facing the company. An additional feature was a series of purpose-built simulations to enable participants to become more aware of their own behaviour and attitudes, and the effect of these on their colleagues. The course was repeated four times, involving 18 supervisors on each occasion.

The third stage built on the success of the awareness-raising course. It involved launching an AL programme. Twelve AL groups were established each with six supervisors sitting on it. Middle managers were made available as group advisers. The clients (that is, those to whom the groups reported) were all from senior management. Each group tackled a common issue brought forward from the awareness-raising course. Supervisors therefore chose issues they considered to be most pressing, such as communication, absenteeism, and cost-effectiveness. Tentative conclusions drawn include signs of attitude change, enhanced adaptability of the company, and financial savings.

Discourse About Consideredness

In the case just recounted the essential value of AL is surfaced. Formal training sessions impart knowledge transfer. The extent to which this is successful depends on the willingness of the presenter to entertain discussion. Discussion and debate set off interaction between people whereby ideas are exchanged, considered and reconsidered. Reconsideration leads to learning and understanding. The amount of learning and understanding achievable is, however, limited by the boundaries of the formal course, say, bounded by a focus on quality.

Awareness-raising sessions provide a more open forum where the learning and understanding is not bounded in the same way. It could be argued that these sessions are necessary to prepare people for a full-blown AL programme. There is a chance for participants to indulge in the moment and engage widely with other participants about roles, responsibilities and issues they are facing. The value here is that participants begin to support participants. Rather than individuals facing their own issues in isolation, there is a collective strength, a combined force of knowledge, expertise, and co-operative relationships.

AL programmes aim to harness this strength and force, and hence give people "power to" make decisions that are well considered. In the case above, supervisors disclosed their thinking to colleagues in group settings. This helped them to think about what to do and how to do it on specific issues they identified. The supervisors were given access to middle managers for company details they normally would not be familiar with. They had senior management as their clients. Overall this process leads to both individual and organisational development.

Action researchers, however, might point out here that there is a number of crucial matters that are not dealt with. First of all, it seems that those involved in the process are not held responsible for taking further knowledge gained inductively in order to establish an ongoing process of knowledge development that has wider public significance. Second, little is said in AL about the relationship between the so-called issue attacker and issue owner. All that we are told is that reporting must be made to the client (issue owner); however, the quality of this reporting process is not addressed. Third, that there may be counter-forces at work that distort the process and influence the output of the process detrimentally so that people feel decisions are ill-considered. Fourth (and perhaps related to the third), nowhere is it explained why discussion need be confined to a collegial debate – the issue of widening the boundary of participation appears not to be problematised in AL. We now turn to AR to find out how some of these matters might be dealt with.

8.4 ACTION RESEARCH

8.4.1 Introduction

Action Research (AR) can incorporate AL practices but places its emphases differently as outlined in this section. There are many accounts and interpretations of AR.[4] One account of some of the arguments and practices in

---

[4] *Systems Practice* has published two special issues that offer highly relevant material which complements our presentation. Volume 9, Issue 1, focuses on group and organisational dynamics with a core theme being Kurt Lewin's contribution to AR. Lewin (1946, 1952) is considered by many to be the inventor of the term Action Research. Contributors are Maruyama, Moreland, Schein, Wheelan, and Weisbord and Jonoff. Volume 9, Issue 2, presents a range of views on AR with a core theme being emancipatory practice. Contributors are Bell, Fals-Borda, Moggridge and Reason, and Whyte. There is also a noteworthy special edition of *Human Relations*, published in February 1993, that explores AR.

AR is given below. The account provides a general overview of AR in advance of focused interpretations[5] that follow.

AR was originally developed by Lewin (1946, 1952) as a way of developing a relationship between social science research and the concerns of people in society. He argued that researchers should help demonstrate the significance of scientific research for improving ways of addressing issues faced in society. The aim was to generate both research findings and action improvement out of the process of research of issues in society. Lewin, as a scientist, was committed to processes of what he saw as scientific testing of ideas; however, his view of this differed somewhat from the styles of hypothetico-deductive research which were being practised by many other scientists.

In AR it is regarded as somewhat inappropriate to formulate initial hypotheses and then use situations to test these. It is more fitting within an AR agenda to pose a central question which the action researcher(s) seek(s) to answer. The aim is to generate insights with involvement from "practitioners within particular, local practice contexts" (Argyris and Schön, 1991: 86). As Argyris and Schön (1991: 86) indicate, AR "takes its cues – its questions, puzzles, and problems – from the perceptions of practitioners . . . [and it] bounds episodes of research according to the . . . local context". Research findings should not be regarded as simply applicable or transferable to other situations. This would detract from the process of (again) taking cues from the local context. However, previous research findings may resonate in new contexts. Hence it is considered incumbent on action researchers to make findings generally accessible so that the wider public may gain insights from studies that have already been undertaken.

The degree to which (and grounds on which) researchers may legitimately challenge participants' views and practices is one of the questions which is still subject to ongoing debate within the AR community. Processes by which confrontation and engagement between views may be facilitated and the role of the researcher in this facilitation are also the subject of contention. In addition, the ways in which researchers can or indeed should address cases where powerful interests apparently block effective intervention toward fairer practice are currently being hotly debated. Broadly speaking, though, it can be said that AR concentrates on facilitating learning and skills development. It identifies critical learning, that is, questioning and replacing mental models, paradigms and/or assumptions that are self-limiting. Ultimately, the goal of AR is empowerment of people to manage their own affairs while contributing to public knowledge.

With AR, there is also an obligation for researchers to make findings and

[5] Our labels for each interpretation of AR do not necessarily coincide with the names given by its key advocates. We have in some cases renamed interpretations to prevent confusion in this text.

insights[6] generated from field work more generally public, and to be accountable as a researcher. This means two things. First, to ensure that those affected by planned changes have a key responsibility for deciding on courses of critically informed action and for evaluating the results (McTaggart, 1991). Second, to use the research process to generate ideas that *may* be of potential use in similar situations. It adds "power to" make considered decisions.

A general overview set out, we now begin our inquiry into interpretations of AR,[7] starting with Participatory Action Research.

8.4.2 Participatory Action Research

William Foote Whyte has named his more recent research Participatory Action Research (PAR). He began his work wondering "how the intellectual contributions of underdogs could be incorporated into the work process in ways that would improve the underdog's lot as well as increase organisational efficiency" (Whyte, 1991b: 2). In the course of his lifetime's work, from *Street Corner Society* (Whyte, 1943) through to *Participatory Action Research* (Whyte, 1991a, b), Whyte has identified three phases of research: from the professional expert, to the action researcher, and then the participatory action researcher (the merits of each are considered in the following discourse about consideredness).

The idea of PAR is that the process of intervention is made useful to the researcher and more enjoyable to practitioners if the social process is expanded to find out and consult with them about possible interpretations of the study.

Whyte claims a special relationship between theory and practice. He notes that the approach adopted in PAR for data gathering considerably influences what can be done with data. Data are drawn from fieldwork and the work of people with whom he shares an intellectual interest. Whyte forgoes thorough literature searches. Instead over time PAR builds up experience-based knowledge. Comparisons are made between cases. Resemblances and differences are noted. Common patterns are detected. Future deviant cases are noted and the pattern modified if deviances are

---

[6] The way in which findings are generated is seen to differ from practices of much so-called normal science; where normally the focus is on survey research and quantitative modelling and where qualitative methods such as interviewing are considered simply as data-gathering devices. In AR the focus is more on qualitative methods which are employed to develop and enrich accounts of what people are experiencing (as they engage in action). It allows for mediation between views so that forms of learning can be enhanced. Insofar as quantitative information is utilised close attention is paid to the way in which it is both collected and interpreted with reference to participant concerns.

[7] This section reviews two members of the family of AR approaches. Other family members that we deal with we prefer to incorporate in discussions on might–right management in Chapter 9.

found. If they are not found then the pattern is further reinforced leading to definitions of structures and processes (Whyte, 1991b: 10).

This knowledge-producing process is defended since "possibilities of studying important changes that would not otherwise occur far outweigh the potential disadvantage of researcher bias through personal involvement in the change process" (Whyte, 1991b: 283). PAR checks claims made with those who have first-hand knowledge. PAR projects are carried out in the field where the action is. Surveys may be used as well but are not relied upon. Projects begin with vigorous discussion when professional researchers and practitioners exchange ideas and opinions. Emphasis is placed on thinking and writing, keeping records, and then rewriting. There is division of labour, sharing out roles and sharing control. "PAR involves practitioners in the research process from the initial design of the project, through data gathering and analysis to final conclusions and actions arising out of the research" (Whyte *et al*, 1991). Emphasis is placed on both social and technical issues.

There are conditions, it is argued, essential to the viability of a PAR project (Whyte, 1991b: 277).

- The professional researcher must be interested in the project.
- The issue must seem important to key members of the organisation.
- The research methods and types of data must appear credible to those participating in the project.

There is also an appeal for complementarism. This is an appeal for space for PAR. "The complexity of the world around us demands the deployment of a variety of techniques and strong intellectual and methodological discipline, not a commitment to the hegemony of a single research modality" (Whyte *el al*, 1991).

Case Study

Two projects are discussed here. The first looks at the way the Xerox Corporation tackled their 1970s decline in international competitiveness in exceptionally favourable circumstances (Whyte *et al*, 1991). The second project, referred to very briefly, outlines PAR under quite unfavourable conditions in Trico Products Corporation with partial success (Klingel and Martin, 1988). At least, these are the observations of William Foote Whyte.[8]

Xerox, based in the USA, enjoyed a monopoly for many years, protected

[8] Another particularly interesting case published in *Systems Practice* is Whyte's (1996) account of PAR in an Eskimo community. Timothy Kennedy helped the villagers to build community solidarity, and from that platform to communicate more effectively with government officials and politicians about the needs and wishes of their community. The story is also about power structures in academia that see as irrelevant or undesirable members of staff with skills in, and who care about, emancipatory practice.

by patents. Between 1970 and 1979, as the patents expired, their share of the world market for copy machines crashed from 94% to 44%. Management, not surprisingly, undertook a comprehensive re-evaluation of structures, policies, and programs. They enjoyed a financial cushion permitting rescue planning over several months.

The program was set up as follows. There was strong mutual respect between management and unions. There was a commitment between the two to develop worker participation. Management therefore did not hesitate to call in the unions at its main copier-production facilities for help with the issue of decline. Personnel researched the experience of other companies which had pursued a similar line. Meanwhile McKinsey and Company were called in to study management and administration procedures and put forward recommendations for change.

Some training of management and union workers was undertaken. McKinsey and Company then set about developing a Quality of Working Life program to tackle issues arising from structures, policies, and programs. A conventional start saw managers and workers concentrating on shop-floor issues and unwittingly missing issues such as labour contracts and management prerogatives and policies. Possibilities for changes at shop-floor level were limited, offering limited life to the program. The challenge was to get from a conventional shop-floor focus to one that had a broader socio-technical and economic focus. This was achieved when management confronted the unions with a crisis.

Management studies demonstrated that the company could save US$3.2 million annually by closing the wire-harness department. The solution was to outsource. The expectation of the announcement was that the parties could begin to discuss how human costs could be minimised and labour relations protected. While this was going on Peter Lazes (ten days a month from McKinsey), who had served for two years as a consultant, trainer and process facilitator, and so was knowledgeable and well trusted, proposed the creation of a cost-study team. The aim was to study possible ways of saving US$3.2 million and hence the 180 jobs that were threatened. This meant a radical form of worker participation – opening up for study all of the costs of plant management charged to the wire-harness department. This included overheads which had always been strictly for management consumption.

Concerns abounded. Unions were worried that changing contract clauses might set precedents that held organisation-wide implications. Management was concerned that privileged financial information would get into the hands of its competitors, and that the process would merely be a costly delay to an inevitable conclusion. Discussion facilitated by Lazes enabled both sides to explore possible consequences of this action and further strengthened the relationship between management and the shop floor, for example through management's respect for quality of information and ideas coming through from the shop floor.

Union leaders selected (following interviews) six workers to represent different levels of skill, experience and functions. Management selected department supervisors and an engineer. These two lots of selection were amalgamated into one cost-study team. The team analysed engineering, business administration and organisational matters. They had an open-ended brief. They found that divisional overhead charges were based upon services not actually being delivered or that could be performed more efficiently within their department. That saved US$0.5 million. Other findings accumulated potential savings of over US$3.5 million. The actual savings achieved hit the US$3.2 million mark although implementation of the changes took longer than anticipated. Cost-study groups were then set up in three new areas where target savings were achieved. Participatory management and union–management co-operation were then spread throughout the division. New practices were established such as a commitment from management that before any lay-offs were announced they would work with the union to set up a cost-study group. Many other changes in working practices became possible in the participatory and co-operative climate.

> At Xerox, participatory action research created and guided a powerful process of organisational learning – a process whereby leaders of labour and management learned from each other and from the consultant/facilitator, while he learned from them. . . . The Xerox success, combined with growing interest in Albany of some Cornellians on employee buyouts to save jobs, led to a 1985 decision by New York State to provide the first solid financing of Programs for Employment and Workplace Systems [of which Whyte became Research Director]. (Whyte *et al*, 1991: 30–31)

The situation facing Trico Products Corporation, another firm in the USA, was similar to Xerox. It supplied windscreen wipers to the automobile industry. Its decline followed that of the automobile industry. Planned management action was to close down a large part of its operations in Buffalo, losing 1,300 jobs, and relocate in Texas and Mexico. Pressure was exerted from the unions, from community leaders, and New York State officials for management to rethink the decision. This concerted effort succeeded in agreement to set up two union–management cost-study teams, with the hope that they would find ways of cutting costs and saving jobs. A third team, established by the union and outside experts, researched the feasibility of building a new, integrated manufacturing facility at Buffalo.

The overall effort to save jobs took almost nine months. By the time recommendations were made, involving new plant teams, management had become committed to the relocation. There had been no commitment from

management that jobs would stay even if cost-study teams identified sufficient cost savings. Management therefore controlled the final decision irrespective of the findings. On the plus side, 300 jobs were saved and a healthy
severance package was agreed for laid-off workers. The future relationship
of labour and management was also improved. The foundation had been
laid for future involvement of the unions in operational decisions and they
gained sophistication and knowledge about finances, production accounting systems, and manufacturing processes.

Discourse About Consideredness

At the outset of this section we mentioned Whyte's progress over fifty years
from professional expert, to action researcher, to participatory action
researcher. Our discourse begins by contrasting merits of these three. The
professional expert makes a study and recommends a course of action to decision makers. The expert can give good advice leading to improved organisational operation, but tends to establish a relationship of dependency
which may lead to superdecisions. This is "power over" the decision-making
process. There is no obvious organisational learning. The traditional *action
researcher* (see Section 8.4.1) Whyte distinguishes from the *participatory
action researcher* by the extent to which participants are "let in" in defining
the parameters of the research process. He suggests that in the former case,
the researcher tends to control the research process and can become the
principal change agent which tends toward superdecisions. The *participatory action researcher*, however, consciously pursues a strategy in which s/he
involves members of the organisation "as active participants in the research
process" (Whyte, 1991b: 5). There is a direct link made here between participatory research and action. Whyte notes that he does not use individuals
as passive informants to be "pumped for data". Individuals in PAR are
active, reading, writing and criticising reports, collaborating in studies, and
providing ideas in this way.

    There is, however, a concern with PAR that the process may be subject to
invisible (intrapsychic) influences that distort the outcomes and therefore
make decisions made feel ill-considered to the participants. For example,
people are often defensive, withhold feelings, and are overly concerned
about themselves and other people or under-concerned about other people.
These feelings people have may impinge on the process of debate and participation and raise doubts about plausibility of induced findings. A more
scientific approach is called for, some critics say. Enter Action Science.

8.4.3 Action Science

Action Science (AS) is the name given by Argyris and Schön (1974, 1985,

1991) to their brand of Action Research. Whyte, in discussing the relationship between PAR and AS, suggests that,

> AS focuses more heavily [than Whyte's PAR] on interpersonal relationships and intrapsychic processes. AS calls for a detached observer to document in detail the intervention process. AS assumes that beginning to learn new ways of thinking and feeling should precede embarking on new courses of action. AS requires the intervention team to gain more control of both the intervention and the research process. (Whyte, 1991c: 97)[9]

Argyris and Schön's description of AS states that,

> AS is a form of action research that, although it shares the values and strategies [of Whyte's PAR], places a central emphasis on the spontaneous, tacit theories-in-use that participants bring to practice and research, especially whenever feelings of embarrassment or threat come in to play. These theories in use we call "Model I". They include strategies of unilateral control, unilateral self-protection, defensiveness, smoothing over, and covering up, of which their users tend to be largely unaware (Argyris and Schön, 1974). And these strategies tend in turn to undermine attempts to implement inventions based on the discoveries of action research; indeed, they often distort the discoveries themselves – all in ways of which researchers and practitioners tend to remain unaware not because of ignorance but because of a skilful adherence to Model I theories-in-use and virtues such as "strength" (construed as dominance or unwillingness to be swayed by others) and "caring" (construed as unilateral protection of others) learned early in life. (Argyris and Schön, 1991: 86–87)

The worry for Argyris and Schön in the face of Model I factors is that social scientists have to wrangle with what seems to be a fundamental choice over rigour or relevance; in other words, choosing either prevailing disciplinary standards of knowledge production or placing temporal priority on relevance to practitioners. They attempt, however, to strike a balance between the extremes by achieving three things: ". . . a way of representing research results that enhances their usability, a complementary way of construing causality, and an appropriate methodology of causal interference" (Argyris and Schön, 1991: 85).

Argyris and Schön are concerned that PAR overemphasises relevance to the practitioners at the cost of rigorous and critical inquiry into "other plausible explanations". They are concerned that seemingly invisible forces tend to be ignored and it is these forces that may well shape the outcomes in PAR. They wish to construct and test plausible alternatives avoiding "obvious interpretations" by seeking out countervailing evidence that reviews

---

[9] Whyte (1991c: 97–98) argues that a feature of PAR is its ability to utilise the process of action itself in order to generate "new ways of thinking and feeling, which [may] further reinforce and support the continuation of new lines of action". He suggests that PAR may be more attuned (than AS) to "creative surprises" arising from engagement in action (Whyte, 1991c: 97).

organisational learning. They wish to present alternative accounts of intervention that propose plausible explanations of organisational change.

AS involves rigour through critical inquiry with a focus on Model I factors that may indeed distort findings observed through a less critical approach. Argyris and Schön ask, How do we really know that "a" caused "b"? Some form of testing is required. "Undiscussables" from Model I may be at work and if not teased out may distort appreciation of causal links. "Obvious interpretations" may simply be the result of (very powerful) defensive routines that prevent learning.

Model I operates as follows. Goals are defined and sought. Action strategies are unilateral involving persuasion and appeal to larger goals. People involved are defensive, inconsistent, incongruent, controlling, fearful of being vulnerable, withholding feelings, overly concerned about self and others or under-concerned about others. The consequences of this are that learning is self-sealing leading to decreased long-term effectiveness. Priority is given to maximising winning and minimising losing. There is a tendency to own and control the task. This leads to a defensive interpersonal and group relationship that yields little help to others.

The tendency is to hold back on generating or expressing negative feelings. There is self-protection. Defensive norms come in to play leading to mistrust, lack of risk taking, conformity, an emphasis on diplomacy, and power-centred competition and rivalry. Consequently there is little testing of theories publicly, although there may be much testing of theories privately. People become oriented also to protecting others from being hurt in a bid to avoid embarrassing situations but this restricts freedom of choice, and leads to low internal commitment and limited risk taking.

AS operates Model II. The goal is to get to grips with addressing organisational defensive routines. To achieve this, situations are designed so that participants can originate ideas and can experience high personal causation. There is minimal defensiveness encouraged through facilitation and collaboration, helping to create choice. Choice becomes informed and freer. Tasks are jointly controlled. Interpersonal relations and group dynamics are kept minimally defensive. This encourages learning where there is questioning and replacement of mental models/paradigms/assumptions that are self-limiting.

There is an internal commitment to choice and constant monitoring of the implementation of choice. Protection of self is encouraged as a joint enterprise and oriented to growth, attacking inconsistency and incongruity. Norms are learning oriented, such as trust and open confrontation on difficult issues. Theories are tested publicly. The claim is that issue management and decision-making effectiveness is substantially improved. That claim is approached again in the case study that follows.

Case Study

Our case comes from Schön's (1983) well-known title *The Reflective Practitioner*. In Chapter 7 of his book (especially pages 226–235 that we follow closely), Schön assesses reflection-in-action using town planning as a vehicle for weighing up decision making through Model I and Model II dynamics.

Schön's case scrutinises a meeting between a town planner, an architect and a developer. The meeting was videotaped. The planner dealt with physical development of the town. He did not actually prepare plans or designs, but acted as an intermediary between local regulatory bodies and private developers who submit proposals for review. Through negotiations in his role as intermediary, the town planner influenced direction and quality of physical development in the town.

The developer submitted drawings and plans for remodelling an apartment building. He wanted to add a couple of apartment units to the building. At a meeting carefully prepared by the planner, the planner reviewed the plans and noted possible violations of the zoning by-law. Under apartment controls 20,000 square feet of lot area was needed but the developer only had 14,341. The planner advised the developer that this would require a variance because the proposal was to add to a multi-family building in an apartment zone where the lots are not large enough. He then prepared the developer for likely examination that the Zoning Board of Appeals would undertake. The planner dealt with negative information by minimising it, making remedies seem straightforward, and enveloping it with good news.

The planner, Schön observed, framed issues arising in his meeting with the developer in a Model I way. The review game he played with the developer became a win or lose one carried out through a strategy of mystery and mastery. For example, the planner decided ahead of time what the developer needed to know. He set up a meeting in his own office, pursued without deflection his own agenda, and used his expertise to reinforce a strategy of control. He prevented reaction to negative information from the developer with tactics that softened or masked impact of criticisms of the plan. He negotiated with the developer in a way that displayed the authority that he denied. He unilaterally controlled impressions that he created in the mind of the developer. So, Schön surmises, the planner created a self-reinforcing system on the foundations of a Model I theory of action. The planner had much of his time consumed in managing a balancing act, manipulating impressions imposed on the developer, and defending himself against the vulnerability of exposure, leaving no time to reflect on issues or his performance.

During the meeting with the planner, the developer decided against going ahead with the project, shocking the planner. The developer was worried that he would have to apply for a single variance. The developer had based his strategy on minimising variances, but had assumed that a single, easily obtainable variance on lot size would not obstruct the project. He ran a private test on project feasibility and decided unilaterally to abandon it since the results looked negative.

The point Schön makes here is that the planner and developer operated in a world where both withheld negative information, tested assumptions in private and attempted to maintain unilateral control over the other person. Consequently, the planner had no idea that his efforts were futile from the moment the developer learned of the need for a single variance. Schön then asks, What might have happened if the planner had operated a Model II theory of action?

If the planner operated a Model II theory of action then he might have been minimally defensive and open to learning. He might have tried to elicit the developer's agenda rather than rigidly sticking to his own. He might have tested the developer's response to the information that a variance would be required. He might have thought things through differently. He might have thought about making his dilemma public. He might have measured effectiveness in his ability to bargain openly rather than how well he performed in his balancing act. The developer in these circumstances might have provisionally confirmed the project with the developer. Let us take this debate further in our discourse about consideredness.

Discourse About Consideredness

As mentioned above, Argyris and Schön (1991) recognise a dilemma in AR, between relevance and rigour. Relevance can be achieved through, say, PAR, because PAR gets stuck into the action right away guiding an exciting process that may surface creative insights while enhancing the process of intervention. Relevance may be only superficial or distorted, however, because intrapsychic defence mechanisms may impinge on the way social processes work in a PAR intervention. Rigour may be needed. A form of rigour is added by AS through scientific analysis of the process, guiding the process so that intrapsychic mechanisms are managed. The case just presented explains by example the sort of findings rigour might uncover. This rigour may, however, be achieved at the expense of relevance. Argyris and Schön know this but still prefer to go for (in their view) greater rigour than PAR. Users of PAR and AS need to be aware of this dilemma.

Nevertheless, AS does offer valuable insights about loosening up the way ideas are changed. It helps to contain defence mechanisms that are built up through organisational life. It helps to change the way of thinking, the way of talking, and the way of communicating. In this sense it is emancipatory and helps to construct a decision-making process where issues are well considered.

Returning to the lobster trap metaphor introduced in Section 8.2, one reason why we get trapped is because we cannot see the trap that we are in.

For example, the town planner was blind to the Model I trap Schön observed he was in. Argyris and Schön show us the trap of the intrapsychy. Science helps to make visible this trap. On the other hand, science may require involvement of professional expertise. Organisations can easily become dependent on professional expertise. For the same reason AS warns us about intrapsychic defence mechanisms, AS must be warned about overuse of professional expertise. We raised the issue of professional responsibility earlier when we mentioned that (some) participants prefer to leave a greater measure of responsibility in the hands of researchers, letting them direct the research through an AS agenda. Participant delegation of responsibility is certainly a factor to be taken into account when deciding the acceptability of such a direction. The danger to be borne in mind is undue reliance on the veracity of the supposedly scientific diagnosis which, just because it has the status of being scientific, is not easily questioned. This danger persists when organisational participants are advised (via AS) to utilise more scientific inquiry to reflect upon their relationships. The problem is that this may become an unquestioned way to define and diagnose defensiveness.

Furthermore, AS in its drive to neutralise or minimise defensiveness of interpersonal relations and group dynamics may be missing opportunities that can arise by facilitating processes of adversarial debate, *thereby* rerouteing people's orientations. Tension created through adversarial debate may generate positive output. Admittedly, facilitation over such a process has to be carefully administered, and appropriateness of an adversarial process in the light of existing political tensions must be carefully thought through; yet, possibilities still exist. The first of the systems approaches reviewed in the next section demonstrates these possibilities have both a theoretical and practical back-up.

8.5 SYSTEMS APPROACHES

8.5.1 Introduction

Systems approaches to issue management grew out of Operational Research and Systems Engineering. Application of these technical and predominantly quantitative methods and techniques to social contexts was largely unsuccessful. While they were apt for landing people on the moon, making war efforts massively efficient, and designing large-scale manufacturing processes, they were found grossly inapt for tackling non-technical social and organisational issues.

Traditional Operational Research and Systems Engineering techniques essentially define (what are considered) problems and objectives and then try to work out the most efficient way of realising them. The main question therefore is, Which technique will help best to identify the so-called problem as it is and then come up with an optimal solution that will solve it? This general process is recommended as if it were unproblematic. The process falls down, however, when issue definition itself is an issue. Then how do researchers and interventionists proceed? This concern arises when messy human-centred activities are the main focus. And even if it were possible to identify the core issue, the process of identifying the most efficient and effective means of tackling the issue again is likely to be contentious. New approaches were developed to address these questions under the heading of Soft Operational Research and Soft Systems.

We have chosen two soft approaches from the wide range available. Our selection represents two possible styles of intervention, each having something original to contribute to our debate about debate. The first style represented is adversarial based and the flag is flown by Strategic Assumption Surfacing and Testing. It utilises adversity between strategies to create conditions for possible syntheses. The second style, represented by Soft Systems Methodology, displays and compares models of purposeful activity as a means of generating debate, leading to accommodation between people which they feel is a workable arrangement.

8.5.2 Strategic Assumption Surfacing and Testing

Strategic Assumption Surfacing and Testing (SAST-Mason and Mitroff, 1981)[10] aims to help seriously challenge accepted modes of doing things in organisations. It carves out space for policy options to be considered that diverge from current practice and normally would not get a (fair) hearing. It promotes rigorous analysis and comparison of all options. It does this by surfacing and challenging assumptions made in the formulation of policy. Alternatives are developed in opposition to one another.

The underlying assumption made by SAST is that organisations are arenas of conflict between groups deliberating views. Organisations therefore are built on tension. An adversarial approach if carefully handled may be able to harness positive output from this tension. The aim is for people to explore the validity and consequences of a strong attack on the assumptions they are making in believing that their preferred strategy or plans will work (in a wide sense of these terms).

The adversarial nature of debate through SAST is best illustrated through

---

[10] In an explication of SAST, from which this review is abstracted, Flood and Jackson (1991a: 121–122) recognise the profound intellectual debt that it owes to the work of C. West Churchman. It is regrettable that we cannot in this volume review Churchman's contribution to contemporary systems thinking since the entire soft systems tradition has been considerably influenced by it (as has the critical systems tradition). We can only encourage the reader to consult the following texts: Churchman (1968a, 1968b, 1971, 1979, 1981) and the Festschrift issue of *Systems Practice* (1988) Volume 1, Issue 4, devoted to Churchman's work.

methodology description. The core idea of the methodology is that designs and decisions are built on assumptions. What is needed is a way of testing the assumptions to see how well they stand up to criticism. Polarised views are assessed in terms of their strengths and weaknesses, are then compared, and from this analysis a synthesised plan for action is formulated. The methodology has four steps: group formation, assumption surfacing, investigative debate, and synthesis.

Group formation. The aim of group formation is to organise people into groups as follows.

- Group people together who share the same (or a similar) view. This means that each view will be strongly supported by its group of advocates.
- Maximise the difference in opinion between the groups. This means that the view of each group will be strongly challenged during investigative debate.

Each group initially formulates a clear and concise statement about their preferred strategy. Once this has been achieved the process moves on to assumption surfacing.

Assumption surfacing. Each group has a clear view about which alternative must be selected. What is not clear in most cases are the assumptions on which that view is based. Unseen weaknesses can often be found when assumptions about the viewpoints are surfaced. The next task, then, is to surface assumptions to be tested. Assumption surfacing employs three quite simple but very effective techniques: stakeholder analysis, assumption specification, and assumption rating.

Stakeholder analysis. Each group must identify key stakeholders on whom the success or failure of their preferred design or decision depends.

Assumption specification. Each group constructs a list of assumptions that they have made about individual stakeholders in trusting that their preferred alternative will work.

Assumption rating. Each group plots the assumptions on a chart. This begins the process of testing how sound they are. It begins to test the alternative as a whole. The chart comprises the following two scales.

- The importance of the assumption in terms of its role in the success or failure of the strategy – from least important to most important.
- The degree of certainty that the assumption is justified – from least certain to most certain.

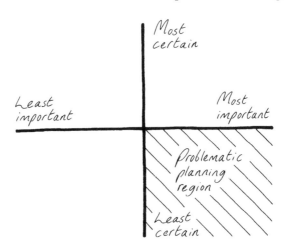

Figure 8.2

The scales are put together to form a chart (see Figure 8.2). Assumptions plotted on the right-hand side of the chart are evidently important. Those in the lower quartile of the right-hand side are risky. These are the assumptions the group is making that are likely to be the root cause of any failure – hence this part of the chart is known as the problematic planning region.

Investigative debate between participating groups is the next step. The groups are brought together. Each group makes a presentation. They explain their alternative and then talk through the results of their assumption surfacing. When each group has completed their initial presentation the facilitator starts a second round of deliberation, this time encouraging reasoned criticism about alternatives. Each group has to defend their strategy against the most penetrating reflections other groups can muster. Opposing groups attempt to show that there are stakeholders who have not been taken into account, or that assumptions plotted on the chart that are not in the problematic planning region should indeed be there. After all groups have been in the hot seat, the groups retire once more to reconsider their assumptions and the alternatives. Assumption modification may take place. Once modification is complete, the groups come together for further debate in the form of synthesis.

Synthesis. The aim of synthesis is to reach a compromise between groups on their alternatives and assumptions. This is a process of negotiation and further modification. A list of agreed assumptions is constructed. Using this list, efforts are made to work out a compromise between the polarised groups. The ease with which this happens is determined by the substantive content of the agreed list.

Two cases are presented below. The first case recounts an intervention in a hospital context where a compromise was achieved relatively easily. The second case recounts a more tensionful yet beneficial use of SAST.

Case Study

The first case reports on a decision to be made concerning substantial capital expenditure on a swimming pool for the social club of a hospital in the Middle East.[11] The location is a crucial factor that influenced considerably the way the intervention was handled. The hospital is managed under a renewable fixed term management contract by Allied Health Company on behalf of the owner, which is the local government. The hospital employs approximately 750 people from a wide range of nationalities, cultures, ethnic groups, and religious backgrounds. There are quite a large number of Western expatriate single female nurses and paramedical staff who are generally recruited through the company's recruitment offices in the UK and Eire.

The hospital moved into new buildings in 1984. A part of these new buildings included a purpose-built staff social club, located on the beach-front adjacent to the hospital. The majority of the staff accommodation is located in blocks of flats situated throughout the city. The social club facilities have been considerably developed over the last few years, including extensive landscaping of the beach-front area with grass and trees forming a large garden area.

Although the club is situated on the beach, many of the staff prefer not to swim in the sea because an extensive area of the beach comprises shingle and pebbles. Also, the amount of tar being washed up had greatly increased since the Gulf War. Tar becomes attached to swimmers' bodies and costumes and is very difficult to remove.

From time to time staff and members of the hospital management team raised and discussed the option of a purpose-built swimming pool in the social club grounds. It would alleviate the issues associated with sea swimming, and might provide an extra attraction helping recruitment of the best trained single female nurses and paramedical staff. Despite these immediate gains, digging a little deeper soon revealed as many disadvantages as advantages, accentuated by the increasingly polarised views of staff members. Two positions therefore emerged generating positive tension in planning, those in support of the argument for a swimming pool and those against; but relations between the people were nevertheless quite amicable. This is a classic situation where SAST can come into its own.

---

[11] The following case is an application written by Bob's colleague Robert Cross, director of the hospital where the intervention was carried out. A full account of the case is given in Flood (1995a: 203–211).

Group formation was relatively straightforward; one group in support of having a swimming pool and one group against. Selecting membership of the groups was, however, problematic. Certain assumptions to be explored might be interpreted as political, racist, sexist, or criticising a religion. It was therefore decided to contain membership within the management team, where there was strong polarisation on the issue anyway, that would act on behalf of those requiring representation. Views of other stakeholders were sought informally and introduced into the exercise by representatives on the management team. This enabled intervention to approximate the ideal of participation while at the same time avoided the issue of negative conflict. These are the realities of managing an organisation in the Gulf region, where there is multi-cultural diversity, having to balance societal, organisational, and individuals' needs equitably without triggering off fruitless conflict and strife.

Assumption surfacing, Assumption specification, and *Assumption rating* were carried out. *Assumption charts* were plotted. The ratings among the group in support of the swimming pool raised only a few potential issue areas that might be of significance. The group were confident in their certainty about the vast majority of their assumptions. The key assumptions of the group against the swimming pool were more evenly spread across the four quadrants. Nevertheless, they too remained confident.

It is interesting to note that up until this stage the two groups were still bullish about their strategies. This is despite the groups undergoing self-analysis in the process of assumption rating and charting, which can lead groups to uncover weaknesses in their strategy. In fact, the two groups felt that they had identified some very important assumptions, and were convinced that they were correct. If nothing else this underlines the strong adversarial and tensionful nature of the strategies of the two groups.

Investigative debate and synthesis. Debate was carried out in several open meetings over the course of five to six weeks. Periods of several days were left between meetings so that groups would have plenty of time to consider the content of debates. This also allowed time for representatives to hold informal discussions with interested parties. Managers put forward their own views and represented the views of other stakeholders who had a stake in the outcome of the debate but who were not included for reasons already explained.

Debate quickly uncovered new stakeholders that neither group had included. In particular a number of fundamentalist groups who stood firm against such proposals on religious grounds had to be included. This added more weight to the position of the group against the swimming pool.

The group against the proposal also pointed out that some assumptions on the chart of the group for the proposal could well turn out to be more problematic than they had initially believed. For example, it was not so certain that the pool would assist that much with recruitment, that learning to swim was important to many people, or that there really would be advantages overall in children being left at the poolside while the parents went shopping. Furthermore, the capital and running costs were very hard to justify and it would not be sensible for the hospital to step out of line with cultural norms of the indigenous population. The group for the proposal acknowledged these concerns and readjusted their chart and viewpoint radically. They eventually dropped completely the idea of a swimming pool.

The group against, however, saw some value in the ideas of the group for the swimming pool that they did not want to lose. For example, more recreational support would help with staff morale and possibly improve recruitment. They formulated a new proposal to harness the worth of those ideas. The proposal requested management to consider utilising financial resources to subsidise use of outside clubs and hotels, while concentrating on utilising hospital social club funds on other more modest ideas that would increase the club's attractiveness to staff. This synthesis ultimately became the foundations of a new strategy that was implemented.

Another use of SAST took place as a spontaneous part of the process of implementation of Local Area Policing (LAP) in York Division, North Yorkshire Police in North England. Bob was charged with leading the LAP initiative through a Steering Committee (a full account is given in Flood, 1995b, and further evaluation in Green, 1995).[12] One of the most important resolutions made by the Steering Committee for LAP was to launch LAP with a pilot on 30/10/94 in the West area; one of four designated areas. This decision was made on 12/10/94. There was much debate with arguments for a pilot set against arguments for all four areas to be launched at the same time.

A meeting of the Steering Committee on 30/10/1994 polarised into two distinct camps; one for a pilot and one for a launch of all four areas at once.

---

[12] LAP was implemented in York Division in four geographic regions as determined by the Steering Committee: West, North, East, and City/Core. Operations were arranged this way with CID supporting each area locally under centralised control. Deliberations of the LAP Steering Committee concluded in a decision to launch in November 1994 West LAP (the West area of York) as a pilot, in advance of implementation of the remaining three LAP areas in 1995. The main feature of the implementation was to ask police constables (PCs, the most junior members of the organisation) to "design" the LAP area to which they were assigned. Implementation involved the PCs of each LAP team going through Idealised Design (see Ackoff, 1974; Ackoff et al, 1984 and Jason Magidson's case written up in Chapter 10 in this book). PCs were organised into small groups and asked to do three things: draw up an operational mission for their LAP, specify the sort of things they wanted to achieve with their LAP, and, on the basis of this thinking, to spell out their plan for implementing LAP in their designated area. Their plans were largely implemented taking into account constraints of co-ordination and budgets.

The majority of people were in favour of the pilot, yet two members, including a nominated LAP Commander, raised genuine concerns about the pilot. The decision, however, began to swing toward the majority, partly because of the pressure of the majority and partly because the majority included the most senior officer. There was no witting use of power, but the culture institutionalised and still at work in the force (although consciously being changed to participatory) moved the decision toward the most senior officer.

At this point Bob stepped in and suggested that the discussion was not penetrating enough and that several matters raised by the minority group had not been fully dealt with. All present agreed that some matters were being swept under the carpet and so agreed to extend the group meeting with an exercise over the lunch period based on SAST.

The two groups formed according to the strategy people believed in. Each group occupied a separate room and followed a standard SAST process. Missions were set, stakeholders named, assumptions about their plans surfaced, rated and plotted. The groups were then brought together for dialectic debate about the two strategies. A negotiated arrangement was agreed upon with all present in tensionful accord with the outcome. All involved concurred with the view that the outcome was substantially improved by following this process which helped to contain tension. The decision was to go ahead with the pilot but to manage carefully resources to benefit implementation of LAP in all four areas.

This paragraph recounts a typical debate from the SAST exercise. There was a danger that launching a pilot now and the other three areas later would marginalise 75% of the Force. In addition, the main idea of the pilot was to run a trial and pass on knowledge from the trial to the other three areas; but this would hardly be effective unless those with experience in the West LAP trial were redeployed at the end of the pilot in other areas so that they could disseminate their knowledge and experience. The trouble with redeployment was that the good work done in establishing West LAP would be undone by fragmentation of the team at the end of the pilot. The group against the pilot were successful in pushing their point that as many officers as possible from the four LAP areas should benefit from the pilot and take away "hands on" experience (if it had to go ahead). There was negotiation on the exact numbers that should be redeployed. The LAP Commander of the pilot West LAP and the minority group were both satisfied to some extent with the arrangements made.

Discourse About Consideredness

Perhaps the greatest value of the York Division exercise in the participants' view was the in-depth understanding generated for all involved about

LAP in York Division. Although the Steering Committee discussed LAP extensively, the level of understanding attained paled to insignificance against that now in place. Having to work out and defend a position on LAP (indeed any position) against the strongest attack that could be mounted from another group grew each participant's understanding of LAP in York Division substantially. This underlines SAST as an extremely effective tool for testing strategies and for raising understanding about issues faced. The policing example also illustrates that SAST encourages careful consideration of positions that may slip by because of, for instance, cultural influences on the decision-making process – such as tendencies to accord legitimacy to viewpoints of those with official seniority.

In the hospital case the main advantage arguably was the consideredness of the final decision following rigorous testing of underlying assumptions of opposing strategies. Stakeholders were identified whose interest and possible influence had not previously been thought through. New assumptions about stakeholders were surfaced and tested. And bearing heavily on the final decision, some assumptions made by the group for the swimming pool were shown to be very important but also more uncertain than they had originally thought.

Comparing SAST to Argyris and Schön's AS raises further points. SAST might in some circumstances incline people toward increasing defensiveness about their positions in a climate where intrapsychic defence mechanisms appear to be firmly entrenched. In such cases it might pay to heed the warnings of AS about negative consequences of intrapsychic defence mechanisms. SAST in such a situation may serve to further polarise opposing positions instead of helping to neutralise them (as a starting point for continued debate). It may serve to further entrench people's sense that they should not declare private agendas, and that they need to protect themselves from invasion by the now clearly defined other team.

Nevertheless, as witnessed in our case studies, SAST does not in all circumstances have to draw out negative aspects of organisational defence mechanisms. In favourable circumstances SAST can encourage an adversarial and participatory style of debate. It allows people to refresh their initial stance by exploiting their capacity to reflect back on this in the light of tensionful confrontation with people who are not like-minded. Benefits accruing from such a process are contingent on *genuine* participation, however. A highly politicised atmosphere may not be most conducive to a SAST process and would require very skilled facilitation. SAST employed in such circumstances could be inordinately damaging. Bob once used SAST in an issue management exercise in Singapore and literally had to prise the hands of one participant from the throat of another (a poor choice of methodology?). Might–right debate is normally more relevant in such circumstances (see Chapter 9).

SAST demonstrably is able in appropriate circumstances to help people to see other people's viewpoints in an informed way. It may help them to see the relevance of those viewpoints. If nothing else, it may help people to understand why people hold the views that they do even if some participants continue to disagree. SAST encourages decision making to be well considered.

8.5.3 Soft Systems Methodology

Research into the application of systems engineering techniques from the mid 1960s led to the development of Soft Systems Methodology (SSM; e.g. Checkland, 1981; Checkland and Scholes, 1990). The research agenda offered a practical way of questioning whether "systems engineering methods could be extended to cover management issues, broadly defined" (Checkland, 1995: 2). Research was carried out through a large number of interventions. The researchers adopted what they saw as a type of AR, although AR

> was felt to be seriously deficient in one important respect. If descriptions of action research were to be more than merely anecdotal accounts of what had happened, it seemed an essential requirement that the researcher declare in advance the intellectual framework within which knowledge in the research situation will be defined. In other words, the researcher must set out the *epistemology* in terms of which research findings will be expressed. (Checkland, 1995: 2)[13]

Methodology was therefore considered to be one of the main outputs of the SSM program of research. "The outcome of the research was a structured process of inquiry" (Checkland, 1995: 5). The process makes use of systems models as ideal systems that stimulate debate about possible intervention. The process constructs and employs verb-based models called root definitions that are developed into systemic diagrams called conceptual models. Debate seeks to establish accommodation between people, making intervention agreeable.

The methodology was reconciled against an interpretive view of social life. Interpretive social theory believes social situations are defined through action concepts. Understanding cannot arise just from observation and theory (surface and beneath-the-surface material analyses of a traditional scientific approach) since any human actor will have reasons, or intentions, that "lie behind" each action. A specific action concept can be transparent only in the context of a certain set of social practices. It is in terms of these that an actor can be said to be doing some particular thing. Beyond observation, we are told, is a set of social practices that can be drawn upon to explain the

---

[13] Some action researchers may consider this comment harsh. Gustavsen (1992) provides a good account of the way in which action researchers have been accounting for their interventions since the 1970s as an alternative to normal science.

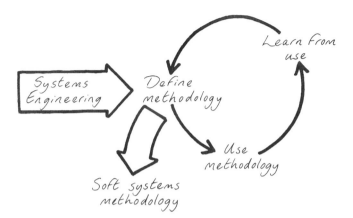

Figure 8.3

action. There is a third, deeper layer that the interpretivist introduces, that of constitutive meaning. Constitutive meaning lies behind social practices. It is in terms of these meanings that people speak and act.[14]

Methodological development (including interpretive reasoning) can be understood in terms of a cycle (see Figure 8.3). Consulting Figure 8.3 we see that "Systems engineering methodology was taken as given; attempts were made to apply it to ill-defined, 'messy' issue situations. The methodology was found to be inadequate for the complexity of the situations addressed, and learning from this experience led to the reformulation of the methodology as SSM" (Checkland, 1995: 4).

SSM aims to engender meaningful debate about organisational issues. The process it advocates may be found relevant when there is no clear-cut issue definition and even to challenge perceived clear-cut definitions. It helps those involved in the process to explore possible ways of appreciating the issue context and to debate possible ways forward which concludes with decision making based on reaching accommodations.

SSM in the 1990s is understood through two modes of operation. Mode 1 sees SSM as a seven-stage process (see Figure 8.4). The process begins when issues are considered problematic. The aim initially is to develop an expression of the issue without structuring it, thus preventing debate, to some

[14] Checkland self-defines his work as drawing on the phenomenological tradition in social theory. It is interesting to note that an ethnomethodological view of the way that people draw on practices to account for their conduct differs from the one advanced by Checkland. Ethnomethodology (originally developed by Garfinkel, 1967, as a way of exploring people's accounting practices) argues that it is not the case that people act in terms of given practices which define how they should operate; it is rather that they are able in social interaction (as a created event) to make their own and others' actions (and words) *appear familiar* by placing them under some familiar category. Hence people are able to make mutual sense of the interaction.

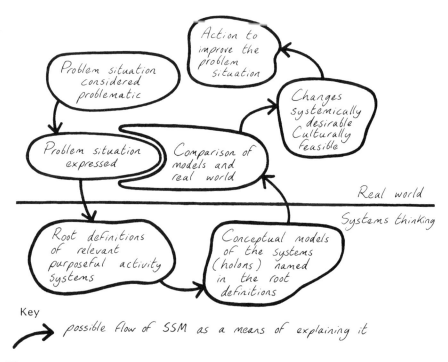

Key

> possible flow of SSM as a means of explaining it

Figure 8.4

extent, from being prestructured by it. Then, relevant purposeful activity systems are generated that hold some bearing to the expression. These relevant systems are explored using systems thinking. The process of exploration uses two sequential techniques called root definitions and conceptual models to develop (some or many of the) relevant systems into models of purposeful activity. These models are then compared to the expression of the real world engendering debate about possible changes that could be made. The systemic desirability and cultural feasibility of the changes are assessed as part of the process. Models are systemically desirable if they are considered to be truly *relevant*. Proposed changes are culturally feasible if they are seen to be *meaningful*. Agreed changes are translated into action to manage the issues.

Mode 2 is a more flexible use of the seven-stage process. Flexibility here means two things. First, intervention can start anywhere in the seven-stage process and can move in any direction. Second, SSM is seen as a set of processes used to organise thoughts about intervention. Mode 1 is more for "neophytes" and Mode 2 more for "sophisticates" (Checkland, 1995: 12). In the case study below we have summarised a (near) Mode 2 use of SSM since this is said to be for sophisticates.

Case Study

We have chosen briefly to review the process of a case taken from Checkland and Scholes (1990: Chapter 9). We have chosen it for two reasons. First, the authors present it as a contemporary use of SSM, mixed but nearer Mode 2, presumably then for sophisticates. Second, they claim that the use "is, perhaps, 'postmodern' SSM" (Checkland and Scholes, 1990: 235). We reconsider that proposition in the section on postmodern debate below.

The case is set in the Shell Group, "at core 'an oil company' . . . engaged in many businesses". Crucial to the group's activities is continual reassessment and updating of technology. Shell has a central staff function, Manufacturing Function (MF), that keeps up with changing and developing technology, decides on research and development programs, advises the Shell Board on policy about technology, monitors performance of production units, and provides rapid response help at the operational level around the world. While perceived to be essential for long-term survival, and here lies the essence of the case, it is difficult to evaluate now the service role being played by MF whose results are perceptible only much later on.

The head of MF, de Vos, considered the need to rethink MF's role and processes. An approach to strategic planning was instigated by de Vos that put the "MF 'vision' fundamentally in question" and surfaced perceived issues that needed dealing with. Checkland was asked to collaborate by introducing SSM into the reorientation of MF.

It was decided to run a series of two-day workshops to which groups of managers were invited. Themes were introduced that came out of previous workshops (including the first stages of the initial strategic planning efforts) adding continuity. Later on workshops were run that included de Vos and his MF management team. SSM was used as a structuring device, helping to make sense of free-ranging discourse. It helped the facilitators "to keep a grip on what could very easily have become a chaotic rambling debate" (Checkland and Scholes, 1990: 270). Many root definitions and conceptual models were formulated. Continuity was enhanced by this use of a common language. Findings were made widely known enabling other people to keep informed.

Following the workshops de Vos announced to all members of MF that "They would soon be taking part in the implementation of a new MF with changed structure and new procedures, a process to which their contributions were sought" (Checkland and Scholes, 1990: 267). The management team selected an organisation structure that embodied the new conceptualisation of MF. At a subsequent meeting de Vos presented the new structure and handed out a booklet that described it and its principles. Over several months details of the structure and processes were filled in with the participation of many MF personnel from across the Function and from many levels.

Discourse About Consideredness

Many of the general advantages SSM offers in terms of debate that it engenders have been presented in earlier parts of our discourse about consideredness. There is no value in repeating points, save to say that SSM, like other approaches to AR, aims to generate much learning and understanding through debate on the way to (with SSM, accommodation-geared) decision making. It is more instructive at this stage of the chapter to compare the way SSM and AR approaches set about achieving learning, understanding and decision making. This we do by first comparing SSM to PAR, then AS, and then briefly to might–right issues (introduced in Chapter 6 and studied in Chapters 9 and 10).

The main parallel to be drawn between PAR and SSM is their common foundation, that research needs to be carried out alongside action in real-world situations and that knowledge can be nurtured in this way. The Shell case study illustrates SSM operating in this way. Knowledge accrued is very different, however. With PAR, knowledge is about specific processes of social situations that may enrich or be enriched by subsequent uses of PAR. With SSM, knowledge is about epistemology in terms of which research findings are expressed. The first main difference then is that the research findings with PAR are induced knowledge about social situations but with SSM they are induced knowledge about methodology[15] (reconciled with the literature on epistemology). Most of the reflections in Checkland and Scholes's (1990) book on case studies, like the one we looked at in brief, are about methodology. Accordingly, SSM can be expressed as a basic process. The essential element of the basic process is development of systems of purposeful activity that can be compared to the perceived real situation. The second main distinction is simply that SSM has been expressed as a basic process and that this process has an essential element of model building and comparison of models with perceived reality.

It is of great value to have a clear expression of the basic process of SSM since the transparency offered encourages further discussion about the process, which we now undertake. Neither PAR nor SSM have addressed the sorts of concern that AS surfaces. AS argues that it is important to be aware of organisational defence mechanisms that can distort the debating process and influence actual decisions. These mechanisms when at work prevent issues from being fully debated in an open and meaningful way. Decisions made therefore are not well considered.

Whyte, as we saw earlier, has defended his position concerning the possible utility of PAR arguing that the process of action itself may generate new ways of thinking and feeling (Whyte, 1991c). Here he suggests that things

---

[15] Theoretical positioning of SSM has been discussed, for example, in Checkland (1981).

can at times sort themselves out in action.[16] Checkland believes, likewise (perhaps too confidently?), that things sort themselves out in the course of SSM-guided intervention. For example, Checkland offers some reference in his account of the case study abstracted above to different moments when people form definitions, but he offers little deliberation about how accommodations were reached.

SSM proponents believe that the crucial variable to be managed is lack of synchronisation of perceptions about reality. They therefore aim as a primary goal to (re)establish mutual understanding between participants, wanting to achieve through accommodation some form of agreement. But it is not possible within their interpretive schema to recognise common-sense events such as interest-based conflict, that may involve people who refuse to budge their positions, and who may employ tactics and resources to get their own way. Or rather, such situations can only be addressed within SSM by hoping that, in practice, accommodations between interests will be achieved in SSM-guided debate. In the Shell case Checkland and Scholes were vague about what was needed to synchronise the views. They were also vague about what the differing interests were, if any. They just intimate that it was not problematic to reach accommodations. Their accounts of SSM make little play on anecdotes as a matter of the policy about how they write up results. Anecdotes, however, can be the point at which an account starts to resonate with people's own experiences.

Checkland and Scholes do not offer much detail about who should participate in SSM and how they might participate. They are rather silent on this point. For example, in the Shell case Checkland and Scholes do not problematise or even attempt to show considerations that led to choice of participants. Surely, failure to address the point must undermine action research when it is based, as SSM is, solely on the interpretive idea of participation of people, and through this, exchange of ideas as the essence of construction and change of social reality.

Furthermore, SSM interpretivism may bring with it relativism, where ideas of social participants are reckoned to be equally valid. It is implied that the facilitator should shy away from passing judgements on these and must simply move toward reaching an accommodation. Relativism is hence tackled by SSM in a process of debate and accommodation seeking. However, it may be argued that if the matter of participation is not clearly tackled then accommodation seeking over relatively equal ideas will be biased. Even if participation is satisfactorily directed, accommodation seeking

[16] Whyte could indeed be seen as subscribing to some kind of complementarist view in that he seems to accept that AR-inclined researchers may need to make considered decisions as to which type of approach should be employed – depending on their understanding of possibilities for relevant intervention in different situations. (See, for instance, his discussion of this in the context of his recognition that AS offers a certain detachment which PAR might not equally provide – 1991c: 97.)

makes no guarantees that biases will be kept out of the debate and decision-making process. To address these issues, it is important to bear in mind that there may be other options for viable action research practice, such as some of those discussed in both this and the following chapter. The considered-ness of the decision to employ some form of SSM (or for that matter any of the processes explored in this and the following chapter) is enriched, we suggest, by taking into account the wider discourse on debate about debate as well as the discourse exploring ways of playing knowledge–power games (investigated in the following chapter).

So, SSM emphasises open debate about methodology employed and offers an explicit account of its own suggested methodological option. This element of debate is important. Debate about methodology through SSM is, however, constrained by adherence to a declared interpretive epistemology in a somewhat non-reflective way (cf. Flood and Ulrich, 1990). The epistemology states that ideas are the prime motive in generating change and that material and economic interests (as experienced) can be accommodated through debate. Hence Checkland and Scholes define politics as a process of reaching an accommodation of interests. However, we suggest that SSM can easily slip into strengthening what AS would isolate as organisational defensiveness; or into maintaining what others might locate as entrenched power–knowledge relations – precisely because it is geared to seeking and encouraging accommodations. Options for facilitative action should therefore consider the kind of argument developed by Argyris and Schön, where conscious attempts are made on the part of the researcher to explicate and attempt to dissolve defence mechanisms that may hinder processes of con-sidered debate. They should consider postmodern efforts to avoid assimila-tion (see our discussion of postmodern debate below). And they should consider, as outlined in our next chapter, options that operate in terms of agendas that, we argue, cannot be assimilated under the SSM banner and its view of human life. In short, our wariness with SSM is its tendency to present itself as *the* option to be activated in all messy human situations. The value that we see in SSM is its suggestion that explicit accounts of methodological processes employed to facilitate debate add to the arena of debate about debate.

8.5.4 Concluding Comment

So far in this chapter we have reviewed some approaches to AR and some systems approaches, which we believe make their contribution in the arena of debate practice. Other approaches from these families are included in the next chapter. It is interesting to note here that, although the two families share ideals of emancipatory practice (through debate and might–right management), there is as yet very little engagement established through, for example, referenced literature (Levin, 1994). Levin, who comes from the AR tribe, made a study of AR and Critical Systems Thinking, and concluded that they are two icons carved out of the same log. He found in conversation with critical systems thinkers that the two "used a different vocabulary, and languages with expressions and words rooted in separate strands of thinking, but we still managed to communicate on important professional issues. I felt strongly that we had a lot in common" (Levin, 1994: 25).

When comparing the two, Levin reckoned AR focuses much on understanding change processes, with Critical Systems Thinking favouring a critical and theoretical and, as this book demonstrates, a practical orientation to systems thinking as the basis for systems development. In this he saw a simplified first conceptualisation of the complementarity of the two theoretical traditions. Levin took things further. Through an analysis of the relationship among theory, people, and practice, an analysis of the AR and Critical Systems Thinking traditions was undertaken. He argued for a common ground that might create the basis for a fruitful exchange of ideas. We hope that this chapter establishes yet further common ground and identifies worthy differences and, along with our discourse on might–right management, has begun the process of fruitful exchange. We now reorientate ourselves by taking AR and systems approaches into the world of postmodern debate.

8.6 POSTMODERN DEBATE

In this chapter on debate practice we enter into play once again with postmodern thought, as we toy with how postmodern debate might proceed. Like defining postmodern organisation, the task of pegging down postmodern debate is not easy. As we said in the last chapter, postmodernism is not supposed to be about clarity of definition – it invites and celebrates ongoing (re)creation of any definition advanced. Postmodernism is about irony and playfulness. Produce an account of postmodern debate but prepare for postmodernists to amuse themselves with it through irony. What a glassy concept! Can we ever know the construction of postmodern debate? Let us cognise.

One view of postmodernism characterises it as destructive. "The postmodern mind seems to condemn everything, propose nothing, as if demolition is the only thing the postmodern mind seems to be good at" (Bauman, 1992: ix). Debate then begins by putting on a pair of boxing gloves. Perhaps this gloomy interpretation is best left on the shelves of the shopping malls. After all, a choice was made in Chapter 1 to resist the dark side and promote optimistic aspects of (modernism and) postmodernism.

Another angle on postmodern debate insists no claim is to be privileged

(Simons and Billig, 1994; 6). Oppressed voices are to be reasserted. Space must be granted for everyone to play their language games. Life becomes a series of experiences. Freedom of expression, however, neglects our imperative of choice. This (naive) interpretation of postmodernism ironically makes judgements at a metalevel about the necessity to keep things open, but it offers nothing in return to help deal with openness, thus laying itself open to be resolved through political dynamics, permitting oppressors to take control (again). Dismal stuff that we have chosen to avoid.

Let us begin again. Let us adopt the proposition that with postmodern debate everything is provisional (including decision making). Debate develops provisional contracts. Debaters are cautious about closing down discussion. Postmodernism wants people to participate on the basis of different experiences. It wants people to participate in different experiences. The worst worry of postmodern thinking is that social settings will remain, or regress into, a closed-down monoculture. Monoculture may well be experienced like superdecisions. The measure of consideredness with postmodernism is the extent to which cautions are given to possible forms of monoculture or superdecision. This process of decision making therefore can only operate through trust and confidence. A case study serves to illustrate some of these points.

Case Study

In the case study illustrating SSM we reviewed in short Checkland and Scholes's (1990) account of strategic visioning for the Manufacturing Function in Shell. In this brief fictional case we revisit the process by running through it ideas of postmodern debate and imagining how the process might skew if carried out through a postmodern quality. In this way we intend to play with postmodern options and their possible consequences for Shell. We also create an image of "postmodern SSM".

It was decided by a fictional postmodernist-oriented Bob and Norma to run a series of workshops for MF to which groups of managers and a sample of customers were invited. The latter were solicited through an advertisement inviting participants (customers) to take part in an entertaining but tensionful exercise in unfamiliar modes of exchange. It was hoped that sufficient people would be lured by their curiosity and would be prepared to utilise their leisure time for this and indeed a large number of customers applied, out of which a random sample was selected.

At the first workshop, proposals were introduced that came out of a previous study that had been run with managers participating in a Checkland-type soft systems intervention. All participants were asked to imagine the consequences of implementing what they took to be the opposite of the proposals suggested through the study. Many of the managers were wary of

Bob and Norma's suggestion that the accommodations which they had attuned themselves to live with (psychologically) were already outdated! They felt that the new study that Bob and Norma were introducing was a little too soon after Checkland had left the scene. But they also were aware that this was a fast-changing concern (that is the manufacturing component of Shell). They thus with some trepidation supported the encounters, but also with curiosity and some giving-up of their normal search for patterns of familiarity.

Bob and Norma facilitated sessions in which they played with the idea that the opposites of the proposals that had been advanced within the Checkland study could be seen as defensible, if one reasoned in a certain way. The challenge was to see how reason could be used to find advantages in the opposite proposals and how indeed a plan of action could be constructed from this. Nearly all the managers and the customers joined in. Tensions arose regarding, for instance, whether the opposites really should be seen as opposites and in what sense they might be seen as perhaps ironically related. Furthermore, tension arose when debaters reckoned some of the proposals had obvious merit over others. Bob and Norma exploited the differences among managers and customers on this score. They also suggested that at the end of the day (literally) some solution would be chosen, whether or not this was regarded as definitively better. If this choice was adopted as a tentative plan of action it was important that managers, as well as customers in this case, did not handle it willy-nilly because they were by now more attuned to seeing just how many uncertainties they were glossing over in adopting any plan. Later on, workshops were run that included de Vos and his MF management team. The participants from the earlier session faced the challenge of presenting their findings as a springboard for continued discussion about ways of planning.

SSM turned around by Bob and Norma was used like a prism to avoid assimilation in free-ranging discourse. It helped the facilitators to construct and at the same time deconstruct root definitions and conceptual models, creating plans held with recognition of some arbitrariness at the moment of their creation. Findings were made widely known enabling other people to keep informed about the somewhat arbitrary character of the planning process at Shell. This, ironically, served to make many of the rest of the staff and also customers more confident. They had sensed that the process of developing plans by relying on the presumed relevance of a defined debating process could not have been workable as presented in a situation of such uncertainty. Many experienced the honesty as refreshing.

Following the workshops de Vos announced to all members of MF that "They would soon be taking part in the implementation of a new MF with changed procedures for 'planning', a process to which their contributions were sought" (as cited in Checkland and Scholes, 1990: 267). This was looked forward to with some excitement but also (again) trepidation. Trepidation was increased as word got round that a number of Greenpeace supporters were insisting on attending too. The latter had come to recognise that the new fragility of the planning process at Shell might make an opening for them to lobby about Shell's oil dumping policy. The national newspapers had leaked news about the way that Shell was making its decisions, as one of the customers who had been attending the initial session was in fact a journalist!

Discourse About Consideredness

With postmodernism discussion bursts into a spectrum of colours as viewpoints pass through a diversity creating prism. Views of people and groups are incommensurable (save for participation in different experiences they offer). The place of discussion is a stadium where people play games. Postmodernism hence questions the extent to which any person or group can get to know the bands of thought on the resulting explosion of viewpoints. It questions, How much do you know?, How do you know?, How do you know you know? This hesitancy when run through processes such as SSM uncover shaky foundations on which decisions are made. For example, on what basis can we claim that accommodations are achieved, or known to be achieved? Are these hesitancies addressed? In what way are oppressive compulsions considered and dealt with? Belief that accommodations between people can be achieved is therefore dismissed as over-optimistic. Accommodations at best are a special, provisional, tensionful case, resulting from postmodern debate.

Accommodations or decisions remain provisional because they are full of tension. Processes previously discussed in this chapter want to unravel and dissolve tension, or, as with SAST, to release and disperse tension. SAST, for example, wants to create tensions but then disperse these through synthetic strategic thinking. Postmodern debate at this juncture wants to create space for further tension which in itself continues a productive process.

Checkland and Scholes (1990: 235) themselves suggest that SSM, as employed in the case we reviewed, "is, perhaps, 'postmodern' SSM in the sense of postmodernism discussed by Cooper and Burrell (1988): SSM is being used to help 'an observer community which constructs interpretations of the world, these *interpretations* having no absolute or universal status'". Our review of postmodern debate has evoked an image that suggests otherwise. For example, Checkland and Scholes (1990: 246), reflecting on the case we reported, say "SSM as such remained unobtrusive to the participants but had provided Checkland [and co-workers]. . . with the feeling they were working to a structure." The structure supplied provides guidelines by which to proceed and puts forward a purpose, which is accommodation. It is here that we locate a fundamental difference between SSM and postmodern debate. SSM wants accommodations to be reached through debate. Postmodernism wants to open spaces for self-invention, which involves forms of play with others. These forms of play and the quality of debate therein cannot be specified by requiring people to submit to a structured process of comparing conceptual models with (perceived) reality as the mechanism for social involvement. As we see it, debate structured in this way and directed by the purpose of accommodating the various viewpoints, and debate toward playful yet tensionful exchange, are different, which is good for diversity management.

With postmodern debate, diversity means preservation and/or creation of difference that keeps open opportunities that we can call upon to explore angles on managing issues. At the end of the conversation, instead of having accommodations, people make personal judgements about the relevance of the exchanges for their different further actions. People decide differently what to do with their appreciation of the conversation and how to act accordingly. However, one possible special case of personal judgement making is that discussants choose to accommodate each other in a way that they can all live with. One special case of accommodation, conversely, is establishment of trust and confidence in each other that permits discussants to participate in different experiences now and into the future. As diversity management states, choice of model(s) and/or methodology(ies) is local in time and space, is widely informed, is provisional, and is always open to further choice.

Postmodernism sees in debate practices such as those introduced in this chapter an ontology that suggests the world is full of people in debate. Related to this is an epistemology, sometimes declared as with SSM, that moulds how research findings are to be presented. Postmodernism, however, wants to deconstruct epistemology and pose alternatives. Alternatives make possible different experiences. One alternative experience is the possibility of conversing with a conscious intention (emotional commitment) to withhold from assimilating thoughts or experiences. Another possible experience is to reminisce over previous experiences and make provisional sense of those experiences as a form of self-management, demonstrating that forms of integrity are possible with postmodernism.

Another positive point about postmodern debate is the provision it makes for people to decide how to treat conversation. Conversation can be a fun event. Conversation can be for mutual support. Conversation can be for one's personal life – or anything else for that matter. It can make debate feel well considered in this way by providing "power to".

"Power over" is a risk that postmodern debate flirts with. Difference may become divisive. It may lead to negative exchanges so that benefits of tension that is encouraged are lost to destructive forces. The tension may then be resolved through power play. Alternatively, divisiveness may lead to people talking past each other, where decisions do not appear to be made. Conversation loses all integrity. Again, decisions are likely to be made through power play. Allowing "power over" means postmodern debate does not serve even its own tentative purposes, for example that of allowing for continued tensionful exchange. In this we observe the dangers of postmodern thought as it penetrates diversity management. Diversity management must manage the dilemma of benefits and dangers that the influence of postmodern thought brings to it.

8.7 SUMMARY AND CONCLUSION

As usual, we conclude the chapter by summarising its substance in bullet points.

- In this chapter we evaluate debate and decision making. Evaluation takes on the following meaning. With power/freedom through debate we mean chances people have to make widely informed and locally contingent choices, given degrees of participation in the process of debate, and the nature and relevance of decisions made in that process. By relevance we mean how well considered people feel are decisions made through the process of debate in the circumstances. Circumstances to us is a holistic concept which admits the need to choose an area of focus. We contextualise decision making to the local (proximal) decision makers in terms of some judgement about who is significantly involved and affected.
- Ways of considering learning and understanding through debate practice within the spirit of diversity management include Action Learning, (and the following two types of Action Research) Participatory Action Research, Action Science, (and the following two so-called systems approaches) Strategic Assumption Surfacing and Testing, and Soft Systems Methodology, finishing with Postmodern debate.
- Action Learning brings colleagues together in group settings. Rather than individuals facing their own issues in isolation, there is a collective strength, a combined force of knowledge, expertise, and co-operative relationships. There are a number of concerns. First, it seems that those involved in the process are not held responsible for taking further knowledge gained inductively in order to establish an ongoing process of knowledge development that has wider public significance. Second, the relationship between the so-called issue attacker and issue owner is not problematised. Third, there may be counter-forces at work that distort the process and influence the output of the process detrimentally so that

people feel decisions are ill-considered. Fourth (and perhaps related to the third), there is no indication why it felt that discussion need be confined to a collegial debate – the issue of widening the boundary of participation appears not to be addressed as an issue in AL.

- Participatory Action Research, the first of two Action Research approaches reviewed in this chapter, makes the process of intervention useful to the researcher and more enjoyable to a range of practitioners by expanding the social process to find out and consult with people about possible interpretations of a study. It generates inductively definitions of social processes. However, the learning process may be subject to organisational defence mechanisms that impinge on outcomes and therefore make decisions made feel ill-considered to the participants.

- Action Science is our second form of Action Research that places a central emphasis on neutralising organisational defence mechanisms that participants bring to practice and research. Unlike SAST, it does not highlight ways of harnessing a positive worth that may accrue from results of tensions springing from these mechanisms. Also, it can be criticised for trading off relevance to the practitioner for scientific rigour. (A research decision to trade relevance for rigor could be experienced as a super-decision by others – unless some attempt to co-define responsibilities has been undertaken in *situ*.)

- Strategic Assumption Surfacing and Testing, the first of two systems approaches reviewed in this chapter, is adversarial – it surfaces and manages conflict. It aims to help seriously challenge accepted modes of doing things in organisations and carves out space for policy options to be considered that diverge from current practice. Alternatives are developed in opposition to one another. A politicised atmosphere where people are inclined to cling to the protection of their favoured position may not be conducive to this process. If this is judged to be the case, it might pay to heed the warnings of Action Science about negative consequences of organisational defence mechanisms. Strong intrapsychic protection mechanisms of the kind that AS suggests may be operable, could further polarise the alternative positions, at the same time entrenching people's defence mentalities.

- Soft Systems Methodology declares its main research findings are induced knowledge about methodology (reconciled with the literature on epistemology). The epistemology states that ideas are the prime motive in construction and change of social reality and that debate between viewpoints can be harnessed to reach accommodations in practice between participant concerns. However, it has a tendency (because of its theoretical underpinning) to regard accommodations that happen to be worked out in practice as being acceptable. It does not venture to offer an account (as does, for instance, AS) of intrapsychic defence mechanisms that may operate to hinder processes of reaching considered accommodations. Nor does it venture to consider power–knowledge complexes that may embody biases at the moment of debate between alternatives. Chapter 9 reviews a range of explanations of a might–right complexion.

- Postmodern debate introduces a form of debate which is not primarily geared to reaching agreements, accommodations, syntheses or reconciliations. It is a form of debate where the definition and purpose of itself is continually opened to deconstruction – to prevent it from taking on a meaning that seems to forbid reworking. Postmodern debate expresses the slipperiness of a clarified definition by continually evading attempts to define its meaning. It does, however, offer a starting point for people to experiment with ways in which they may use conversation to engage with one another, and in this sense the concept and practice of debate is not empty of meaning. Postmodern debate, we suggest, may operate in any sphere of society as people experiment with ironies which offer new types of insight. In this chapter, we described its operation in a fictional case of Shell Oil decision making. Many might argue that this is not a locality where postmodernist-oriented authors would choose to operate. However, the definition of the significance of postmodern thought (which for them may indeed bar involvement in an oil giant like Shell) is, we suggest, itself ambiguous. Involvement in helping to generate fragility of consciousness in one of the international giants *may* be a place where postmodern-oriented thought could (*inter alia*) make a contribution. It depends how the notion of contribution is defined. And this leads us back to the issue of how we may engage in debate about the meaning of considered decisions. This chapter was aimed at outlining and discussing various ways in which the notion of debate toward considered decisions has been grappled with by a number of researchers including postmodernist-oriented ones.

In this chapter we have presented our interpretation of six approaches to debate practice. A discourse about consideredness has been developed as the chapter progressed. We have shown different proposals for debate management leading to enhancement of "power to" in decision making. We found that many cases of fruitful debate practice occur where co-operative relations exist (or at least can be generated/nurtured through facilitator involvement) between participants (e.g. the Xerox and Gulf hospital cases). As soon as this spirit breaks down, giving rise to a politicised atmosphere where people struggle to control the situation in terms of their own definition, then the purpose of debate practice too begins to crumble away (e.g. Trico Products Corporation). There could be a case to be made for might–right practice, the theme of our next chapter.

Chapter 9

Loop 3.
Might-right _Management:_ _Why?_

9.1 INTRODUCTION

In Chapter 7 we reviewed ways people are able to discuss process design and organisational design, surfacing some issues for people to take into account when considering the relevance of forms of design to their circumstances. Chapter 8 did the same sort of job for debate management, for people who enter a process that deliberates over courses of action, expecting decisions to be attainable without people being overly defensive about their initial opinions. What seems to be missing to us is a reflexive loop that stimulates contemplation about how people undertake design management and debate management; a loop that we call might–right management. This loop allows us to reconsider design management and debate management in terms of news that may switch attention to knowledge–power play. In this chapter we explore four ways (entailing eight approaches) to might–right management: (two approaches to vitalising educational practices) Dialogical Intervention Strategy and Critical Systems Heuristics; (two approaches to nurturing self-reliance) Collaborative Inquiry and Self-reliant Participatory Action Research; (styles of) Reconsideration of Social Processes; (and three approaches to intelligent protest) Right in Protest Through Communicative Rationality, Might of Strategy in Protest, and Novel Protest. We preface these approaches with a discussion about the might–right complex.

9.2 ABOUT MIGHT–RIGHT

When we discussed the relevance of forms of design in Chapter 7, we purposely did not problematise how any conception of relevance itself can be defined. For example, a reflexive loop could problematise the might of an appeal to imperatives that buttress a preferred conception. Or, such a loop could problematise the right of appeal to forms of science and/or forms of agreement that buttress a preferred conception. In these and other ways, the process of knowledge creation that defines what is relevant is subject to might–right scrutiny.

When we discussed the issue of consideredness in Chapter 8, we purposely did not problematise how any conception of well consideredness can be defined. There are practical implications of such conceptions. For example, a reflexive loop might problematise in Action Science political factors, beyond intrapsychic factors, that confound efforts to open space for meaningful public debate about modes of thought. Indeed, scientists, by virtue of the power of status that they can introduce as professional researchers, may initiate or sustain a knowledge game that entrenches an imbalanced style of human relationship. Likewise, when reviewing Soft Systems Methodology, we kept largely in abeyance questions that need to be raised that address the researcher's involvement in defining whether fair accommodations were likely to be reached. In these and other ways, the process of knowledge creation that defines what is well considered is also subject to might–right scrutiny.

Both design management and debate management are enriched when they have to account for issues surfaced through the reflexive loop of might–right management. Sharpened attention to the might–right problematique enhances diversity management in the following ways.

- Researchers and interventionists are better equipped when choosing (a) design and/or debate model(s) and or methodology(ies) to recognise that wider might–right issues could be accounted for by choosing options such as those discussed in this and the next chapter.
- Researchers and interventionists are better equipped to decide that their most useful contribution could be to manage might–right issues straight away by choosing options presented in this and the next chapter.
- More generally, researchers and interventionists operate in the knowledge of possible astute action that might–right management emphasises.

In Chapter 6 we introduced a form of graph that promotes evaluation of practical and research efforts aimed at issues of power and freedom. In Chapter 7 the graph is contextualised to evaluate design management showing that the relevance of designs in the circumstances can be explored by raising questions about superstructure and no structure. In Chapter 8

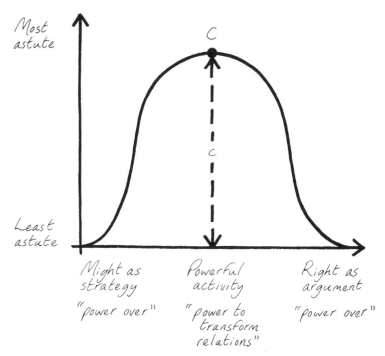

Figure 9.1

the graph is recontextualised to evaluate debate management exploring consideredness of decisions made in the circumstances by raising questions about superdecisions and no decisions. For this chapter on might–right management the graph is recontextualised to evaluate might–right management (see Figure 9.1). Evaluation here translates as follows: with power/freedom through might–right management we mean chances people have to act and choose, given power people have to make widely informed and locally contingent choices about transformation of social relations, and the nature and relevance of designs and decisions made in that process. By relevance we mean astuteness of judgement made in the circumstances. Circumstances to us is a concept that allows us to operate in terms of a chosen focus of attention. Here we focus on transformation of social relations and we contextualise such transformation to the local (proximal) decision makers.

Processes generating relevant designs or well-considered decisions can easily move away from the ideals just mentioned if the processes do not cater for questions raised by the might–right problematique. Might–right management (re)vitalises a concern for political effects of adopted epistemologies. Figure 9.1 therefore sets a further ideal of "astuteness of judgement".

This can be explained in practical terms. Design management and debate management between them ask in the circumstances, Are we doing things right?, and, Are we doing the right things? Might–right management asks, Is rightness the right of appeal to forms of science or presumed agreement, or the might of an appeal to imperatives, that buttresses a preferred conception?

Before indulging in options we put forward as examples of might–right management, we wish to launch our discourse on might–right management. To do this we indicate how the discourse views interests. We ask the following, In what way does might–right management help us to review the question of interests from a political and epistemological angle?

9.3 MIGHT–RIGHT AND THE QUESTION OF INTERESTS

The arena of discourse labelled "astuteness of judgement" comes at the question of interests from a different angle than either structuralism (a perspective introduced in Chapter 6 to stimulate discussion about design management) or intersubjective decision making (a perspective introduced in Chapter 6 to stimulate discussion about debate management). In structuralist discourse, theory and practice are oriented toward structures that serve collective interests. With intersubjective discourse, interests are made an issue as interested parties define their concerns and arrive at reconciliation, accommodation, or celebration of differences.

In might–right management a different question of interests is raised. The question is, Why should alternative power relationships be pursued without relying on structures to serve collective interests; or on processes to generate reconciliation, accommodation, or celebration of differences? Or phrased more directly, Why should we aspire toward relations with each other that enable reconsideration of games of knowledge production in society?

The question of interest here is couched in terms of revision. Patterns of relationships are revised to challenge games of knowledge production entrenched in society – so as to establish more attractive power relationships. Attention is concentrated on reasons why we ought to fight to preserve the might–right arena of discourse that makes possible exploration of knowledge–power configurations in society. We now begin our exploration of options for might–right management beginning by introducing our options for might–right management.

9.4 OPTIONS FOR MIGHT–RIGHT MANAGEMENT

There are many, many issues of concern when it comes to might–right management. We have chosen four ways (entailing six approaches) that represent the many issues. First, we explore educational revitalisation. This is done by elucidating two methodological processes: Dialogical Intervention Strategy and Critical Systems Heuristics. Cases investigating practical interpretations are run through. Second, two processes for nurturing self-reliance are reviewed. Collaborative Inquiry and Self-reliant Participatory Action Research help to enhance quality of social relationships and build self-reliance for mainly vulnerable social groupings. Again, cases are given.

Third, we introduce briefly Reconsideration of Social Processes that tackles knowledge–power networks in society, noting that this book is one case that undertakes such reconsiderations. Fourth, we think through the significance of intelligent discourse when choosing to import forms of Protest in society. Our own contribution to the might–right complex proposes oblique use of models and methodologies from design management and debate management, but is deferred to Chapter 10 where it is fully elaborated.

These four ways (entailing six approaches – not forgetting our own contribution in the next chapter) of keeping alive the discourse of might–right management may incorporate elements of the others in practice. Our categorisation only accentuates a particularly prevalent focus in each approach. This helps in the management of diversity, aiding recognition of a wide span of possible choices. Also, note that categorisation in this chapter roughly corresponds to the five bullet points on pages 72–73 that introduce the typology of power advanced in Chapter 6. Preparation work completed, we now turn to vitalising educational practices.

9.5 VITALISING EDUCATIONAL PRACTICES

9.5.1 Introduction

An important and widely researched and practised way of might–right management is to revisit educational practices with the purpose of rethinking processes of knowledge production in society. This pushes for new forms of knowledge production in society and may include efforts to influence formal educational practices, formalised in schools and universities, and/or attempts to revitalise informal educational settings. Dialogical Intervention Strategy (DIS) is one approach designed to target (and/or create) such educational arenas. We review DIS below and provide an example of DIS set in the people's education movement in South Africa. Other initiatives set up possibilities for education encounters outside of formally defined educational institutions as could, for example, Critical Systems Heuristics (CSH). We review CSH after DIS and provide an example of it that investigates quality standards in the UK's National Health Service.

9.5.2 Dialogical Intervention Strategy

Dialogical Intervention Strategy (DIS) aims to influence educational practices by exposing through practical means, implications and applications of transforming patterns of undialogical interaction in the following way.

- *Consensus* – where people fail to make provision for continued opposition.
- *Accommodation* – defined as either toleration of difference without the effort to engage critically with alternatives; or as a consultative stance in which knowledge production practices are glossed over.
- *Manipulation* – where groups of people impose their definitions of reality on others.
- *Elimination* – where groups of people believe they need to liquidate a particular set of meanings and (sometimes) people who uphold those meanings.

To tackle these undialogical interactions, Hölscher and Romm (1987) proceed through four phases.

In the *first phase* as a starting point for investigation the researcher chooses and isolates issues that s/he regards are of concern in society. Modes by which people conceptualise the issues are thought through. In some cases people may have chosen to ignore them as issues – which in itself is an approach toward them (i.e. a dismissive approach).

In *phase two*, the researcher confronts participants with his/her account of their meaning patterns and the way that these relate to other people's meaning patterns. The researcher also brings into the discussion further ideas and information about the issues if s/he feels that these are relevant. At the same time the researcher tries to introduce the notion of dialogue as an attitude to the world and to other people through both theoretical discussion and practical example. Here, Freire's (1985) conception of dialogue is a significant inspiration.

In *phase three* the researcher brings together some of the arguments presented. This may be done through a face-to-face encounter, or as mediator, or a sort of go-between. The goal is to develop a practice of receptivity to encounter opposition. In this process new ways of rendering the world meaningful will emerge; ways which still incorporate recognition that other people may not share the same outlook. The researcher may confront (groups of) people who seem unwilling to take seriously other people's opinions. S/he may decide on a repetition with them of the processes of phase two. However, this may be assessed as unfruitful, in which case s/he may decide that it is necessary to sideline the group and exclude them from continued mediations. The problem is that in doing so s/he may (appear to) be endorsing exclusionary practices. It is important in terms of DIS practice that both the researcher and other people with whom s/he is working at least recognise this as an issue (see Hölscher and Romm, 1987; Romm, 1996).

The *fourth phase* co-involves researcher and participants in the process of institutionalising new ways of organising and practising education, infused with a consciousness of accountable action amid the continued display of difference of vision. What accountable action means for participants may also be considered in this phase, with a focus on responsible use of power. A dilemma arises for the researcher if people selected or appointed to oversee the arrangements are unable or unwilling to find a balance between responsibly exceeding while still accounting for conceptions of other people. The researcher could activate counter-power as an antidote to this, but this is not guaranteed to generate patterns of more discursively attuned action in society. Issues and solutions of this sort have to be considered.

Application of DIS within the people's education movement in South Africa provides our case study.

Case Study

The DIS context was self-defined by proponents as a nascent people's education movement. McKay (1990) examined the people's educational movement in South Africa in the late 1980s and early 1990s.[1] She met participants involved in formulating education policies, high school students and teachers. She listened to and mediated between them. New ways of addressing issues on the policy agenda of the people's education movement were considered.

McKay asked classes of students, from several schools, chosen through purposive sampling, to write an essay entitled, "My ideal school". She undertook content analysis of the essays, characterising and coding content thematically. Themes were used to activate discussion, especially around issues with a high level of emotional intensity of expression. Themes became the basis for group interviews with students; to probe further their perceptions, to activate discussion between them, and to evaluate their responses to ideas that she brought into the discussion.

Some ideas that McKay brought forward in the student group interviews were surfaced in conversation with teachers, parents and policy makers. Some were personal, arising from her teaching experiences. Some ideas were her interpretation of theoretical literature.

McKay organised interviews with a selection of teachers. The aim was to uncover issues of concern to them and how they would respond to other people's ideas, including her own, in the educational arena. Results of these

---

[1] The people's education movement was influenced by the fact that it represented a critique on the apartheid education regime. At the same time the movement wanted to offer an education policy that would be consistent with the demand for democratic knowledge construction.

discussions were then fed into the people's education movement. In this process she both challenged and accepted challenges from people in the movement. For example, at one point she challenged one quarter's belief that the way teachers handled their positions in the schools was a faulty link in the chain of implementation of a people's education agenda. McKay suggested that what she called "teacher bashing" was not conducive to preserving the dignity of teachers. Nor was it likely that telling the teachers how to implement agendas and blaming them for subsequently not implementing these agendas would contribute to their sense of dignity or to their efforts to deal with problematic issues they faced.

McKay learnt in the process what kinds of issue were relevant to participants. She enriched her awareness of possible contributions she could make toward the people's education movement. She moved on to planning.

McKay located schools where it was possible to suggest retraining teachers while inviting the input of students in the knowledge-creation process (McKay and Romm, 1995: 106–111). She also became involved in literacy training, for example, as requested by some trade unions for their members. After the South African government elections in 1994, McKay set up an adult basic education training unit at the University of South Africa with support from the Ministry of Education. Adoption of DIS-type practice ensures that the capacity for astuteness for all concerned is a quality that continues to have relevance.

Discourse About Astuteness

McKay knew her participants had to recognise power play entrenched in defining South African reality if transformation on the level of social relations was to occur. Efforts had to be made to redress modes of knowledge production that had served to uphold oppressive relations (McKay and Romm, 1992: 20–22). Issues at stake were not seen primarily as solvable via structural solutions nor indeed a democratic process that made provision for a plurality of different interests (design and debate management, respectively). Issues touched the core of educational practices which, if perpetuated, would surely serve a society built upon cultivating monological reactions. The intention was to provide an educational basis for turning around these reactions, helping citizens to recognise ways that they could participate in redefining reality. And leaders may become sensitive to the demands of people to participate in construction in that reality, along with their established responsibilities.

However, a series of challenges to McKay's work jump off the page. Why should we regard the standards of dialogue utilised in DIS desirable or even feasible? How can these standards be grounded? Is it sufficient that McKay claimed to cover the range of moral considerations available to her at the time? And why did she choose a course of research and action committed to nurturing dialogical capacity? In defence, we suggest that nurturing dialogical capacity is acceptable as a way of doing research as long as the researcher's involvement and impact in creating and using definitions of dialogue is recognised and does not become unduly impositional.

Another series of challenges may immediately strike the reader. How closely did McKay's research approximate her own agenda? Was it acceptable that she assumed a position on issues, for example, about "teacher bashing"? If so, what renders it so? In defence, we suggest that relating research involvement to responsibilities as a citizen can be considered acceptable for researchers. For example, this may be legitimate when defining courses for action. McKay operated a commitment to respect teachers' dignity in the process of "retraining" them, toward an enriched sensitivity to notions of dialogical knowledge production. Acceptance of her judgements depends only on the degree to which imposition of and commitment to actions that felt right were astutely weighed against the danger of rightness taking on characteristics of solidity.

There is, however, no scale for measuring astuteness in a once-and-for-all fashion. It is only possible to reflect, both during the action and *post facto*, on judgements, thus keeping alive awareness that DIS is intended to foster. Discussion about handling might–right issues *in situ* can never be closed, for this then implies a regression into the finality of presumed right answers. Such concerns must be taken on board by other approaches to revitalising educational practices, such as Critical Systems Heuristics, our next feature.

9.5.3 Critical Systems Heuristics

Critical Systems Heuristics (CSH: Ulrich, 1983, 1991, 1994) aims to influence educational practices by exposing the use of argument that often benefits those already advantaged in organisations and society. CSH wants to expose how planning can be led by exclusionary rationalities. Those who are worst affected by the plans are often excluded by the way arguments are presented and processed. Ulrich (following Habermas to a large extent here) suggests that the division between apparently factual details and normative ones that arise in everyday language often *conceals normative claims behind empirical propositions* (Habermas, 1969; Ulrich, 1983). This means that the general populace become by and large excluded from penetrating or locating the normative content of what is being presented as fact. The important requirement for Ulrich is to enhance involvement of the worst affected in information gathering and use. This form of argument should include concerns raised about likely consequences of the plans and attendant moral concerns about who is to benefit, raised by people who may be affected. Argument in this sense must form a part of social planning.

Ulrich offers a set of 12 questions that he believes will aid critical inquirers wishing to investigate and, where appropriate, shift the processes by which plans are implemented and evaluated. The questions are asked in two modes (see Tables 9.1 and 9.2). The "is" mode explores things as they currently stand with the actual client. The "ought" mode explores things as they ought to be with interested and disadvantaged parties as clients. A number of potential clients are looked at through the "ought" mode. Results from the "is" and "ought" modes are critically cross-evaluated leading to re-education of participants, especially focusing on the means of knowledge production in society.

Ulrich hopes to acclimatise both planners and affected participants to practise critically heuristic argument to the greatest degree possible in the

Table 9.1   The 12 Boundary Questions from CSH in the "is" Mode

(1) Who *is* the actual *client* of S's design, i.e. who belongs to the group of those whose purposes (interests and values) are served, in distinction to those who do not benefit but may have to bear the costs or other disadvantages?

(2) What is the actual *purpose* of S's design, as being measured not in terms of declared intentions of the involved but in terms of the actual consequences?

(3) What, judged by the design's consequences, is its built-in *measure of success*?

(4) Who is actually the *decision taker*, i.e. who can actually change the measure of success?

(5) What *conditions* of successful planning and implementation of S are really controlled by the decision taker?

(6) What conditions are *not* controlled by the decision taker, i.e. what represents *"environment"* to him or her?

(7) Who is actually involved as planner?

(8) Who is involved as *"expert"*, of what kind is his or her expertise, what role does he or she actually play?

(9) Where do the involved see the *guarantee* that their planning will be successful? (E.g. In the theoretical competence of experts? In consensus among experts? In the validity of empirical data? In the relevance of mathematical models or computer simulations? In political support on the part of interest groups? In the experience and intuition of the involved?, etc.) Can these assumed guarantors secure the design's success, or are they false guarantors?

(10) Who among the involved *witnesses* represents the concerns of the affected? Who is or may be affected without being involved?

(11) Are the affected given an opportunity to *emancipate* themselves from the experts and to take their fate into their own hands, or do the experts determine what is right for them, what quality of life means to them, etc.? That is to say, are the affected used merely as means for the purposes of others, or are they also treated as "ends in themselves", as belonging to the client?

(12) What *world view* is actually underlying the design of S? Is it the world view of (some of) the involved or of (some of) the affected?

Table 9.2 The 12 Boundary Questions in the "ought" Mode

(1) Who ought to be the *client* (beneficiary) of the system S to be designed or improved?

(2) What ought to be the *purpose* of S, i.e. what goal states ought S be able to achieve so as to serve the client?

(3) What ought to be S's *measure of success* (or improvement)?

(4) Who ought to be the *decision taker*, i.e. have the power to change S's measure of improvement?

(5) What *components* (resources and constraints) of S ought to be controlled by the decision taker?

(6) What resources and conditions ought to be part of S's *environment*, i.e. not be controlled by S's decision taker?

(7) Who ought to be involved as *designer* of S?

(8) What kind of *expertise* ought to flow into the design of S, i.e. who ought to be considered an expert and what should be his or her role?

(9) Who ought to be the *guarantor* of S, i.e. where ought the designer seek the guarantee that his or her design will be implemented and will prove successful, judged by S's measure of success (or improvement)?

(10) Who ought to belong to the *witnesses* representing the concerns of the citizens that will or might be affected by the design of S? That is to say, who among the affected ought to get involved?

(11) To what degree and in what way ought the affected be given the chance of *emancipation* from the premises and promises of the involved?

(12) Upon what *world views* of either the involved or the affected ought S's design be based?

circumstances. This form of argument enables people to state their case by appealing to *both empirical and moral considerations*. Ulrich believes critical heuristics will lead to better planning (presumably facilitated by persons who can play a part in assessing the fairness of the process). He also believes that institutionalisation of critically heuristic argument makes it difficult for powerful interests to legitimate their own practices in terms of reasoning, by sleight of hand, that conceals its normative biases. Their field of operation has to incorporate a moral component operating via fair(er) practice, taking into account wider concerns in social planning.

Case Study

We now present a brief account of a project undertaken in 1993 and 1994 involving Wendy Gregory, Norma Romm, and Mike Walsh (from the Centre for Systems Studies at the University of Hull). The project was carried out in a region of the UK's National Health Service (NHS; see Gregory *et al*, 1994, and 1995, in Bob's *Solving Problem Solving*). Our interpretation follows.

The primary purpose of the project was to create an arena for multi-agency dialogue in a region of the NHS around the topic of quality management. A key element of the project was to develop competencies in what it means to engage in fair argument. This is an informal educational practice. The researchers as facilitators set up a series of 27 workshops including: purchasers of health services, manager providers from two provider trusts, nurses, mixed professionals, Community Health Council members, and users from the Royal Sheffield Institute for Blind People and Visually Impaired Person's Group. The facilitators alternated so-called peer group meetings with multi-agency ones in which peer groups were represented. They (like Ulrich) drew on Habermas's idea to organise argument around four criteria: comprehensibility, sincerity of speakers, moral claims based on judgements of acceptability, and empirical support for statements. These validity checks were translated into four easily comprehensible questions (see below) that were presented to participants at the beginning of the project. They helped to raise competencies in conversation about quality standards in the NHS.

- Do you understand what is being said?
- Is the speaker being sincere?
- Is the speaker's point acceptable to you?
- Do you agree with the speaker's use of information and/or experience?

Participants were informed that these criteria could be applied to question any statement made. Checking in terms of these criteria was implemented less forcefully than either Habermas or Ulrich might. For example, the co-workers emphasised the need for greater accountability rather than consensus of opinion, in line with what we value in diversity management.

The researchers as facilitators structured conversation around a set of issues regarded as relevant to the topic – quality standards in the NHS. They utilised questions springing from the 12 tabled above to help direct the discussion. In the process of facilitation the researchers got directly involved by offering challenges to statements being made in group discussion. This facilitative stance was chosen to counteract discussion around the official display of supposedly unviolable information. It was shown by example how such information could take on a different significance if new experiences were introduced into the discussion.

Space does not permit a detailed account of the discussions that arose in the project nor how the researchers chose how to proceed. Suffice it to say that workshops progressed on to a final set of multi-agency group meetings where proposals for action were worked out.[2] This led to a final encounter

---

[2] Soft Systems Methodology (SSM) verb-based proposals were developed in the debating process, but the process proceeded more in line with the facilitators' conception of the significance of Critical Systems Heuristics. For this reason we suggest that elements of SSM were utilised, but in a support role.

open to all participants involved in the project. The facilitators regarded the final encounter as a defining moment in the project, which we summarise below to illustrate how discussion and argument proceeded.

Discussion revolved around vitalising communicative capacities in the NHS. It was noted by many participants that the skill to address a diversity of concerns was lacking. Readdressing relationships between parties in the health service required concentration on developing these capabilities. This might help revive the reliance of an operation that had become increasingly geared primarily to producing statistical displays of good performance as the prerequisite to financial support by government. This mode of operation in some senses imprisoned staff and was detrimental to the quality of health care provided. One function in the NHS discussed was the Community Health Council (CHC).

How to promote the CHC as a way of increasing patterns of accountability was explored. Could the CHC or other elected members of the public become non-executive members of the NHS trust boards? Disagreement surfaced as some felt that the boards should be open only to trained members of the public. Others felt that competence was less important than communicative qualities. Some CHC members said they needed support from the health authority to make possible their presence on trust boards and to make the presence welcome, even, or especially, as a constructive critical voice.

Further issues were raised. For example, the nature of so-called competition between trusts was discussed. Did competition lead to more effective service? Competition did not seem to some participants to allow users to have more say in defining the quality of services. A counter-view pushed co-operation among health providers as a better way of serving the community.

Discourse About Astuteness

It is of course difficult to judge *post facto* how successful a project has been when the purpose is to shift people's consciousness and generate possible new ways of thinking and acting. Many participants who responded to an evaluation indicated that they had shifted perspective, had made relevant contacts, and had become more aware of new ways of working together. Nevertheless, it can be argued from a cynical perspective that we should doubt whether the project contributed to the kind of large-scale alterations of orientation that may be necessary to transform patterns of relationship existing in the NHS. However modest, we suggest that inputs can help people including those deemed more privileged to grapple with issues that they find imprisoning, for example in terms of budgetary constraints. It helps to open space where new forms of relationship begin to be envisaged. And this space opens up by continued practice of new forms of argumentation so that more opportunities for these kinds of practices can be generated for other researchers, facilitators, and practitioners.

The researchers as facilitators operated through a rationale that they saw as different from most other research taking place in the NHS at that point in time. They distanced their project from those which focused primarily on finding out using design management methodologies whether goals of efficiency as defined by statistically created data were being met. They also tried to shift the focus of some of the softer projects being undertaken using debate management methodologies. They wanted to introduce a wider educational arena (see Romm, 1994b, for one interpretation).

In order to proceed with the critically heuristic agenda, the researchers had to ensure that the sponsor (the health authority) was willing to support the agenda that modes of relationship needed to be transformed. To this end, Wendy Gregory and Mike Walsh gathered an array of data, using interview and questionnaire procedures, which in the eyes of the sponsor could warrant both financial and symbolic support to the project. This did not mean that the agenda of the project was subsequently seen in exactly the same way by the sponsors and the researchers. The researchers were aware that the health authority was prepared to sponsor a project aimed broadly at trying out a methodology for enhancing communicative encounter between stakeholders in the NHS, including patients in the process. Nevertheless, the researchers dealt with the research question in a novel and even unpredictable manner from the point of view of the sponsor (and indeed some of the workshop participants).[3] The researchers had to balance the pull of the sponsors toward generating tangible results for care in the region, and pull of the research agenda, wanting to open up a broader remit by revisiting forms of argument used in processes of confrontation between participants.

It can be argued, however, that the critically heuristic argumentative form placed undue emphasis on fairness of the process of argument itself. For instance, reliance on processes of sound argument excludes or mutes to some extent, say, patients who were not prepared for these forms of exchange. Did they become unduly disadvantaged by reliance on forms of sound argument valorised in the project? The research project tried to cater for this by holding peer group meetings as a forum to practise forms of argumentation. The researchers decided to concentrate in this project on critically heuristic argument as the forum by which better social relations could be sought. And while it might be averred that this may have disadvantaged the vulnerable, it could be seen more optimistically as an

---

[3] In justifying the way things advanced, we pointed out in our report that this mode of proceeding has its roots in what Gouldner (1965) called a "clinical" approach to applied research. In such an approach the researcher confronts the research question in a way that allows new light to be cast on its definition.

opportunity for them to practise the skill of argument increasing their sense of dignity and their knowledge about forms of social argumentation. Another angle for commentary is that the process might have been unduly confrontational. Critical heuristic argumentation, it may be claimed, can and should give way to processes of encounter whereby games of knowledge production are more playful. This may allow another route to participants to transcend the narrowness of exclusivist visions. Discourse on these possibilities is to be welcomed in diversity management and does enrich options to be considered. Considering these options makes it more likely that an interventionist enhances astuteness of judgement in might–right management. Another option for might–right management is to nurture self-reliance, as we now find out.

9.6 NURTURING SELF-RELIANCE

9.6.1 Introduction

The work of collaborative and participatory action researchers seeking to establish self-reliance, experiments with practices of human inquiry and action. The approaches set up cycles of reflection and action in which co-researchers become involved, including professional researchers and other participants in society. We discuss two types of self-reliant research. The first is Collaborative Inquiry that addresses the relationship between epistemological and political concerns as part of the process of inquiry. The second is Self-reliant Participatory Action Research where sites of self-reliance are generated as part of a process of shifting patterns of social relationship. In both cases, the aim is to create forms for activating new social relationships by concentrating on fresh ways of co-generating knowledge construction as an ongoing process.

With Collaborative Inquiry, if all goes well, inquirers, including those deemed more privileged, become sufficiently emancipated to embrace concerns of other people by self-reflection on limitations of their previously insular conceptions. The hope and proposal is that, even among participants whose outlook would normally forbid co-inquiry meetings, or would have turned them into places for a contest and bargaining rally, new ways of confronting their relationships will become unravelled. Examples of this form of Collaborative Inquiry include Brown (1981), Krim (1988), Reason (1988, 1991, 1994) and Moggridge and Reason (1996).

With Self-reliant Participatory Action Research, co-inquiry as an ideal directs the process of action research, but particular attention is paid to increasing capacities for self-reliance among those thought to be most vulnerable. Self-reliance is pursued as a form of human relationship in which empowerment becomes more evenly distributed among people in society. This in turn is linked to a resistance to top down homogenisation of ways of life in society. The arguments and practices of Collaborative Inquiry and Self-reliant Participatory Action Research are discussed in turn. We begin with Collaborative Inquiry and focus on Reason's arguments and practices to illustrate what this option involves. We then discuss the purposes of Self-reliant Participatory Action Research, depicting this with a case study and offer an account of its potential global significance.

9.6.2 Collaborative Inquiry

Reason (1994: 41) describes his work on the "methodologies of human inquiry" as a way of training individuals and developing the community toward a consciousness of future participation. In Collaborative Inquiry researchers/participants are seen as co-researchers involved together in inquiry and action. He suggests that the discipline of human inquiry should aim to liberate both individuals and communities and should "hold open the tension between individual and community that contributes to the development of both" (Reason, 1994: 41). He argues that the process of inquiry he endorses is a way of providing significantly different perspectives that lead to new ways of exploring issues. In this process it should not be assumed that Collaborative Inquiry is a tension-free activity for participants. He emphasises that Collaborative Inquiry of the kind he endorses

> can be an upsetting business. It is my experience that research which . . . authentically challenges the way those involved conduct their lives raises all kinds of emotional issues which are ignored or denied by conventional research doctrine. . . . [It is] a clear advantage if an inquiry group [participants in the project] has available to it a degree of emotional competence so that personal distress can be appropriately managed. (Reason, 1988: 28–29).

Part of the significance of encounters within an inquiry group is recognition by participants that challenging favoured ways of conducting their lives may involve some distress. The rewards of Collaborative Inquiry come only if co-inquirers find a way of dealing with these emotions. Rewards come in the form of better ways of living together. Reason believes that the kinds of power parties bring into the encounter cannot be ignored in the process of directing the inquiries. Power may need to be problematised explicitly to allow participants to redress power dynamics. For example, it may be necessary to point to sites of privilege as a prerequisite to encouraging "the privileged to emancipate their own lives in order to be free to respond to the needs of the oppressed as they experience them themselves" (Moggridge and Reason, 1996: 163). The inquiry process wants to open up new possibilities for quality encounters that realise "greater effectiveness and greater justice" (Moggridge and Reason, 1996: 163). Quality encounters mean framing and reframing reality in successive cycles of reflection and action.

Reason proposes four phases to activate his preferred process of reflection and action. The process encourages participants to deconstruct favoured theories and practices. The process is meant to be a co-operative one in the sense that reflection and action respond to mutual deliberation and mutual engagement with experiences. The four phases follow, with Reason's (1994: 43) annotations.

- Phase 1 – presentation by co-inquirers of knowledge and ideas that they have and their view of the purpose of the inquiry process in which they will be engaged.
- Phase 2 – engagement in a set of agreed actions, recording and interpreting the process and outcomes of their own and each other's experience.
- Phase 3 – further engagement with experience, to develop more "openness to what is going on and so free of preconceptions that they see it in a new way" (Reason, 1994: 43).
- Phase 4 – reassemblement of co-inquirers to "consider their original propositions and questions in the light of their experience", and as a result of this reassemblement they may "modify, develop or reframe them and pose new questions" (Reason, 1994: 43).

The cycle between the phases of action and reflection is repeated several times. The inquiry is ideally finished when the initial questions are fully answered in practice, or presumably when these are reframed (Phase 4), thus reaching new resolutions of issues raised. An example of Collaborative Inquiry in action now follows.

Case Study

The context for the Collaborative Inquiry was a multi-disciplinary health clinic (Marylebone Health Centre – MHC). It consisted of general medical as well as five types of complementary practitioners. At the time Reason was recording the Collaborative Inquiry project (see Reason, 1991) the complementary practitioners holding sessions at MHC were a homeopath, an osteopath, a practitioner of traditional Chinese medicine, a psychotherapist and a masseuse.

The participants had agreed to institute arrangements geared toward empowering patients by involving them in discussions about health care. The stated claims of the clinic were to offer a multi-disciplinary approach and to empower people to take control of their own health and well-being. It was thus decided that the MHC initiative should be explored by the clinicians using a co-operative inquiry approach facilitating learning from the opportunities and issues facing the multi-disciplinary venture. In initial reflection meetings it was agreed that issues in the management of power were central to the conduct of the clinic. This applied to the management of power between the practitioners as well as to their relationships with patients. The purpose was to find ways to explore issues, including the issue of their relationship with patients, and share power in appropriate ways while at the same time attacking entrenched power bases that might have developed. They were operating in the light of a wider scenario in which social debates about legitimate medical practices might indeed effect the very survival of some of their practices.

Reason suggests that the case study may be treated as an opportunity to consider a possible application of Bateson's (1972) theory of learning. In this case, the practitioners concerned could learn not only (Bateson's Learning I) how to apply a type of medical practice, or (Learning II) how to relate this to the principles of the theory underlying that application, but also (Learning III) to recognise that alternative practices are available and that it is possible to move between them. This third process of learning implies a "shift of comprehension and of consciousness that permits a more encompassing view of practice" (Reason, 1991: 149).[4] However, this requires a detachment from any position that allows for the possibility to "move with . . . ease between them [the alternatives]". The important requirement Reason suggests would be the ability to develop and work with metaframeworks that encompass in this case "the different clinical frameworks of the group members [that] show their relationships and enable clinicians to move with some ease between them".[5]

In the case study, Reason suggests that struggles over the legitimacy of viewpoints offered, and over differences in formal power held, could not be ignored (especially in a context where complementary medicine is already experienced as undervalued). The process of evolving a culture that might support the management of paradigmatic conflict was shown to be difficult in this case. Reason proposes two ways of addressing these: a realistic and an idealistic strategy.

The first strategy, which Reason calls realistic, is to try to find a way of expressing deep paradigmatic conflicts, so that when the conflict erupts it is not just glossed over as personal or professional pathology. Finding the language to make manifest the way that this deep conflict may express itself is one step toward managing power in a more astute fashion.

There is a second strategy, labelled by Reason idealistic. An idealistic

---

[4] Reason's (1991) reference to Bateson's Learning III processes bears some resemblance to our conception of shifting attention between points of foci and choice making as we triple loop. Learning III is linked up with what we call a capacity for reflexivity as described in Part 2 of this book.

[5] As indicated in Part 2 of our book, we have suggested that triple looping involves some kind of metaframework that allows people not to become too attached to any prefavoured view. In this sense it requires a certain detachment that resonates with Reason's thinking.

strategy tries to move beyond the sporadic expression of conflict to a higher level of group operation. Time is devoted to thinking about and addressing factors (such as sources of power) that may imbalance discussion; but time would also have to be devoted to cultivating attitudes of nonattachment. In this way parties may learn to emancipate themselves by paying attention to paradigmatic differences and ways of addressing these differences.

Throughout this process participants must recognise that their power and potency have to be redefined so that neither participant is trying to control the situation in terms of a prefavoured conception (of reality). Prefavoured conceptions can be buttressed by built-in biases in the social and political system. In this way the system may open up, ideally, to forces other than a simple power play which, when left unmanaged, is likely to continue largely unaffected. But this is an idealistic strategy (recognised by Reason as such) and to operate with some conception of the ideal still may put interventionists in a situation where they have to make judgements, e.g. the judgements concerning to what extent they must try and operate the realistic versus the idealistic view. Reason leaves this case study open for the reader to think through these options.

Discourse About Astuteness

Reason (1994: 44) notes that the ideal of Collaborative Inquiry is not always achieved fully in their practice. This indeed is one of the reasons why astuteness of judgement may be called for by those involved. For example, as suggested in the above case study, astuteness of judgement may require ways of moving between the realistic and idealistic way of addressing "the situation" – all the time aware of the management of power in our terms as the management of a might–right complex.

In a further write up of some of their work, Moggridge and Reason (1996) argue that this work points embryonically to possible new ways of generating co-working, built on new forms of human inquiry. However embryonic these efforts are, we suggest that it is relevant for researchers to develop possible new forms of inquiry to shift styles of human relationship. It may be argued that the more theoretical and practical work done in this field, the less easy it will be for those inclined to pursue predefined agendas to legitimate their ways of doing things. This indeed seems to be the hope of authors proposing the potential of Collaborative Inquiry as a means of energising alternative forms of human relationship.

Research of the kind suggested by Moggridge and Reason (1996) in some ways is experimenting with subversion of entrenched knowledge–power games. Sometimes, however, research may be seen as too immediately oriented to generation of resolutions between partners without building up the capacities of the more vulnerable. Building up capacities helps people to participate more confidently in inquiry and action cycles. It makes more possible astuteness in these cycles. Authors whom we name Self-reliant Participatory Action Researchers focus more on this component.

9.6.3 Self-reliant Participatory Action Research

Fals-Borda and Rahman's work is a classic representative of Self-reliant Participatory Action Research (SPAR). The main thrust of SPAR is to employ action research to nurture self-reliance as a mode of human relationship. The intention is to operate "in defence of multiple and cherished ways of life and for resistance against homogenisation" (Fals-Borda and Rahman, 1991: 33). They are inspired by the plight of so-called less-developed countries.

Discussing Asia, Latin America and Africa, Rahman (1991: 16) argues that ways of fostering self-reliance as an antidote to power–knowledge relationships experienced as oppressive may vary, depending on circumstances. Rahman suggests that in Asia and Latin America forms of class confrontation combined with socio-economic initiatives to improve the short run livelihood of the people are crucial. These tackle oppression at the micro level when problems are most acute. In a number of African countries, by contrast,

> people's collective action takes the form more of socio-economic initiatives. These often confront or assert *vis-à-vis* those state bureaucracies and technocracies that seek to impose their ideas of "development" (modernisation) – ideas which typically are alien to the people's way of life and culture and are often also destructive of the physical environment. The people's own initiatives seek to promote their authentic self-development. . . . Additionally, these areas are often addressed to negotiating with or challenging the relevant state organs for better service in areas where they are supposed to serve. (Rahman, 1991: 16)

Rahman goes on to say that promoting an authentic people's movement means stimulating "awareness raising" as a priority. This means awareness of the capacity to transform the relations of knowledge (Rahman, 1991: 17). While professionals, along with the knowledge and insights they bring to bear can be consulted, professional opinion must be treated as an input in a dialogue rather than a package of knowledge to be handed on. A crucial part of the process of empowerment is subverting any top-down form of knowledge relationship. It is important to bear in mind the history of the way in which patterns of power have been buttressed by forms of knowledge creation and to act consciously to shift these patterns.

Rahman makes it clear that the process of transforming relations of knowledge production means people self-developing by engaging in socio-economic initiatives. The two efforts go hand in hand. As people begin to self-develop in ways not envisaged by the models, ideals and ideologies traditionally handed down to them, so they discover their capacities to introduce alternative knowledge relations in the social arena. They escape traps laid by presentations that bring with them practical realities and necessities. They play a part in negotiating or challenging the way in which they attain support from, for example, state bodies (Rahman, 1991: 16). They shift their relations with these bodies so that the bodies play a supportive role rather than sticking to predefined criteria that declare what services are apparently possible. The character of the services and the way that these are provided take on a new dimension.

Fals-Borda (1991: 21) extends the point saying that struggles to generate "genuine accountability to the people is not merely a matter of formal institutional structures but also, critically, of people's self-awareness and the promotion of this awareness, and people's self-confidence to assert their self-awareness as their political statement". The focus of Fals-Borda and Rahman's collective effort SPAR is on sustaining awareness that underpins any notion of democracy: awareness of the moral requirement to participate as knowledge equals in society and awareness of the possibility of people taking initiative as an exercise of freedom (Rahman, 1991: 22). This may create preconditions that shape development of leaders who are more likely to recognise and to be responsive to knowledge equals. However, vigilance must be maintained to guard against the possibility of "degeneration" (Rahman, 1991: 23).

What contribution can professional researchers make to achievement of self-reliance? Rahman (1991) says that this question is still under consideration. Fals-Borda says that research involving professionals must be a collective process rather than a task to be dealt with by a set of researchers who define the research agenda, define the process of research, and interpret results. The focus is rather on confirmation of ideas achieved through "dialogue, discussion, argumentation". Hence data collection involves, primarily, methods such as "meetings, socio-dramas, public assemblies, committees, fact-finding trips and so on" where the relevance of information is subject to collective argumentation (Fals-Borda, 1991: 8).

Clearly, researchers (even so-called external ones) who are prepared to practise the types of knowledge relationships that have been outlined by, for example, Fals-Borda and Rahman, are not to be ignored. They can play a part by enriching appreciation of options open to people as a minimum (see Fals-Borda, 1996). Aid given by researchers to facilitation and animation in the process of generating increased self-reliance is a relevant contribution. Of course, this does not mean that the question of their involvement can easily be settled. For example, is the researcher's purpose to widen the range of concerns to incorporate perhaps more than just immediate ones about achieving short-term benefits? Or is the researcher's purpose to generate through research an agency on the part of the participants in which they feel equipped and skilled to make astute judgements that address their social involvements? Perhaps these issues can be further illuminated through the following case study.

Case Study

Our case is set in Tanzania where Maghimbi (1990a, 1990b, 1995) worked with co-operatives, attempting to enhance their self-reliance as part of the process of tackling knowledge relationships in society. Norma was engaged on an extended basis in discussions with Maghimbi about his work. Maghimbi (1990a) highlights the way in which the Tanzanian government policy of collectivisation of rural production (crystallised in the Arusha declaration, 1967) threatened to undermine the co-operative movement in Tanzania. With the declaration, the collective came to be officially defined and practised through state enforced definitions. Maghimbi argues that, instead of building on the movement, the policy thus ran counter to it. The policy, he continues, could not be implemented successfully because it failed to resonate with the way in which peasants by and large wished to define themselves as farmers. They would gladly be involved in a co-operative movement in order to, for example, procure seeds and fertilisers, organise marketing, transport crops and so on. They were not, however, inclined to work for a so-called collective system which they saw as controlling them by government policy dictates (Maghimbi, 1995: 43–44).

Maghimbi details processes by which the co-operative movement was brought under the control of the Tanzanian state under the guise of ideological reschooling in which people were taught the (supposed) value of collective production. The policies of collective rural production were presented as traditional Tanzanian values. Maghimbi (1990a: 367) doubted this. To the contrary many of the peasantry in Tanzania were willing to interpret their traditional lifestyle as conducive to a people's capitalism in the countryside, where people could have individual access to land while engaging in co-operative activities as needs arose. Maghimbi illustrated this with the existence of a strong co-operative movement of this sort in Tanzania before and in the aftermath of the Arusha declaration.[6]

Some peasants openly resisted attempts to move them to collectivised villages under a policy of villigisation. Others resisted in passive mode. Maghimbi identified potency in passive resistance. As he says, many "simply did not pick the nuts" (that is the cashew nuts for collection by government officials) (Maghimbi, 1990b: 95). The peasants with enhanced self-reliance and, indeed, self-confidence felt increasingly able to protest in these ways.

[6] Maghimbi (1990a: 223) argues that it is possible to use co-operatives as people's institutions and it matters little whether they are called capitalist or socialist.

Nyerere assumed another influential role in the late 1980s following his Presidency of Tanzania. He chaired a Commission to debate issues central to development in less-developed countries. The Commission emphasised the importance of cognitive participation when defining options for development. It stated that "leaders who refuse to listen to any but their own voices soon exhaust their leadership potential. . . . Participatory development is thus a must" (South Commission Report, 1990: 227).

Enforcement of a directive relationship over the peasantry (*inter alia*) was not sustainable. Maghimbi (1995: 46) indeed argues in regard to Tanzanian directives that the government's policy on this issue has never been clear and that "we can only so far describe these changes as wavering and staggering or muddling through policy". Co-operatives could not be controlled by enforcing a clientele relationship in which the government offered returns as rewards for obedience to fulfilment of policy. New relationships started to emerge. Co-operatives began to redevelop a basis of self-reliance, a platform from which they could participate in defining kinds of support they might need. Maghimbi (1990a) outlines some of the ways support was sought. He also shows how the regeneration of the co-operatives required rethinking of the categories of capitalism and socialism (Maghimbi, 1990b). Farmers helped create development options for the country. Their involvement in vitalising what Braun (1991) called a people's economy was premised on *cognitive involvement* in astutely thinking through their own significance in the development process.

Discourse About Astuteness

Maghimbi's action research with co-operatives in Tanzania locates points where erosion in people's exercise of initiative can be evidenced. It also shows that it is possible to regenerate people in such circumstances by enhancing their self-reliance. Maghimbi and small farmers were able to define ways in which co-operatives could impact on development policies. This meant aiding co-operatives to reorganise themselves in line with co-operative principles that participants were committed to, although, of course, there were still practices under discussion as the research work continued.

Those involved, as Maghimbi describes it, attempted to shift their input in the development process into terms that permitted negotiation of their relationship with bodies like state institutions. This got caught up in a struggle over the way the process of development would be officially envisaged. A way of operating was carved out that was not initially (or perhaps ever?) welcomed by the state. Shifting co-operative–state relationships away from dependency toward self-development is likely to be a continuing struggle. This struggle requires continued astuteness by those who are trying to resist attempts to frustrate grassroots community-based institutions.

Discussion on SPAR so far has concentrated on issues of self-development in so-called less-developed countries. Similar kinds of initiative are relevant in so-called developed countries where issues to be tackled are different. Two authors who make this point are Vanderplaat and Giddens. Their views are outlined below.

Vanderplaat (1995) in her article entitled "Beyond Technique" discusses evaluation of social programmes in Canadian social policy. They may become infused with a "commitment to social empowerment and a vision of social justice" (Vanderplaat, 1995: 83). Rather than accepting the society's "prevailing social, political, and economic orientations, this type of intervention . . . refers to social actions which seek changes to existing social relationships and institutions" (Vanderplaat, 1995: 84). Continuing, Vanderplaat says the intention is for people to "produce change within and to their environment rather than themselves being an object of change-producing strategies", for example by being the receivers of technically led social programmes. The importance of mutual help and building solidarity is underlined. Solidarity in discourse refers to what she would see as instantiated, to a greater or lesser extent, in "public participation projects" characterised by "strong social supports, skills and self-esteem". As an example she refers to the way in which the health promotion policy of Health Canada came to adopt a "programming strategy which subscribes to the concepts of public participation, enablement and empowerment". She argues that while translation of the principle of "empowerment-based social programming" is not easy, elements of this can be found in Health Canada and other similar initiatives.

Vanderplaat (1995: 85) is aware of difficulties connected with addressing what she calls the "unequal distribution of discursive power". She feels that it is precisely as a counterpart to this that "empowerment-based social programming" becomes significant. Her description of the potential of such initiatives concurs with the argument developed in the case of co-operatives in Tanzania discussed earlier. The contexts of these initiatives means that in practice the way self-development is pursued has to be adjusted accordingly, but the principles and purposes are similar.

In *Beyond Left and Right*, Giddens (1994: 147) also highlights the potential significance of practices combining self-reliance with emancipatory purposes. He describes their significance in, for instance, the USA and the UK, noting the psychic discomfort which may be generated "as individuals become dependent on systems of provision which they recognise as alien and over which they have no control". It is not surprising, he says on page 147, that people tend to take a "manipulative attitude toward them [these systems]" for their dependence on the wider society is accompanied by "exclusion from participation [in the community]". Giddens (1994: 153) discusses the cultural demoralisation which ensues and argues that a (re)definition of "positive welfare" may be needed to shift the terms of social discussion. He suggests on the same page that "most welfare measures are designed to cope with events once they have happened, rather than at origin" and this is one of the roots of their failure. Difficulties arise often because "resources are being organised in ways which are more and more inappropriate to the problems they were set up to meet". In such situations it is necessary to consider the import of what Giddens calls positive welfare. This is not necessarily tied only to initiatives taking place within a single nation-state, for there are many concerns that indeed transcend state boundaries (Giddens, 1994: 156).

Giddens sets out a set of traits that he believes could characterise an "alternative development" approach which offers a way of redefining priorities. This draws on the kind of self-development initiatives tabled by other authors that illustrate a myriad of instances over the globe. The over-all purpose as Giddens sees it is to offer a challenge to the way in which welfare systems, often associated with modernity, tend to exclude partici-pation of those dependent on it. People's involvement then becomes reduced, by and large, to mere adoption of a manipulative stance where they attempt to manipulate the system in order to extract benefits. Giddens (1994: 158) prefers to challenge this by questioning entrenched patterns of modernity rather than generalising them and attempting to extend them to so-called less-developed countries. Traits for an alternative development draw on literature that has a quest for emancipatory self-reliance, coupled with nurturing solidarity by setting up support systems. He refers, for example, to the way in which indigenous social movements and self-help groups all over the world have come to engage positively, rather than re-actively, forces transforming their lives. He cites the Seventh Generation Fund developed by American Indian activists as an example. "The purpose of the programme is to ensure that policy decisions are considered in terms of their potential impact on the seventh generation; and at the same time to foster self-reliant economic development" (Giddens, 1994: 159).

A significant feature of Gidden's alternative development is that the meaning of development is essentially linked to the promotion of "self-reliance and integrity". He says, "self-reliance may sometimes entail the production of markets, but it refers mainly to the reconstruction of local solidarities and support systems" (Giddens, 1994: 160). The Tanzanian co-operative case study could be referenced here. An example given by Giddens, however, explores setting up a bank in Bangladesh to offer loans mainly to poor women. Many subsequently became self-reliant. Pay-back to the bank was 98%.

He also refers on page 162 to possible improvements to health care through responsible participation. He goes on to discuss ways in which family ties may provide relevant support systems as long as they avoid entrenched patriarchal practices. However, Giddens does not mean to imply that examples like these are relevant in all circumstances but, he notes, they count among the cases of development processes built on self-reliance and integrity. Alternate development must therefore be sensitised to local demands. Local demands in turn must be astutely sensitised to intervention from the state, business and international organisation. But, how can these "big battalions" be reasoned with?

Vanderplaat and Maghimbi would perhaps argue that part of the task of empowering people is to locate ways in which dependency on the big battalions is reduced. They provide examples of how to turn around entrenched ways of defining social realities and attendant social practices. An option they do not emphasise is to concentrate on development of a theoretical language by which to rethink the practice of forms of sociation. This rethinking may form part of a process that shifts power constellations that otherwise serve to define the limits of what is possible in society. The next section picks up this theme.

9.7 (RE)CONSIDERATION OF SOCIAL RELATIONSHIPS

In one sense this book provides an input into the debate about what social relationships could amount to. It may be considered a case of the kind of enterprise that is explored in this section. Diversity management is an invitation for people to relate to one another in an accountable way that still leaves open maximum choice for people to define and live in terms of a reality that they feel is theirs.[7] Diversity management as a theory does not want people to feel unduly controlled by social constructions. A myriad of social theorists have turned their attention likewise to evoking possible ways of generating better relationships; or at least for undercutting those relationships believed to stifle unnecessarily people's will to avoid assimilation. The deliberations we focus on in this section are Foucault and his postmodern work, followed by a comparison of this with Habermas's critical modernist argument, rounded off with reference to a sample of researchers who have entered this theoretical field.

Foucault's postmodern work is often cited for its importance to deconstruction of familiar definitions of sanity, sexuality, truth, self-hood and so

[7] The standard that we indicate forms the backdrop for this book is a standard that we believe can help to generate better relationships. At the same time the standard allows us to address issues of structure and widens processes of decision making. This is not to say that the standard is set in concrete and is incontestable. In Part 2 we present a discussion where as far as possible we account for the standard we have adopted.

on. Foucault's work carries out detailed historical interpretation that evokes a sense of non-universality of such definitions. Gutting (1989: 283) says that Foucault's historical work is crucial because it opens space for subverting "forms of expert knowledge (psychiatry, criminology, economics, etc.) that tell us that the changes [to forms of social relationship] we envisage are simply not possible". Space is created for "examining [criticising] such claims of impossibility . . . thereby clearing the path to liberation". Hoy (1986: 136–137) points out, though, that the notion of power that informs Foucault's historical studies may be too broad and that it becomes difficult "to speculate about whether future power configurations might be better". The charge of broadness (vacuity?) of Foucault's notion of power is some-times linked to the claim that "Foucault's studies are too empirical and historiographical, and not sufficiently theoretical" (Hoy, 1986: 136). This is precisely the charge levelled by Habermas, who argues that Foucault's work does not allow us sufficiently to conceptualise what better relations might involve (see, for example, Habermas, 1986b).

Simons (1995) asserts that Foucault's conceptualisation of power relations does implicitly include a regulative principle for the assessment of political regimes. A regime, she notes, "is judged [by Foucault] unfavourably as dominative if it minimises the possibilities for strategic reversal and thereby confines practices of liberty. . . . The regulative aim should be to pursue games of power . . . played with a minimum of domination" (Simons, 1995: 94). Although Foucault is wary of generalising what possibilities exist for playing such games, he implies that inventions can be made possible within power relations (see also Barker, 1993: 80–81).

Habermas constructs a theoretical discussion around communicative rationality as a form of human sociation. In this undertaking he offers a detailed account of the way in which "the public sphere" as a forum for moral deliberation, over issues of collective concern, has become histori-cally eroded by party politics and interest group associations (see in par-ticular Habermas, 1989: 181–235). He uses these studies to substantiate a theoretical vision of communicative power (as Arendt, 1986, calls it) as a basis for generating legitimate use of power (Habermas, 1986a: 85).

This is not to say that Habermas accepts fully Arendt's conception of how communicative power may operate. He feels that Arendt ignores the con-ditions of the modern world by envisaging "a state which is relieved of the administrative processing of social problems; a politics which is cleansed of socio-economic issues; an institutionalisation of public liberty which is independent of the organisation of public wealth" (Habermas, 1986a: 83). Habermas reckons that compromises have to be made in the light of these conditions. His views of this are discussed in the next section where his conception of the potential for protest against the current momentum of forms of modernisation led by standards of economic and administrative efficiency are elucidated. Despite differences in Foucault's and Habermas's work about the status of the content of theorising over options, both we regard as "underlabourers" (to use Gutting's term, 1989: 283) in clearing the ground for discourse about fairer forms of social relationships.

Another discourse that tries to cut into our concerns about human living in society from a different angle (recently drawing heavily on MacIntyre's *After Virtue*, 1981) is that of Fuenmayor and Lopez-Garay (Fuenmayor and Lopez-Garay, 1991; Fuenmayor, 1995; Lopez-Garay, 1995). They have concentrated on (re)generating historical studies as an essential component of efforts to uncover the parameters of the specific epoch in which we seem to be enmeshed, as a prelude to altering its mode of patterning our responses to the world. They consider it essential to provide a historical setting as a prerequisite to overcoming the instrumentalist mentalities and the impoverished view of moral choices that characterise the current era (as they see it). The researchers provide a methodology that invites people to review themselves in the light of this setting. They see their methodology generating conditions for a process of truth seeking as a (new) way of conducting our relationship with the world. The methodology is called Interpretive Systemology.

Interpretive Systemology aims to lend credence to, and to operationalise, a search for what may be called holistic sense as a way of confronting the world (Fuenmayor, 1991: 489). It opens the space for people to reach for transcendence as they gear themselves to a continual process whose only end (that is, purpose) is the search for truth. This is constituted in the search process as an infinite sequence of unfolding interpretations of phenomena. The methodology sets an example of how truth-seeking may be undertaken as a process aimed at enriched understanding and comprehension. It is a process that can be applied to any phenomenon in society (e.g. a planning corporation, an educational institution, or a field of study, such as organisational studies).

The phenomenon is seen as essentially a realm of possibility that unfolds through its being presenced in many interpretive contexts (Lopez-Garay, 1991: 491). A set of such contexts is explored by way of example (in any particular study) to show how the phenomenon may be unfolded in different interpretations, and what likely practical consequences (as responses to the phenomenon) are implied by each of the interpretations. These interpretations are then linked in a process of comprehension which builds a narrative to explain the variety of unfoldings, in this way attaining a greater sense of the way that the phenomenon is created through the series of unfoldings. Fuenmayor and Lopez-Garay consider it essential that Being is seen as constituted through the unfolding process, and thus as defined as a never-ending de-becoming process (Lopez-Garay, 1995). Its becoming is forever being adjusted by subsequent unfoldings. History here is thus defined as the arena in which Being is inextricably linked to its having been (become) and its about-to-be. The only way of making this process materialise is through constructing a narrative structure as a sense-making event. Fuenmayor (1991: 486) explains the methodology of Interpretive Systemology as follows. It has two main phases. The first phase, understanding, involves designing a range of contextual systems (contexts of meaning) to highlight a variety of points of view of a (chosen) phenomenon. Efforts are made to interpret the phenomenon under study in the light of each of these contexts. The explicit results of interpreting the phenomenon in each context of meaning are developed. In the second phase, comprehension, a debate between these contexts is orchestrated conceptually and an attempt is made to develop a framework that contains a number of contextual systems. Comprehension aims to embrace a truing process, as a search for holistic sense, which is developed by making sense of the variety. Seeing this is part of the process of unfolding of the phenomenon.

Fuenmayor and Lopez-Garay suggest that a way of life attuned to operating this methodology offers a search for truth (and goodness) which is far removed from instrumentalism that they see as characterising modes of relationship in the current era. They side to a large degree with MacIntyre's argument concerning a turning point in our history. MacIntyre makes reference to the collapse of the Roman imperium. He (tentatively) highlights a parallel between the collapse of the imperium and the collapse of current civilisation. MacIntyre is not totally gloomy, however, since he observes that at the time of the collapse of the imperium there were local groups who, maybe unwittingly, fought to preserve moral virtue in their local circumstances. They did not identify with the imperium. This salvaged civilisation through the Dark Ages. The hope is that local forms of community will also see us through the collapse underway and the new Dark Age that we are in. MacIntyre (1981: 263) appeals to local forms of community "within which civility and the intellectual and moral life can be sustained through the new dark ages".

Fuenmayor and Lopez-Garay (as MacIntyre) do not go so far as to appeal to a form of communitarianism in which (MacIntyre's view of) moral virtues can be fostered. They go along with MacIntyre's suggestion that it is the general lack of consciousness of our (Dark Age) predicament that constitutes part of our predicament (MacIntyre, 1981: 263). Fuenmayor and Lopez-Garay leave open the question of what may constitute some (astute) way forward in the face of the entrenched reductionism of thought which they have located as patterning our current way of responding to the world. What they concentrate on doing, via a theoretical mode of activity, is evoking a (holistic?) sense of a potential new order of thinking and being (Fuenmayor, 1995) which they presumably invite us to participate in constructing and constituting.

As we see it, their view of knowledge production as a never-ending process of truth seeking offers an interesting alternative to both the Habermasian and Foucauvian positions as we have presented them here. It is an alternative that has implications for human living in the world. Instead of appealing to the Habermasian view of consensus, or to the Foucauvian view of games of strategy as a way of diverting excessive domination, they appeal to new forms of orientation to the world in which our patterns of response are enriched by our continual search for holistic sense. This by implication may make a difference to the conduct of our way of life in society, although the co-workers expressly shy away from any proposal of this sort.[8]

In summary, we suggest that reconsidering our relationships in the context of reviewing processes of knowledge creation in society is a relevant activity. It does lay some groundwork that allows us to keep alive a discourse about new forms of social relationship. These exercises invite people to rethink modes of human sociation. They are a (strategic?) necessity for discussion and action aimed at subverting and shifting current ways of life. Theoretical discussions may in turn be linked to protest in society and it is to this that we turn our attention.[9] The next section investigates the option of talking about and/or engaging in protest as a way of transforming knowledge-power–relations.

9.8 PROTEST

9.8.1 Introduction

The discourse of might–right management may suggest that people engage in forms of protest. By protest we mean expressions of dissatisfaction as qualified below. Protest in society is often self-defined as an effort to alter, primarily, social structures seen as unduly constraining. Or it is self-defined as an effort to assert one's right to participate more fully in communication processes. Or it is presented with disdain with no attempt by the protester(s) to offer an account of the larger significance of their protest. We

---

[8] They consider their work not primarily directed at reconsidering social relationships, but at indicating what it may mean to search for holistic sense. The former may be a side product of the latter.

[9] It is worth noting here that MacIntyre (1981) is concerned that in the new Dark Age, protest is too narrowly conceived as a search for the fulfilment of rights. In this way protest becomes too utilitarian. We agree with him where protest is instrumentalised as a way of extracting benefits; however, we argue in the next section that we should not rule out the relevance of protest to keep alive concerns about self-invention against all-encompassing systems of thought. Our argument may be somewhat incommensurable with that of MacIntyre's! We believe, however, that his insistence that incommensurability is a feature of emotivism of the new Dark Age, where positions are supported through emotion, already fails to cater for possible ways of addressing (in)commensurability between his and our positions (see our discussion on the notion of (in)commensurability in Chapter 1).

recognise the potential relevance of all forms of expression of protest and their import within various arenas of discourse. However, we concentrate on expressions that nurture a quality of self-reflection that dovetails with our discourse of might–right management. This means protest that penetrates as far as transforming knowledge and power games in society.

Both Habermas and Foucault may be regarded as central figures who have activated discourse around might–right protest. As noted in Chapter 6, Habermas's texts tend to over-valorise the right in the force of communicative reason. Foucault's texts tend to endorse the might of powerful strategy as a form of protest. We give credence to each of their views. We believe, however, that the extent to which the right of communicative rationality becomes unduly powerful and conversely the extent to which the might of strategic power is relied upon, are issues that require astute judgement. We suggest that both Habermas and Foucault provide starting points for the import of protest as a way of transforming entrenched patterns of social response but leave it to our readers to judge for themselves, astutely, whether the charge of excess levelled against them can be upheld. The following discussion provides further background reading on this matter.

This section, then, reviews Habermas on "Right in Protest Through Communicative Rationality" and Foucault on "Might of Strategy in Protest". There are of course many other innovative vehicles that help us get to and change knowledge and power games in society. To illustrate this point we turn to fiction, to "Novel Protest", which promises the sort of innovation and change that diversity management promotes.

9.8.2 Right in Protest Through Communicative Rationality

We proceed with a discussion of Habermas's argument. Habermas argues that the strength of communicative rationality can be used to provide an antidote to unnecessary domination. Domination ensues when patterns of action are both practised and legitimated only in terms of economic and administrative standards of rationality. Habermas believes that "legitimation" conceived in the narrow terms of instrumental rationality serves to exclude thought about collective needs that cannot be satisfied within formal systems of economy and state (Habermas, 1979: 169).[10]

Habermas has a (varying) ambivalent position when it comes to potency of communicative rationality in influencing systems of economic and administrative organisation (Cohen and Arato, 1994; Spaul, 1996). Habermas

---

[10] Habermas sees the radical import of apparently isolated protest initiatives in terms of their more general relevance for rerouting somewhat the course of a "modernisation" geared primarily toward more efficient functioning of systems. He sees the expression of dissatisfaction with the current mode of operating with the party system as a signal of protest against an administratively oriented democracy (see, for example, Habermas, 1979, 1986a).

is keen to reverse the profit-dependent instrumental mentality that dominates work, lifestyles[11] and social policy. The trouble is, Habermas senses,
counter-initiatives have only a stalemate siege-like impact on the systems of
economy and state. Deadlock sieges may grip events in this way but do not
influence their course in any significant way. Options left open to reverse
pervasive standards of economic and administrative reality in Habermas's
view become restricted to informal economic arrangements, self-help
groups and small democratic communities (Rajan, 1993; Spaul, 1996).

An "offensive model" might, however, provide a further option (Cohen
and Arato, 1994). This option can be employed to reconsider the relationship between (economic and administrative) systems and (people's cultural
and social) lifeworld contexts. New Social Movements (NSMs) may have
the sharp edge needed to challenge tendencies in systems of formal economy and state. NSMs means "the various public protest and collective
action groups which have promoted 'single issues', such as ecology, feminism, peace, etc." (Spaul, 1996: 319). NSMs look "inwards toward the lifeworld and the development of forms of association, co-operation and
communication, but also outwards toward the economic and political systems in the hope of influence and reform" (Spaul, 1996: 328–329).

Seen in this light "the politics of influence and inclusion denote the
claims of new social movements that their counter-initiatives be recognised
as valid within the political process, and that the discursive force generated
by them may validly shape the political agenda" (Spaul, 1996: 329). The
politics of influence and inclusion shifts the pattern of relationships away
from one where "roles are imposed on citizens and clients of the economy
and state" (Spaul, 1996: 329). Initiatives by citizens that imply a withdrawal
from loyalty to the system are both a challenge and an indication that systems can function on different premises. System contexts can be responsive
to lifeworld-generated pressures for reform.

Spaul looked for evidence to support this angle on communicative rationality. He makes reference to the Brent Spar case in Europe, 1995, when pressure from Greenpeace impelled a turnaround in the oil giant Shell's decision
to sink a redundant oil platform. Greenpeace made public issue of this on
the grounds of predicted unnecessary pollution. Subsequent accounts show
ironically that Shell's scientific data supporting their form of disposal as
least pollutive was probably right, yet media pressure instigated by Greenpeace impelled them to reverse their decision. Nevertheless, in this Spaul
sees evidence that

> public debate and concern for a range of dubious business practices, ranging
> from environmental responsibility to investment in countries with poor

[11] This is a manifestation of what Habermas calls the colonisation of the "lifeworld" by the
"system" (briefly mentioned in Part 2 of this book). Consult Brand (1990) for a good introductory discussion.

human rights records, has resulted in the development of a set of standard means by which business can signal to their consumers their stance on environmental and ethical issues . . . Such signals are created in response to lifeworld pressure (focused by organised environmental and consumer groups) and indicate a willingness to respond to such pressure, but they are also thoroughly integrated into the market logic by which business inevitably works. (Spaul, 1996: 330)

So, Habermas's dual concept of system and lifeworld reinterpreted through the offensive model may lead, Spaul contends, to accommodations where as a matter of course the system and the lifeworld resolve their different standards. The terms of the accommodations, however, are most likely to be the subject of continuing conflict, in part because of the market logic.

Our position is to keep alive discourse in the face of coercive forces and so we find Spaul's right in protest through communicative rationality relevant. We refer back to examples introduced in Chapters 7 and 8 to make our point. It is crucial to keep alive discourse about, say, policy that leads to retrenchment of staff. Retrenchment is often legitimated by the system as a necessary effort to downsize to make more efficient and viable operations as a response to growing (global) competition, benchmarking, and other forms of erosion on the profitability of organisations. In the face of this system rationality, How can the lifeworld promote counter-initiatives? Perhaps it is only when the issue is raised in the wider social arena that it becomes possible to exert pressure on the logic of downsizing? Vitalisation of a counter-rationality may require lobbying for socially responsible business practices. The offensive model takes the issue into the organisational and social arena. A decision to downsize buttressed by an appeal to the logic of survival in a competitive environment therefore becomes open to scrutiny. The second (less successful) case of Participatory Action Research in Chapter 8, the case of Trico Products Corporation, may be better thought of as an example of a possible case of the offensive model since downsizing was not prevented in the short term but system rationality could be seen to be influenced in the longer term. We now turn to Foucault's work on protest, that shows some similarity with Habermas's ideas.

9.8.3 Might of Strategy in Protest

Foucault (e.g. 1984) shares with Habermas a desire to transform the way that power and truth games are played out in social contexts. Foucault, however, treats Habermas's regulative consensual principle of discourse as too strong. Foucault portrayed a critical role that intellectuals can play to "dissipate what is familiar and accepted, to re-examine rules and institutions . . . [and] . . . on the basis of this re-problematisation . . . [the intellectual may] . . . participate in the formation of a political will in which he [*sic*] has his role as citizen to play" (Foucault, 1990: 265). Foucault thus wants to nurture a political will to protest against pervasion of "the familiar and accepted". This differs from Habermas in both vision and outcome.

Power relations for Foucault involve a continuous process of adversarial struggles and confrontational strategies. Power relations are characterised by "agonism", a process which involves "strategy, reaction and even taunting, as in a wrestling match. Agonism may be as serious as political domination or as light as child's play. It permeates all the different types of relationships (economic, familial, communicative and sexual) within which power relations are immanent" (Simons, 1995: 85). Foucault stresses that resistance allows for experimentation with ways in which power games can be played out; resistance here being legitimised by the possibility for further resistance (Simons, 1995: 86).

In one of his interviews with sexual choices as the theme, Foucault identified contexts where agonism is at stake. The question is

> whether the system of constraints in which a society functions leaves individuals the liberty to transform the system. . . . A system of constraints becomes truly intolerable when the individuals who are affected by it don't have the means of modifying it. This can happen when such a system becomes intangible as a result of its being considered a moral or religious imperative, or a necessary consequence of medical science. (Foucault, 1990: 294)

For Foucault an intolerable situation arises when restrictions become so sedimented that the possibility of altering them seems to be foreclosed.

Foucault suggests that transgressive practices point to new forms of human relationship. In the case of homosexuality, its challenge to society opens up "the prospect that gays will create as yet unforeseen kinds of relationship that many people cannot tolerate" (Foucault, 1990: 301). He says his own involvement with "other members of the gay community" is shaped by a wariness of imposing his "own views, or setting down a plan or program. . . . [since] . . . I don't want to discourage invention, don't want gay people to stop feeling that it is up to them to adjust their own relationships by discovering what is appropriate for them" (Foucault, 1990: 302). The game is to generate new forms of relationship, practised with the minimum of domination which, in this way, contributes to a wider political agenda. This strongly suggests a critique of political processes that may "entail opposing networks of power and rationalities of government" (Simons, 1995: 103).[12]

[12] Simons (1995: 106) suggests that Foucault's argument in this respect can be seen to resonate with the feminist one that the personal is political. She is aware that many feminists accuse Foucault's work for being too ungendered. Despite this, she thinks that his theoretical focus allows for questions of concern to feminists to be posed. However, Hartstock (1990: 164) argues that Foucault's argument refuses to allow for ideas of progress to be entertained and she feels that it is *this* which represents a threat to the feminist movement.

Foucault, however, does not embrace a static or unified position that threads through all his texts. At times he concentrates on acts of personal transgression and prides himself on the fact that this may not have ramifications for the way that broader political processes in society pan out (Simons, 1995: 103). At other times he claims political significance of his and other people's transgressive practices insofar as they seek alternative forms of governance. The way, then, people relate to each other becomes a directly political question (Burchell, 1991: 145). Whichever, Foucault has certainly raised some intriguing issues for our discourse on astuteness in the domain of might–right management. This discourse continues below with a novel account of protest.

9.8.4 Novel Protest

There are many innovative ways in which protest can be lodged that lie outside of social theory as such. As an illustration of this we have selected a novel that explores state coercion. The novel is Coetzee's (1982) *Waiting for the Barbarians*. Coetzee was born in Cape Town, South Africa. His book, we argue, shows novel writing as a form of intelligent discourse to be reckoned with. It exploits another way of locating the problem of insular mentalities and their madness by ironising, in Coetzee's novel, the way that the anonymous Empire constructed its view of so-called barbarians. Before entering further discussion on this matter, let us review Coetzee's story (drawing on the sleeve summary).

For decades the Magistrate has run the affairs of a tiny frontier settlement, ignoring impending war between the barbarians and the Empire whose servant he is. The Magistrate implemented the laws of the Empire faithfully, sometimes sensing an absurdity, but always reconciling this against the need for order. He was seeing out the last few years of his administrative position.

Colonel Jolls has just arrived as the novel begins. Jolls is from the Third Bureau which is the most important division of the Civil Guard. Jolls's mission is not to be discussed. Enough said that it was launched under emergency powers. With the arrival of Jolls and his team of interrogation experts, though, the Magistrate finds himself jolted into sympathy with their victims – until the barbarous treatment of prisoners of war finally pushes him into a quixotic act of rebellion, and thus into imprisonment as enemy of the state. The Magistrate's imprisonment led to both physical suffering and humiliation as he was tortured and subsequently mocked by the previously respectful inhabitants of the frontier settlement.

Jolls's glorious mission, however, collapses as forces the Empire exerts have the reverse from desired effect. Forays into the wilderness beyond the frontier lead to debacle. At the end of the novel a few surviving troops, including Jolls, hurriedly pass through the settlement on return to the safe houses of the Empire. The frontier is then left waiting for the barbarians (but from which direction?).

Coetzee's novel arouses thoughts and emotions of many sorts. The novel is a form of protest about the sinister nature of states that impose a system rationality over people. The novel as passive protest explores the Magistrate's active protest against barbarous treatment of what he has always experienced as relatively innocuous peasants eking out an existence. This exploration touched Nadine Gordimer who wrote that "Coetzee's vision goes to the nerve-centre of being. What he finds there is more than most people will ever know about themselves. And he conveys it with a brilliant writer's mastery of tension and elegance." For Gordimer the novel is an experience of self, looking from the outside in, and is protest for self-emancipation.

The exploration also hit home with Bernard Levin who wrote, "Mr Coetzee knows the elusive terror of Kafka [the nightmare quality of the writings of Kafka]", illustrating that he experienced the novel as a strong protest against the instrumental nature of Coetzee's invented (and all such) Empires. For example, the book can easily be interpreted as Coetzee's comment on South Africa under apartheid as well as a conscience-raising enterprise against all oppressive regimes. Through Coetzee's novel it is possible to sense anger as a legitimate emotion. There is a right of anger, found in a blend of emotion and reason. In this way Coetzee appeals at an emotional level. He appeals to conscience.

There are also direct lessons to be astutely reasoned with in Coetzee's argument. Three most obvious ones follow. First, he is making a point about the self-defeating nature of oppression. All is relatively stable until the Empire starts to exert barbarous force. The force feeds back on them so that, by the end of the novel, the frontiers of the Empire are left ragged and the Empire exposed to attack. This is a poignant metaphor for leaders of societies, organisations and other social groupings. Second, protesters learn that there are both passive and active forms of protest. Third, novel writing also questions the importance of drawing a line between fact and fiction. The crucial question on this score is, Does this fiction resonate in a particularly poignant way with any aspects of the reader's reality? If so, then what action should be undertaken? With these and other lessons "under the belt", it is now time to sum up our view on protest.

9.8.5 Concluding Comment

This section shows some of the ways in which protest initiatives can enter the discourse of might–right management. We point to ways in which protest is a response to mighty systems that seem to forbid subversion. In this way protest can keep alive moments of subversion and may aspire to strategic reversal of sedimented systems of operation. We also draw attention to the communicative force of protest initiatives in society. This highlights and activates the potential for more communicative rationality. Of great importance and in keeping with diversity management, we argue that any engagement in protest must astutely manage forces pulling toward mighty strategy on the one hand and the glitter of reason on the other hand.

9.9 SUMMARY AND CONCLUSION

The main points of this chapter are summarised below in bullet points that act, like in the other chapters, as our conclusion.

• In this chapter we evaluate might–right management – a reflexive loop that stimulates further contemplation from another angle about design management and debate management. Evaluation here takes on the following meaning. With power/freedom through might–right management we mean chances people have to act and choose, given power people have to make widely informed and locally contingent choices about transformation of social relations, and the nature and relevance of designs and decisions made in that process. By relevance we mean astuteness of judgement made in the circumstances. Circumstances to us allows interventionists to choose an arena of focus and in this case the focus is power–knowledge transformation contextualised to the local (proximal) decision makers.

• Might–right management can be explained in practical terms. Design management and debate management between them ask in the circumstances, Are we doing things right?, and, Are we doing the right things? Might–right management asks, Is rightness the right of appeal to forms of science or presumed agreement, or the might of an appeal to imperatives, that buttress a preferred conception?

• The question of interests for design management orientates theory and practice toward structures that serve collective interests. For debate management, interests are made an issue as interested parties define their concerns and arrive at reconciliation, accommodation, or celebration of differences. For might–right management, the question of interests asks whether relations can be established between people that enable reconsideration of games of knowledge production in society.

• Ways of considering social transformation through might–right management within the spirit of diversity management include (the following two types of educational revitalisation) Dialogical Intervention Strategy, Critical Systems Heuristics, (and the following two ways of nurturing self-reliance) Collaborative Inquiry, Self-reliant Participatory Action Research, followed by Reconsideration of Social Processes, (and the following three types of intelligent discourse about protest in society) Right in Protest Through Communicative Rationality, Might of Strategy in Protest, and Novel Protest.

- Dialogical Intervention Strategy, the first of two types of educational revitalisation reviewed in this chapter, aims to develop educational practices by exposing through practical means implications and applications of transforming patterns of undialogical interaction.
- Critical Systems Heuristics is our second way of vitalising educational practices, that aims to influence educational practices by exposing the use of argument that often benefits those already advantaged in organisations and society.
- Collaborative Inquiry, the first of two ways of nurturing self-reliance, aims to train individuals and develop communities toward a consciousness of future participation.
- Self-reliant Participatory Action Research is our second way of nurturing self-reliance where the main thrust is to employ action research to nurture self-reliance as a mode of human relationship. This is done by concentrating initially on the capabilities of the more vulnerable people in society.
- Reconsideration of Social Processes explores and seeks ways of transforming knowledge–power networks in society.
- Right in Protest Through Communicative Rationality, the first of three forms of protest reviewed in this chapter, draws on the strength of communicative rationality to provide an antidote to unnecessary domination.
- Might of Strategy in Protest is our second form of protest, that wants to nurture a political will to protest against pervasion of "the familiar and accepted".
- Novel Protest is our third form of protest that shows novel writing as a form of intelligent discourse to be reckoned with as it explores another way of locating the problem of insular mentalities.

In Chapter 9 we have covered a wide range of approaches to might–right management. Our own contribution to the might–right complex proposes oblique use of models and methodologies from design management and debate management. We have chosen to deal with this in a chapter of its own. It is individualised in Chapter 10.

Chapter 10

Loop 3 Continued. Enhancing Emancipatory Practice

10.1 INTRODUCTION

In this chapter we explore an option for might–right management that amounts to redirection of models and methodologies in terms of purposes not normally associated with them and not provided for in the theoretical underpinning proposed by their proponents. We call this kind of option the oblique use of purposes. Before we discuss what we mean by oblique use it is necessary to clarify our argument about non-eclectic mixing of options – within and between our three loops.

First, let us consider how we have addressed the question of the relation between types of option within our three loops. Chapters 7, 8 and 9 isolated models and methodologies and some other approaches that aid design management, debate management and might–right management. We showed that if action options from any of these loops become linked, that is combined in some way, the purpose of one option is likely to be dominant. Other models and methodologies operate too but are not of primary significance. Here, choice often arises by default to a preferred way of intervention that reflects a dominant underlying theory. It is thus preferable, we argue, to be explicit that one approach is operating in a dominant role.[1]

---

[1] The language "dominant" versus "support" models and methodologies comes from the Total Systems Intervention argument that we introduced in Part 2. The reason that one model or methodology will become dominant is because they operate in terms of different theoretical underpinnings (as shown again in Chapter 6). To combine means therefore that consciously or unconsciously something is being prioritised.

Other approaches are then known to operate in a support role. The quality of choice is thus open to further evaluation.

Practitioners in triple loop learning are always faced with choice; choice to prioritise design issues (How?), debate issues (What?), or might–right issues (Why?). The need for choice between loops arises because the management of issues is linked up with the way core issues are problematised. In the light of this, people have to judge whether to tackle issues as issues of structural irrelevance, or as needing more considered debate, or as a lack of astuteness in the way in which knowledge construction is being perpetuated via dominant forms of argument and/or the way in which tactical plays of power seem to forbid readdressal of social relationships. There is (in)commensurability between the loops.[2] They simply cannot all be mixed in the hope that somehow they will deal with the whole situation. The only way a more comprehensive appreciation can be gained is by the interventionist reflecting upon the kinds of core issues that they are choosing to emphasise as they move toward a choice of loop. The interventionists' choice of core issues is also a choice of core loop through which they commit their action (and this is what we mean by being systemic!). If links between options are being operated, however, these must be reflected upon so that dominant loops do not come to operate by default.

So, we have argued that purposes of design, debate, or might–right management can be served by activating one of the loops in a dominant role. Now we wish to add another option for action. It is the option of redirecting the purpose of a model or methodology in terms of principles and purposes not provided for by its usual theoretical underpinning. We call this "oblique use" of models and methodologies. We offer this option within diversity management because we believe that it offers a way of working with models and methodologies that may, at times, be defensible.

We build up our defence of this by first considering the oblique use of design and debating models and methodologies to tackle might–right management issues. We suggest that although these approaches are not fundamentally equipped to address might–right issues, it may be defensible in certain circumstances to use their frameworks obliquely to begin to tackle such issues. There may be cases when head-on attempts to tackle might–right issues using options developed in Chapter 9 are considered to be less than astute in the light of the primary purpose of might–right management. In such cases, oblique use of models and/or methodologies from Loop 1 or Loop 2 may become a relevant option. We then go on to suggest that any model or methodology can be used obliquely to aspire towards the purpose of a loop not domain to its normal theoretical underpinning. We evoke this

---

[2] This is not to say that we consider there to be commensurability between options *within* these loops (How?, What?, and Why? arenas). Comparisons between such options themselves require *creating* meeting points for discussion in the discourse as part of the process of deciding how to proceed within the loop. The management of (in)commensurability here again requires recognising that knowledge judgements about situations faced cannot be divorced from practical choice making.

idea as worthy of general consideration, although we do not have space to offer further examples and must leave this instead for our readers to cognise.

10.2 DILEMMAS FOR TRIPLE LOOP LEARNING

A dilemma arises for triple loop learners when facing issues of power manifested in the coercive force of strategy and/or the coercive appeal to obvious right practices. Tackling these head on may prove to be problematic. Those with power,[3] whose position may be shaken if questions such as Who benefits and why? are asked, could strongly resist the process. Interventionists therefore may be reluctant to ask such questions in the belief that those who have (or believe they have) power will ignore their involvement or deny access to them. Interventionists should be wary of simply disregarding powerful actors in the face of this type of response.

Oliga (1990) notes that true opportunities for initiating educative enlightenment or empowerment may often seem an unrealistic possibility given strong political and ideological forces which, he argues, exist in most organisations. Payne (1992) comments on Oliga's dilemma: "even committed critical systems theorists as educators or consultants face a difficult task in actually initiating a 'contracting' process leading to CST [Critical Systems Thinking]". Payne continues, talking of slowness and uncertainty of bringing about change unless "organisational leaders become convinced to initiate modes of discursive rationality with which they are presently unfamiliar".

Cummings (1994) similarly points out that we need to recognise that the desire to offer a practical model or methodology to address coercive contexts may at times come into conflict with resistant forces. There is a dilemma. He argues that at the time when the interventionist identifies issues of power as coercion being of primary concern, it often will seem unlikely that a Why?-type intervention is possible because of likely resistance on the part of more powerful people. He questions what guidance, if any, (critical systems) theorists give to resolve this dilemma.

Taket (1992) raises different doubts about interventionists' possible reluctance to employ Why?-type methods. She points out that Why?-type intervention is not (yet) a well-worked-out option. This has consequences for practice.[4] It means that the Why? option is a relatively weak one and in practice is much less likely to be used than might have been the case.

This raises a number of key questions as follows. Can issues of power

---

[3] As noted in our discussion of power in Chapter 6, we do not define power as linked solely with positions or commodities of power that seem to define the powerful. We can indeed never be sure what power the different parties have, for people can always express their power in unexpected ways (see also Romm, 1994a: 333). Nevertheless it may be necessary at times to isolate power holders as part of the process of defining intervention possibilities.

[4] Although we would argue that Chapter 9 in this book has made what we call Why?-oriented approaches a much better worked-out option than was the case in 1992.

and domination be addressed only if alternative sources of power can be found for the interventionist? Are there alternative sources of power? Should the interventionist take on the role of attempting to generate a stable base of alternative power before reconsidering relations with "the powerful"? Should work be refused? Should the interventionist make the best of it using How?- and What?-type approaches? And what does all of this mean for the relevance of emancipatory practice and diversity management? These questions are addressed in the next section.

10.3 CURRENT RESPONSES TO THE DILEMMAS

Currently there are a number of responses to the dilemmas just mentioned. None are fully satisfactory; or rather, all can be seen to be accompanied by "bad news" (see Gouldner, 1980: 18). Responses include the following ones.

- Press forward with a Why?-type agenda by invoking intervention that highlights the need to raise ought questions as a way of shifting social asymmetries – even if this means that defensive mentalities on the part of all the participants (including the more powerful ones) may become entrenched as one begins to raise these questions directly. This type of Why? practice could be operative in, for instance, our options called Revitalising Education Practices in Chapter 9, and in some of the work of those whom we have called collaborative inquirers engaged with might–right management. Oliga's caution about prospects for educative practices is relevant here.
- Refuse to continue or even begin with work that involves "the powerful" if it is deemed impossible to raise Why? issues. Withdraw from all involvement with them and thus (supposedly) support the disadvantaged – even though it is possible that the disadvantaged's perspectives may have been better incorporated within the political dynamic if one adopted a more mediating role. Some of the practices for Self-reliant Participatory Action Research verge on refusal to engage with "the powerful".
- Concentrate on developing some theoretical historically informed vision of future possibilities for more attractive power relationships hoping that people may be touched by this somehow – even though this may offer only a distant hope. Our discussion in Chapter 9 about conceptual underlabouring activity is relevant here.
- Consider options for developing protest initiatives and advising others in the community to continue with whatever forms of protest they can imagine in order to provide an antidote to what is regarded as intolerable power play on the part of "the powerful" – even though in this process the interventionist recognises that s/he may not have to bear the brunt of

many of the unintended consequences that might follow. It may be apt to
review our discussion of protest in Chapter 9 in the light of this proviso.

• Press forward and continue to work in the situation with clientele that
includes all the stakeholders and make the best of it, accepting some principles of diversity management such as those which elevate the question
Why? have to be temporarily sidelined – even though one understands
this to be a primary issue of concern.

The first four bullets suggest that interventionists press forward with some
kind of Why?-type agenda while attempting to support as their key client
the most vulnerable (in Ulrich's terms, 1983: 393). If the intervention fails to
be of any benefit to the most vulnerable, then the interventionist may consider the task fruitless. The fifth bullet has the interventionist wishing to
adopt a Why?-type agenda when s/he perceives the pressing need for
might–right management. However, s/he assesses the practical difficulty of
pressing forward with such an agenda in the face of perceived resistance of
"the powerful". S/he decides that s/he cannot adopt a Why?-type
approach but may use other models and methodologies which are available, such as design or decision-making ones, to operate practically in the
situation. This means operating at the expense of diversity management
principles. Such a possibility leaves the framework of models and methodologies intact and ensures that practical work is done, but ultimately means
that interventionists fail to adhere to the principles of diversity management in practice. It is not a valid use of diversity management.

These types of response appear to leave diversity management and
indeed triple loop learning on rather shaky grounds. It seems that in situations where might–right management is deemed to be of primary concern,
diversity management and triple loop learning are accompanied by risk taking that the interventionist cannot easily justify as necessarily worthwhile (in
terms of the question, Why fight?). That is not to say that risk taking can ever
be avoided. Risk taking has to proceed in the light of possible bad news and
also in the light of other possibilities (themselves admittedly not risk free).

The above analysis, however, omits to ask if there is another as yet
unrecognised response. We believe there is and offer our option as a suggestion for when other options discussed in Chapter 9 are considered
unfeasible or counterproductive. Of course, there is no guarantee either that
the option that we put forward here will fill the gap for might–right management, but it is another option which means greater diversity. It is also an
option that we can demonstrate has resonance with accounts of intervention as we will show later.

We realise that there will also be those who argue that the whole point of
Why?-type principles of action is that they are not to be judged in terms of
outcomes generated, but in terms of principles served. In this case, the
dilemmas arising from difficulty of implementation would be less acute.

This glossing over of the dilemma, though, must respect that some people find adherence to principles insufficient and are determined to recognise that experienced outcomes are relevant to Why?-type reasoning.

10.4 A NEW RESPONSE TO THE DILEMMAS

We now argue that there is indeed another response, one that accounts for the way in which interventionists may proceed when might–right management is judged to be of the greatest concern but where a direct use of a Why?-type approach is considered untenable. The new response argues that models and methodologies with their immediate and given purposes can be used to address purposes other than those provided for in their usual theoretical underpinning. For example, an interventionist may choose to use a design-based or debate-based model or methodology obliquely to fulfil, say, a Why? purpose. Such a choice occurs when s/he regards the Why? purpose as primary, yet recognises that this is not catered for through the purposes of design and debating approaches, but recognises furthermore that it cannot be tackled successfully with a direct Why?-type approach. This means confronting the perceived core might–right issues from a less direct angle.

The oblique use of a model or methodology to aspire to some purpose other than its immediate and given one must be differentiated from claims by, for example, systems designers and debate-facilitating interventionists, that they already address all issues. Oblique use of a model or methodology does not amount merely to developing what Jackson (1991) calls their critical kernel. We suggest that in the case of design options, explosion of the critical design kernel still prioritises design principles as the precondition for social existence with consequent implications for intervention. And in the case of debate facilitation the same story holds. An oblique use, however, means operating, say, design or debate facilitation in the knowledge and through the principles of an alternative agenda. We offer and interpret two practical examples to illustrate this option. We also suggest that might–right options could themselves be employed obliquely in some circumstances, that is, shot through with How? or What? principles.

10.5 TWO EXAMPLES OF THE NEW RESPONSE

10.5.1 Introduction

We will now review two practical examples that we have chosen as the basis for our discussion. The examples deal respectively with an oblique use of cybernetics (the VSM) and then a soft systems approach (called Interactive Planning – IP).[5] Neither example is purely our own, but we have been in contact with the interventionists concerned who find our interpretation of their work satisfactory. Neither intervention was carried out with an oblique use of model or methodology explicitly in mind. We are aware that purported illustrations which necessarily involve interpretation provide no final proof of their relevance to an argument. At the end of the day, however, we strongly suggest that an oblique interpretation of these two cases is a plausible one.

10.5.2 Oblique Use of Cybernetics

The VSM, outlined in Chapter 7, we interpret has an immediate and given purpose to design an effective organisation. Our claim in this chapter is that it is possible to use the VSM *obliquely* to address might–right issues. This means investigating effective design with the intention of tackling another issue; the issue of how to centre organisational life around fair(er) knowledge–power play in terms of our contextualised might–right management graph (Figure 9.1). We suggest that in order to address *this* issue using the VSM, it must be decided to proceed from an oblique angle in the knowledge, and through the principles, of a Why?-type approach. The following example serves to clarify this point.

The original interpretation of this example is written up in Flood and Zambuni (1990). Our current explanation throws more light on the case by providing a reinterpretation of how the intervention may be understood. Flood and Jackson argue (1991a: 110) that in any complementarist-based study, it is "usual to combine its use [the use of VSM] with attention to the culture and political metaphors". Here they acknowledge that VSM on its own is not equipped specifically to pay attention to such issues. What we suggest in this case is that the so-called attention to the political metaphor (and concentration on tactical plays) was instantiated by redirecting the VSM in terms of this attention. A VSM analysis is normally tempered in use with attendance to other issues. We suggest that a neat explanation of what occurred in the case is that it was recognised that might–right issues had to be addressed because of the way that the mighty were strategising. A choice was made to address this by using the VSM, but attending mainly to issues of coercion and corruption through principles and purpose normally associated with a Why?-type approach. We call this attendance an oblique use of the VSM approach. This interpretation of the case, we believe, is a plausible one.

The intervention occurred in a major tourism services group. The country

[5] Readers may be able to consider other design or debate models and methodologies as re-directable in similar fashion. We chose these two cases (using VSM and IP, respectively) because we were able to check our interpretation with the interventionists helping us to account for our categorisation of them as oblique usage and because we found them apt examples as illustrative cases.

in which the intervention was carried out had suffered from poor economic growth and political instability. The society was beset by significant amounts of corruption. The standard of education for most citizens was rather basic. This has an impact on the capabilities of those working at the lower levels in organisations. An almost inevitable result is that management style in such a country becomes corrupt and tends to be autocratic. The interventionists imaged the organisation as suffering in this way. Most employees felt generally unhappy, neglected, and even victimised. For example, the most lucrative jobs were always given to a privileged few employees. Management acted with autocratic policies. A challenge which the interventionists felt important was to introduce a more liberated democratic style for lower staff levels with the aim of improving management overall. In other words, the context was judged to suffer from ineffective organisation, but it was also judged to be driven by tactical plays of power and hardened mentalities and so choice of a Why?-type approach would have been appropriate.

Instead of using a Why?-type approach, however, a cybernetic model was chosen. In discussion with participants, managers included, the pressing and primary need that surfaced was to install an organisation that could provide necessary services and survive, and would be equitable. It would survive only if it were equitable. Hence a cybernetic model could be drawn in and operated through Why?-type principles to help aspire to Why?-type goals. What occurred is that managers and others were introduced to a vision of equity via a VSM-type of design. The interventionists' involvement in educating members of the organisation toward the new proposed structure and participating in the way information was handled therein was coupled with a rising sense in the lower echelons of the organisation of their own potency in sustaining a new ethos.

The apparent solution may be seen to be cybernetic. According to some interpretations the organisation was merely redesigned employing the VSM. The operational divisions broke up the old corrupt organisation. New procedures for co-ordination and control were implemented. The procedures put in place ensured that lucrative jobs could be shared out fairly. Overall, the design had an impact on autocracy and corruption because of the VSM's critical kernel.

Another plausible explanation, however, is that the VSM was used obliquely. The main purpose of the exercise was to deal with corruption and coercion through the education practices that accompanied and indeed led the intervention. The process was about developing new visions rather than primarily new structures. Or rather, the process was about developing new visions with structure being used to support this process.

Despite this practical illustration, some cyberneticians may continue to stick with the former type of interpretation of the general utility of a cybernetic approach. They may well argue that cybernetics, say the VSM, can tackle all issues; issues of design, debate, and full and equal participation in organisational life. They may maintain that these are in principle accounted for within the proper use of the approach. They may claim that the example given actually demonstrates this.

But diversity management holds its view that this cannot be the case. Cybernetics on its own is primarily geared to treating intervention as grounded in the fulfilment of needed functions. It offers a design which makes provision for these functions to be met. It is not adjusted in itself to the purpose of activating a new ethos that tackles knowledge–power plays. What is preferable, then, if knowledge–power gaming is considered particularly problematic, is to proceed in terms of the rationale that we are developing in this chapter. What can be achieved through this rationale beyond the immediate output sought is encouragement for people through an oblique vision to become less defensive about their positions. There may be the beginnings of a shift in consciousness across the organisation.[6]

10.5.3 Oblique Use of Soft Systems

Interactive Planning (IP), mentioned in Chapter 8 though not explicated there, has an immediate and given purpose as we see it to engender meaningful debate about issues faced. This enhances learning and understanding and hence aims to improve consideredness of decisions establishing agreed working arrangements. In Ackoff's terms, interventionists must first formulate the mess (including obstruction analysis), and then organise means planning, ends planning, resource planning and choose options for implementation of agreed changes. This is achieved by facilitating a discussion around ideals to be pursued (idealised design). As with other soft approaches that we discussed in Chapter 8, it does not directly problematise events in terms of uneven power among the participants. This lack of guidance to interventionists about involvement in such scenarios may be due to the IP belief that when the design process focuses on ultimate values, surprising amounts of agreement are normally generated, that is, surprising even to the participants (cf. Ackoff, 1979: 192; and 1993: 406–407). "Problems dissolve." The theoretical framework of IP suggests that people can expect to find surprising amounts of consensus when stakeholders are brought together in debate. IP aims to find and capitalise on this consensus.

[6] Some critics may point out here that our discussion above can hardly be considered relevant to the general aims discussed in Chapter 9 under the banner of might–right management. They may argue that the focus here on a specific organisation would need to be significantly extended if general patterns of knowledge–power play are to be readdressed in society. We have two comments to make in this regard. The first is that working in a specific context to generate an (embryonic) shift in people's practices may make a vast difference in the lives of some involved people and should not be shunned on the ground that the chosen place of action was too narrow in scope. The second comment that we make is that of course the VSM, as any model, can be used to focus on larger systems (even whole societies such as in Beer's work in Chile – see Beer, 1981). Our argument on oblique use can be applied likewise in such cases.

Bearing in mind this soft purpose, we suggest that it may be possible to use IP obliquely in terms of purpose from the might–right loop even though the situation may be less than conducive for fair agreements through soft processes of debate. The logic developed in this chapter suggests that in cases where participation in a debate is less than sufficiently dialogical, an interventionist may use some form of debate-facilitating approach. This form, though, would be shaped by an oblique use with the purpose of addressing issues of coercion. An example which we reckon illustrates the oblique use of IP now follows.

The example that we discuss is taken from a paper in *Systems Practice* that describes some very interesting examples of the use of IP (Magidson, 1992).[7] Our presentation sticks closely to the original since Magidson's effort blends well with our point. The use of IP is arguably carried out with Why?-type principles at the fore as we shall soon see.

Magidson's case deals with problems in communities in inner-city Philadelphia. Typical inner-city problems plagued communities, such as homicide, rape, robbery, aggravated assault, burglary, larceny, auto theft, and arson. Some community volunteers decided to do something about the matter. They started a grass-roots movement consisting of people frustrated with the efforts of government and determined to do something about it. The government were reluctant to alter their own practices. Their resource base was strengthened by the fact that they were seemingly responsible for defining what projects to fund and it was they who could eschew proposals if these did not fit their predetermined ideas. The grass-roots movement decided to review their own situation and make improvements. Interact, the organisation employing Magidson, were enlisted to participate in the process of improvement.

The process began with obstruction analysis and right away we can see Why?-type principles flowing in. Four interacting categories in which progress is necessary if society is to develop were considered: the political–economic (scarcity of resources), the scientific (lack of relevant knowledge), the ethical–moral (areas of conflict), and the aesthetic (vision of a desirable state and belief in the possibility of its realisation). This exercise was conducted first so that obstructions standing in the way of community volunteers were problematised. Let us pick up on one obstruction and follow it through the intervention to demonstrate the way Why? principles prevailed.

An obstruction in the political–economic category was a maldistribution of wealth that reduced the quality of services supplied to the citizens of Philadelphia. Many of Philadelphia's services are budget–based, and funding comes from decision makers whose objectives are frequently in conflict with those who need and use the services. The requirements of these

[7] Actually, System Dynamics (e.g. Wolstenholme, 1993) was used too but in our terms only in a support role.

decision makers frequently do not match the requirements for successful community development. The funding structure for providers of youth services (e.g. community and recreation centres) was therefore felt to be obstructing development. Success depended on whether they met requirements of decision makers, for example, in government agencies. If proposals did not match the interests of decision makers who allocate funds, they were likely to be rejected.

Adopting IP's idealised design, community volunteers assumed that their neighbourhoods had been destroyed the night before and that they were designing ideal neighbourhoods with which they would replace them today (i.e. there were no obstructions assumed except technical feasibility and sustainability). The participants specified characteristics that they felt ought to exist ideally in their neighbourhoods. After the group specified the (56 idealised) characteristics, they developed two means of more closely approximating their ideals. Pride coupons was one of them.

The Pride Coupon Program was designed to promote a variety of quality activities through which youths could develop their talents, be recognised for doing so, and derive satisfaction in the process. Also, it was intended to eliminate the obstruction of the current funding system that had resulted in poor services to youths and to address the scarcity of meaningful, legitimate, after-school activities.

The essence of the idea (and tactic) was to turn the funding structure on its head so that the service providers depended on demand. This could be accomplished by subsidising the users of services and allowing them to choose from which service providers to buy. Each provider's income therefore comes to depend on how many youths purchase from them. Preference is indicated through choice. This arrangement dramatically increases the quality and variety of services and reduces waste. Youths spend vouchers called pride coupons at a youth activity organisation of their choice. Providers are reimbursed by submitting the coupons they collect to a fund established by donations from foundations, corporations, government agencies, and private individuals. Organisations put in place through political interest but which raise no interest in the youths, receive no demand and become financially and socially defunct.

In short, as we see it, the IP process of idealised design was redirected in terms of Why? principles, establishing a relationship between the stakeholders that enabled the use of counter-tactic, coupled with fresh ways of confronting and turning around patterns of (inter)dependence. Here we see echoes of what we called in Chapter 9 Self-reliant Participatory Action Research. This revises both tactical and knowledge-construction practices as a route to fairer social relationships. Self-reliance in this case led people to undercut the funding structure and its attendant rationality. It diverted entrenched patterns and allowed for more manoeuvring space on the part of those affected. The way in which this occurred, we contend, was by employing IP in an oblique fashion.

Our interpretation of this example is likely to attract the following responses. Proponents of a soft approach may argue, just as proponents of cybernetics might in the previous example, that their preferred approach *is* capable of tackling issues that we have ascribed to might–right management. The example just given may be claimed to demonstrate this. We argue, however, that soft methods have not provided practical evidence to support claims that debate processes as such can be engendered in the face of knowledge–power issues (as highlighted in the case where rationalities held by the government have become set into hardened patterns). This, we suggest, is due to the underlying theoretical belief that reaching agreement between stakeholders is unlikely to be problematic, and that when it is, processes for dealing with might–right issues can be designed into the system (cf. Ackoff, 1979: 192; and 1993: 407). Ironically, if Ackoff is to be believed, the way forward when there is resistance from certain clients in a soft systems intervention is to begin to use it in an oblique mode of operation.

10.5.4 Concluding Comment

The examples in this section briefly review practical cases where we suggest both cybernetic and soft approaches have been used in the oblique fashion argued for in this chapter. We now put in place both moral and theoretical justification for the oblique use of models and methodologies.

10.6 MORAL AND THEORETICAL JUSTIFICATION

This chapter has thus far argued (using two practical examples) that a purpose aimed at addressing might–right issues can be served by the oblique use of, for example, cybernetic and/or soft systems approaches. This is provided that the interventionists are aware of the principles they are using to drive the approach and hence adjust it to serve the redefined purpose. We believe that this argument has moral and theoretical justification as well as a practical justification put in place in the last section. Moral justification is given first and thereafter we discuss a possible theoretical justification.

A moral basis for the oblique use of approaches to tackle might–right issues comes from the responsibility interventionists have when facing the sort of dilemmas that we referred to above. In confronting these dilemmas we suggest that it is incumbent on interventionists to consider at least the oblique option that we have presented – as an option. The interventionist has to decide whether it may be possible to address what s/he regards as a pressing issue of might–right management via an oblique use of a model and/or methodology not apparently designed for this purpose.[8] We suggest that the range of choice becomes extended through our introduction of the oblique-use option. The possibility of oblique use also may help to sensitise people, *inter alia*, to ways in which coercion may manifest in society – a sensitivity which in turn affects ways of appreciating might–right management as an issue to be addressed.

A possible rejoinder by critics of our new response may be that, in any case, interventionists are aware that they may combine models and methodologies. Hence the whole diversity management framework that has been set up is artificial anyway. In practice, people may combine, say, How?-type and/or What?-type approaches with Why?-type ones to address issues, including what we call might–right issues. The idea of using an approach obliquely, it may be argued, is hardly different in practice with what interventionists do anyway.

As outlined in Part 2, we do not see such eclecticism as constituting good practice. We suggest that mixed combinations have to be carefully thought through to avoid principles and purposes becoming dominant by default. In practice, interventionists may use one approach according to *its* logic and then eclectically add on others without considering or confronting competing theoretical underpinnings. This means that a serious confrontation with competing possibilities is occluded.

Our argument is that it is morally preferable that interventionists decide how and for what purpose they will be using any approach. If they see their own operation of models and/or methodologies through the framework that we have described, they have to make the choice about *how* they will address the issues. Practitioners cannot leave it to some supermarket-like pick'n'mix of models and methodologies and hope that in this way they somehow will tackle effectively all issues faced. They may have to decide that while they are using, say, a cybernetic approach, they need to use it *in a specific way* in order to address obliquely issues of might–right management. And likewise with the use of a soft approach, or indeed any approach, at any point in an intervention.

As mentioned above, there is also a theoretical defence for adding the oblique-use option for tackling might–right management. This defence cannot easily be separated out from our moral defence, for it is tied to our moral commitment. The defence could run as follows. One can draw

[8] A number of authors have commented that proponents of, say, cybernetic and soft approaches seem not to appreciate issues of coercion as distinct ones that need to be addressed (e.g. Gregory, 1993: 51). This may be because, as we have explained above, their model or methodology is not designed specifically for this purpose. Their perception of issues is framed by what they believe they *can* address. The option of oblique use that we have presented here may be relevant insofar as it helps to increase sensitivity to issues being appreciated that otherwise might have been glossed over.

on and extend Habermas's (1982: 227) suggestion that coercive non-communicative action may be self-destructive. For that matter one could draw on Foucault's remark too that forms of violence may be regarded as self-destructive (see Barker's, 1993: 81, commentary). In other words it may be pointed out, as Romm has expressed it, that:

> people wishing to "play the power game" in the human world often find that such thinking-and-acting is self-destructive, because people have to rely on others and are, therefore, never self-sufficient. Imposed plans, which are imposed on people perceived to be less powerful, are often not fulfilled in the way they were intended by the "imposers". (Romm, 1994a: 332)

It is possible that people may realise that their power is fragile and that others may wish to become involved in defining reality. This may prompt them to become open to encounter with other arguments. In other words, recognition that other people may undercut their imposition may prompt people toward more dialogical communication, or at least to some openness toward other people. This is the space which, as shown above, we believe diversity management and triple loop learning can exploit and develop. These encounters may shift the control mentalities associated with coercion, but through procedures that open rather than close agendas that generate options for rethinking action.

Although the oblique agenda wants to address in moral terms those with official power – requiring them to be fair(er) for moral reasons – we recognise that there is also an opening for triple loop learners to proceed strategically on this matter.[9] In a context where the powerful may resist a normatively oriented intervention programme, there still may be an opening for some sort of intervention which the interventionist may consider strategically preferable to the other responses offered in Chapter 9. Recognition by "the powerful" of possible self-destruction reduces the need to focus directly on questions such as, Who benefits through designs or accommodation through debate and why?, a focus which may meet with resistance. It then becomes possible to proceed using models and methodologies such as cybernetic or soft ones to evoke options that reassess practices generating more symmetrical power–knowledge gaming.

The argument so far has centred on the oblique use of models and/or methodologies to aspire to essentially Why?-type goals. This is where the oblique idea was born. The argument, however, can be broadened into one that enhances the process of choice of models and methodologies in intervention. We now outline an enhanced choice process.

[9] Ironically the interventionist may act strategically in terms of, in this case, a Why?-oriented agenda to address what some clients may regard as strategic issues of success. This reasoning is becoming prevalent in systems thinking, for example, being the cornerstone of a new argument about facilitation from a critical systems perspective (see Gregory and Romm, 1996).

10.7 ENHANCING THE PROCESS OF CHOICE

The discussion above has made out a case supporting might–right management through both oblique and direct intervention, that is, when it comes to the actual purposes being pursued. Discussion concentrated on oblique use of Why?-type approaches. We conclude the chapter, however, by arguing that all model and methodological options can be employed to serve purposes other than their immediate and given one, that is, other than the purpose normally given by the immediate users. This means that just as one can use VSM and IP obliquely to attain a might–right purpose, so too can one use any approach as a framework that embraces a purpose not normally ascribed to it.

For example, there may be occasions when interventionists use a Why? framework of action to pursue the purpose of design or an accommodation between participants. They may feel that they need to raise the issue of, Who benefits and why?, in order to press toward a design or accommodation for effective action. Where such a decision is taken, an interventionist could be said to be using a Why?-type approach obliquely. It would not then be expected that non-dialogue (unargued-for mightiness) or pseudo-dialogue (failure to question given forms of argument) would be dominating the situation. This means that use of a Why?-type approach would be guided by other expectations.

Let us consider the use of, say, an approach such as Critical Systems Heuristics (CSH; Ulrich, 1983) as an illustration. As explained in Chapter 9, CSH asks 12 questions to find out whose interests "are being/ought to be" served. We suggest that these questions could be asked when participants are more or less equally equipped to participate in, for example, defining an ideal arrangement for future collaboration. In such a situation one could argue that although the methodological framework of CSH could be utilised, it could be dominated appropriately and defensibly by the purpose of, say, IP. This would mean that the CSH approach, which is normally underpinned by a theoretical expectation of non-dialogue or pseudo-dialogue, would in this case be redirected and dominated by guiding principles and purpose springing from a soft approach. Again, we would call this domination of the framework an oblique use of a methodology.

This abstract example has paved the way for rounding off discussion about enhancing the process of choice in diversity management. When choosing models and methodologies, then, interventionists are faced with options such as which one(s) to use. But they also have options about how to use them. These choices must be defended as interventionists decide how best to tackle the issues. Appropriateness of choice rests on the interventionist(s)' conception of the circumstances of which they are by definition a part.

Of course, this does put a responsibility on the shoulders of interventionists to defend their choices and work with them. This may finally lay the diversity management framework open to the charge that it has now become too complex to be of help to interventionists. This, we suggest, is not altogether a fair commentary. As we see it, the oblique response enhances the choice making and simplifies the overall process because it clarifies what can be done.

The enhanced process of choice in diversity management can be put across diagrammatically. Figure 10.1 shows the relationship between the three main purposes of types of intervention. This was the understanding held prior to our new option. The figure pictures how an interventionist may move from one type of approach to another in any direction at any time, depending on circumstances. It pictures types of approach being used according to their immediate and given purpose.

Figure 10.2 extends Figure 10.1 with three straight lines that represent the oblique use of models and methodologies. For example, it shows how the normal application of How? and What? models and methodologies can be dominated by a Why? purpose when oblique use seems justified in the circumstances. This applies to all purposes and hence all models and methodologies. The lines are directed with arrowheads. Each line has two arrowheads, one at either end, meaning that it is possible to move in both directions of the line. There are six possible oblique uses of types of model and methodology shown in Figure 10.2. An oblique use occurs when a model or methodology of a given type is drawn along any one of the arrows, piercing a model or methodology of another given type that it is directed at, and dominating it, as depicted at the tip of the arrowhead.

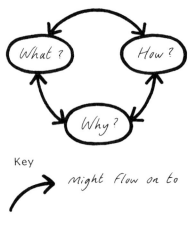

Figure 10.1

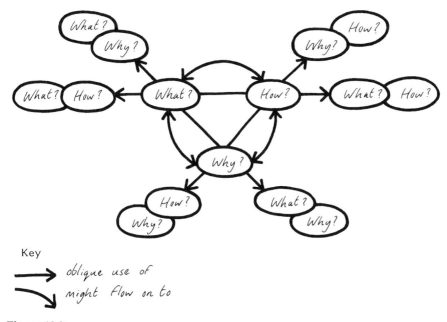

Key

⟶ oblique use of

⤵ might flow on to

Figure 10.2

Domination here means that a chosen approach is operated according to the immediate and given principles and purpose of another one.[10]

10.8 SUMMARY AND CONCLUSION

As is the style in this book, we will now round off Chapter 10 with the main points and findings summarised in bullet points.

- In this chapter current intervention practices are explored focusing on choice of model or methodology. After careful analysis we recognised that there are dilemmas here for triple loop learners. Dilemmas occur when interventionists are faced, for instance, with choice of Why?-type approaches and the direct use of their immediate and given purpose. Direct use may threaten the powerful and attract their perfidious influence so that it is not possible to develop an anti-coercive agenda. The options offered in Chapter 9 then may need to be reconsidered. In the light of such deliberations we offer a possible alternative response – as another option that may be considered relevant in certain circumstances.

---

[10] We are using the word domination without implying association with oppression as is its normal use. We thus flavour the usual meaning of the word with an alternative agenda. It is an oblique use for our purpose.

- The alternative response is to use models and methodologies obliquely. This means, for instance, that How?-type and What?-type approaches can with careful handling be used to aspire to the purpose of a Why?-type approach. Two practical examples are given in this chapter exploring an oblique use of a cybernetic and a soft approach dominated by a Why? purpose. We believe that our interpretation of the two examples throws new light on them and the way they have been used. It also provides a framework to guide reflection on choice making on the part of interventionists. We have concentrated in this chapter on issues connected with might–right management and have offered our cases for oblique use in these terms. But we also wish to extend the argument to enhance the process of choice in diversity management more generally.
- We present our argument on oblique use as an initiative in intervention that we believe is possible because of the complementarist argument that shapes up the process of diversity management. Complementarism along with our understanding of the oblique use of models and methodologies provides a suitable and morally defensible way forward for cybernetic and soft systems approaches to be used in coercive contexts where power–knowledge gaming is regarded as particularly problematic. This involves redirection at that time according to the demands on interventionists to pay proper attention to what it may mean to act appropriately. We also do hope that some of our arguments will serve to sensitise those normally wedded to one or another approach to other options based on some contrasting theoretical self-understanding.
- Our argument about the possibility of oblique use is based on the suggestion that interventionists have the reflexive capacity to learn from many theories by opening up to news they announce. This capacity creates options for oblique use by interventionists incorporating some news not normally received when tuned to one theoretical position. It is this capacity that may allow someone deciding to employ, say, a cybernetic approach to indeed use it, but with self-understanding not normally domain to the approach.
- We have in this chapter offered suggestions for extending and enhancing the process of choice in diversity management and triple loop learning and have in this way tried to open up further debate about model and methodology choice in intervention.

Chapter 10 completes our review of the three loops of triple loop learning. The chapters at times hint at moving between loops and at other times make it clear that this must be so in the kind of reflexive, or complementarist, approach we are promoting. This alludes to a meta-discourse with meta-learning about meta-management. Now it is time to bring these necessities to the surface in our penultimate chapter on triple looping.

Chapter 11

Contours of Triple Loop Learning

11.1 INTRODUCTION

In Chapter 11 we crystallise out defining tips from our discussion on the three loops of triple loop learning. Sketching a line of argument linking these tips draws the contours of triple loop learning. These contours are sketched out below.

11.2 TRIPLE LOOPING

In our role as cartographers we now set about drawing the contours of triple loop learning. Triple loop learning is about increasing the fullness and deepness of learning about the diversity of issues and dilemmas faced. It is about ways of managing them. It is the dénouement of single loop learning and double loop learning.

Single loop learning will be most familiar to the reader as means-end thinking. Ends are set and then a search begins for the best means of meeting those ends. The general issue is, How should we operate to meet best those ends? Other definitions of ends are either not recognised or not valued. The consciousness of single loop learners is non-reflexive leading to an obsession with the best means to meet their defined ends. Single loop learners are task oriented, oriented exclusively to identifying the best means to meet their defined ends. Identification of ends and the best means to achieve them is not considered to be problematic. Single loop learners are isolationist in this way. We recognise three main types of single loop learning, each one being an obsessive use of one of our three loops (see Figure 11.1).

The first type of single loop learning in broad terms is about process

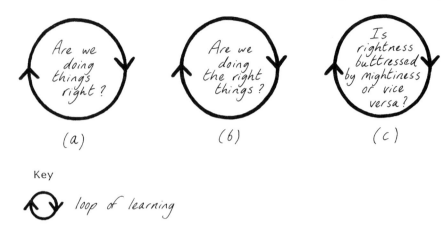

(a)   (b)   (c)

Key

loop of learning

Figure 11.1

design and organisational design (Figure 11.1(a)). Subject areas include process-based approaches like Business Process Reengineering and Quality Management as well as a range of design proposals that create structural arrangements within which processes flow. The centre of learning asks, *Are we doing things right?* The question is clearly, *How* should we do it? Ends, for example, with Business Process Reengineering are to defunctionalise organisations and rebuild them on a small number of core business processes. The means then is a search for a radically improved set of processes to do this, measured in terms of efficiency. For Quality Management, broadly, speaking ends are to make customers happy. The means then is incrementally and continuously to improve the efficiency of the processes that produce the ends. For people concerned with organisational design, the ends come in the form of models, each claiming to offer the most effective rules of organisational design. The means are a search for principles of implementation to produce the right way of achieving those ends.

The second type of single loop learning in general terms is about processes for debate (Figure 11.1(b)). The subject domain is some sort of interpretive-based intervention. Interpretive-based intervention is a reaction to the obsession with finding structuralist solutions that preclude the intersubjective-debate processes necessary to define, for example, quality. Interpretivism recognises that definition of ends and means is problematic because there are many different viewpoints on ends and means. A new centre of learning is set that asks, *Are we doing the right things?* This specific question in other words is, *What* should we do? Yet this is subsumed within the wider task-oriented question, How can we achieve our ends and means? Ironically, new ends and means are set. Ends become accommodations or reconciliations between people. The means becomes a participative, open and free debate. Intervention is then a participative process where designs for organising processes and structuring arrangements are debated and broadened by issues introduced through interpretive thought such as cultural phenomena. The whole process, however, is dominated by an obsession with the redefined ends and means.

The third type of single loop learning reflects a concern with power–knowledge dynamics (Figure 11.1(c)). The subject domain is fair(er) practice. The reaction here is to the obsessive foci of design-based and debate-based intervention. Definition of ends and means from the How?-type obsession is considered to be problematic because it runs the risk of definition production with results that are unfair to some, if not many people. Furthermore, the means of debate pursuing a What?-type obsession are considered to be problematic because debate is easily distorted by, say, coercive forces, meaning that it is not open and free, is not participative, and is not fair on those who are coerced. A new centre of learning is set that asks, *Is rightness buttressed by mightiness, or mightiness buttressed by rightness?* This specific question in other words is, *Why* should we do it? Yet this is subsumed within the wider task-oriented question, How can we achieve our ends and means? New ends and means are set. Ends are forms of fair(er) practice. The means are ways in which fair(er) practice can be achieved including ways of education, building self-reliance and protest (all set out in Chapter 9). The process is dominated by an obsession with these ends and means. Design and debate approaches consider these ends and means problematic because they are regarded as ideologically based and not scientific.[1]

Clearly, there is much conflict over what is the right centre of learning to adopt. Each loop attempts to win people over, demonstrating its superiority by attempting to solve the dilemmas it is shown to face by the other two loops. However, one attempt to overcome the conflict is a reconciliation between the first two types of single loop learning, the How?-type and the What?-type. This reconciliation is the most likely one since both centres of learning share a grave concern that intervention based on subverting forms of knowledge oppression is too ideologically based and is not scientific. The reconciliation is known as double loop learning (see Figure 11.2).

Double loop learning attempts to interplay the centres of learning embracing design and debate practices by asking, Are we doing things right and are we doing the right things? There is a bid to preserve the How? and

---

[1] The complaint is that knowledge-generation processes provided by natural and/or social science are disregarded in the obsession with seeing knowledge–power relations. It therefore becomes impossible to judge the quality of any knowledge or learning. This is considered to be ideological by critics of Loop 3. However, might–right contenders counter-argue that ideology arises because people fail to problematise knowledge–power connections. In terms of *this* definition of ideology, both design and debate interventionists ironically become embroiled in ideology.

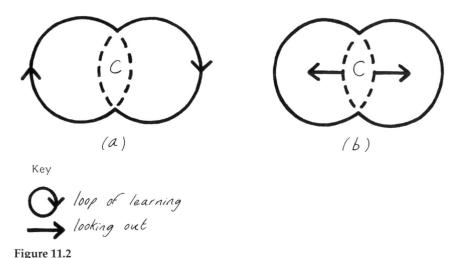

(a)   *(b)*

Key

○ *loop of learning*

→ *looking out*

Figure 11.2

What? centres that the two questions bring forward respectively, thus de-emphasising the task-oriented nature of intervention. Intervention moves a step forward in a reflexive direction by facing up to choice between the two centres at any one time. There is a new consciousness as interventionists loop between the two centres of learning (Figure 11.2(a)). There is limited complementarism.

Double loop learners can and do slip into another less reflexive consciousness. Rather than looping between the two centres of learning, consciousness gets stuck in the middle looking out (Figure 11.2(b)). There is double vision and blurriness. Practitioners receive news from the two centres but do not try to manage it in order to act without defaulting into one of the two loops. They then clear their vision by acting according to the means and ends of a dominant loop (their preferred one) and denature the other loop either by subsuming it or by annexing some of its means. These are forms of imperialism. Figure 11.2(b) depicts the lack of reflexivity. It depicts an operation of consciousness, "looking out" in terms of given premises, that is unwilling to reflect back on its premises.

Another consciousness is the pragmatist or eclectic one where vision remains blurred. Practitioners go ahead with any means within their immediate vicinity that they can focus on. They reach whatever ends they stumble on. The direction they blindly follow is often, however, a well-walked one that leads to a dominant end point as argued in Chapter 2. This too implies a failure to exercise the capacity of reflexivity.

Triple loop learning wants to establish tolerance between all three centres of learning and preserve the diversity therein. It does this by bringing together the three questions from the three loops into one overall aware-

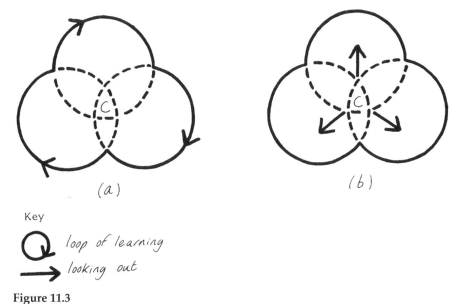

(a)   (b)

Key

Q̲ loop of learning
→ looking out

Figure 11.3

ness, Are we doing things right, and are we doing the right things, and is rightness buttressed by mightiness and/or mightiness buttressed by rightness? Intervention is no longer task oriented since How?, What?, and Why? centres, that the three questions bring forward respectively, come into consideration at any one time as a basis for responsible choice making. There is a new reflexive consciousness as interventionists continually loop between the three questions (Figure 11.3(a)). The looping helps people to develop a discourse for each centre of learning that enables them increasingly to become widely informed, especially as the discourse is related to (insoluble) issues that they face in their lives. Triple loop learning then manages the model and methodological diversity of the centres of learning that in turn enhances management of the diversity of (insoluble) issues to be dealt with. Triple loop learning links into a triple loop the three centres of learning. Triple loop learners loop around these three centres of learning. In this way triple loop learners operate intelligently and responsibly. Their whole consciousness becomes more than the sum of its parts, encouraging awareness of dilemmas involved when addressing issues such as those introduced above.

Triple loop learners can slip into another less reflexive consciousness just like double loop learners can. They too are capable of getting stuck in the middle looking out (Figure 11.3(b)). Looping ceases to happen or never gets started. They get triple vision and much blurriness. They either clear their vision by becoming imperialists or become stumble-in-the-dark pragmatists.

The contours of triple loop learning are now drawn and it remains for us to summarise the main ideas.

11.3 SUMMARY AND CONCLUSION

We conclude Chapter 11 with a quickmap of the contours of triple loop learning in the form of bullet points.

- There are three types of single loop learning each with a different centre of learning. There are specific questions asked respectively for each centre. Are we doing things right? Are we doing the right things? Is rightness buttressed by mightiness and/or mightiness buttressed by rightness? But each question is fixed on the task-oriented quest to do its own things right. The centres of learning are not reflexive. Or, put differently, attention becomes fixed on a single loop with over-confidence in its way of learning.
- Double loop learning has two centres of learning asking, Are we doing things right and are we doing the right things? There is partial reflexivity. There is limited complementarism. There is a danger of slipping into imperialism or stumble-in-the-dark pragmatism.
- Triple loop learning is about increasing the fullness and deepness of learning about issues and dilemmas faced and ways of managing them. It wants to establish tolerance between all three centres of learning and pre-serve the diversity therein. It does this by bringing together the three questions from the three loops into one overall awareness, Are we doing things right, and are we doing the right things, and is rightness but-tressed by mightiness and/or mightiness buttressed by rightness? Triple loop learning links into a triple loop the three centres of learning. Triple loop learners loop between these three questions. In this way triple loop learners operate intelligently and responsibly. Their whole consciousness becomes more than the sum of its parts. This is our brand of complemen-tarism.

Our argument for diversity management is secured in Part 2. Our case for triple loop learning is made in Part 3. It remains for us to summarise the inspiration for diversity management and triple loop learning in Part 4, our closing remarks.

PART 4
Beginning

Chapter 12

Closing Remarks

It seems a strange thing that this planet of ours keeps spinning on its axis and rotating round the sun, as far as we know, relentlessly, presumably unknowingly, despite everything. Despite the human joys and tragedies that it is host to. Despite the monotony that the human race has created for itself. Despite the freaky escapes people invent and believe in. What a weird planet!

Just listen to the voices: "The world is real!"; "The world is a discussion!"; "The world is just damned unfair!". What loopy worlds we have created. Worlds that encircle and entrap our lives. Worlds that are worlds apart. Worlds that are in conflict. Modernism versus postmodernism. Soft systems versus hard systems. You versus us. And ultimately, what does this achieve for you or us? What does it achieve for soft systems or hard systems? What does it achieve for modernism or postmodernism? Hegemony? So bloody what! What a bloody waste of time! If it was not for the fact that hegemony means "power over" we could sit back in our jeans and tee-shirts and laugh at it all.

"Power over" is not at the end of the day a laughing matter. It means no structure, or superstructure, or no decision, or superdecision, or the force of might or right. It means feeble attempts to solve dilemmas. It means in its most potent forms no choice for people. It means we are stuck in one loop or two. Ironically it means we are not loopy enough. Looking at Figure 12.1 we see the human race is in danger of getting stuck in World One. We want to live in World Two.

World Two is the world of diversity management and triple loop learning. It is a world where power is facilitative and is "power to". It is a world of relevant designs, considered decisions, and astute judgements over might–right issues. It means people have chances to make widely informed and locally contingent choices in the process of managing dilemmas that characterise organisational and societal affairs through triple loop learning. It is as loopy as you can get.

Diversity management and triple loop learning is an ideal. It is an ideal that hands over to you choice making about your own life. It is an ideal that recognises the fragility of reality. It is not a bad ideal as far as we can see. It is not a bad deal to make. The deal is to work toward tolerance of differences. The deal is to nurture a value in people's minds about differences. The deal reckons survival and imagination depends on differences.

This book was in large part made possible by the differences between us, the authors, and by the tolerance we had for each other. Differences abounded. There were differences in academic training; one in holistic thought and the other in social theory. There were differences in the languages we spoke accounted for by different academic training that we have enjoyed. There were differences in the extent and nature of the practical experience we had; one mainly with experience in the world of organisational enterprises and the other mainly with experience in community and societal affairs. One of us has a physical disability. There were differences in gender to handle; one of us shaped to some extent by a male paradigm and the other to some extent by a female paradigm. There were differences in our backgrounds; one brought up in the psychedelic sixties in the UK and the other brought up in the face of apartheid in South Africa. There were many other differences. Our tolerance of these differences and management of the tensions that surfaced is at the same time an example and vindication of diversity management and triple loop learning.

And so we appeal to you to give serious consideration to our argument. For how much longer can the human race struggle on faced with polemical devices chaining the species to polemical adversarial relationships? Polemical relationships lead to a lack of tolerance. Polemical relationships lead to splintering. Polemical relationships lead to brawls. Polemical relationships lead to war.

For how much longer can human beings struggle on faced by the same old ways? Freud's (1973: p. 193) observation that the greatest desire of every human being is to find one way, one *Weltanschauung*, by which to order their lives, is a scary one. One way leads to assimilation. One way leads to complacency. One way leads to *ennui*. One way leads to nausea.

When scanning the universe of theories the messages most commonly picked up say that human beings are doomed to polemical and one-way struggles. These are messages from the dark side. We have chosen to resist the dark side. We have chosen to explore a different terrain.

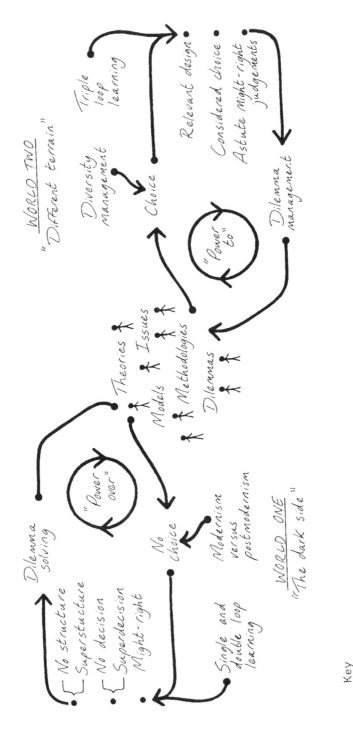

Figure 12.1

References

Ackoff, R. L. (1974). *Redesigning the Future*, Wiley, Chichester.

Ackoff, R. L. (1978). *The Art of Problem Solving*, Wiley, Chichester.

Ackoff, R. L. (1979). Resurrecting the future of operational research. *JORS*, **30**, 198–199.

Ackoff, R. L. (1981). *Creating the Corporate Future*, Wiley, New York.

Ackoff, R. L. (1993). Idealized design: creative corporate visioning. *OMEGA*, **21**, 401–410.

Ackoff, R. L. (1994). *The Democratic Organisation*, Oxford University Press, New York.

Ackoff, R. L., Vergara, E. and Gharajedaghi, J. (1984). *A Guide to Controlling Your Corporation's Future*, Wiley, New York.

Ackroyd, S. (1992). Paradigms Lost: Paradise Regained? In (eds) Reed, M. and Hughes, M., *Rethinking Organisation*, Sage, London.

Adorno, T. W. *et al* (1969). *The Positivist Dispute in German Sociology*, Herman Luchterhand Verlag. English translation, 1976, Heinemann, London.

Ahrne, G. (1994). *Social Organisations*, Sage, London.

Aldrich, H. E. (1992). Incommensurable Paradigms? Vital Signs From Three Perspectives. In (eds) Reed, M. and Hughes, M., *Rethinking Organisation*, Sage, London.

Altieri, M. (1987). *Agroecology: The Scientific Basis of Alternative Agriculture*, Westview Press, Boulder, Co.

Arendt, H. (1986). Communicative Power. In (ed.) Lukes, S., *Power*, Basil Blackwell, Oxford.

Argyris, C., and Schön, D. A. (1974). *Theory in Practice*, Jossey-Bass, San Francisco.

Argyris, C. and Schön, D. A. (1985). *Strategy, Change and Defensive Routines*, Ballinger, Cambridge, Mass.

Argyris, C. and Schön, D. A. (1991). Participatory Action Research and Action Science Compared. In (ed.) Whyte, W. F., *Participatory Action Research*, Sage, Newbury Park, Ca.

Ashley, D. and Orenstein, D. M. (1985). *Sociological Theory: Classical Statements*, Allyn and Bacon, Boston.

Babüroglu, O. N. and Ravn, I. (1992). Normative action research. *Organisation Studies*, **13**, 19–34.

Bachrach, P. and Baratz, M. S. (1962). Two faces of power. *American Political Science Review*, **56**, 947–952.

Banner, D. K. and Gagné, T. E. (1995). *Designing Effective Organisation: Traditional and Transformational Views*, Sage, Thousand Oaks, Ca.

Barker, P. (1993). *Michel Foucault: Subversions of the Subject*, Harvester Wheatsheaf, Hertfordshire.

Barnard, C. (1938). *The Functions of the Executive*, Harvard University Press, Cambridge, Mass.

Bauman, Z. (1992). *Intimations of Postmodernity*, Routledge, London.

Bateson, G. (1972). *Steps to an Ecology of Mind*, Chandler, San Fransisco.

Bealer, R. C. (1975). Theory and rural sociology. *Rural Sociology*, **34**, 229–233.

Beer, S. (1973). *Designing Freedom*, Wiley, Chichester.

Beer, S. (1981). *Brain of the Firm*, Wiley, Chichester.

Beer, S. (1985). *Diagnosing the System for Organisations*, Wiley, Chichester.

Beer, S. (1989). The Viable System Model: Its Provenance, Development, Methodology and Pathology. In (eds) Espejo, R. and Harnden, R., *The Viable System Model: Interpretations and Applications of Stafford Beer's VSM*, Wiley, Chichester.

Benhabib, S. (1990). Epistemologies of Postmodernism: A Rejoinder to Jean-François Lyotard. In (ed.) Nicholson, L. J., *Feminism/Postmodernism*, Routledge, New York.

Benton, T. (1977). *Philosophical Foundations of the Three Sociologies*, Routledge and Kegan Paul, London.

Bertalanffy, L. von (1955). General Systems Theory. *Main Currents in Modern Thought*, **71**, 75–83.

Bhaskar, R. (1993). *Dialectic: The Pulse of Freedom*, Verso, London.

Bhaskar, R. (1994). *Plato Etc.*,Verso, London.

Bleicher, J. (1982). *The Hermeneutic Imagination*, Routledge and Kegan Paul, London.

Boddy, D. (1981). Putting Action Learning into action. *Journal of European Industrial Training*, **5**.

Bohr, N. (1932). Atomtheorie und Naturbeschreibung. *Atomphysik u. menschliche Erkenntnis*, **I**, 10.

Boulding, K. E. (1956). General Systems Theory – the skeleton of science. *Management Science*, **2**, 197–208.

Bourdieu, P. (1975). The specificity of the scientific field and the social conditions of the progress of reason. *Social Science Information*, **14**, 19–47.

Brand, A. (1990). *The Force of Reason*, Allen & Unwin, London.

Braun, G. (1991). The Poverty of Conventional Development Concepts. Edited and published by the Institute for Scientific Co-operation at Tübingen in conjunction with numerous German universities and research institutions, *Economics, Biannual Collection of Recent German Contributions to the Field of Economic Science*.

Brown, L. D. (1981). Participative Research in a Factory. In (eds) Reason, P. and Rowan, J., *Human Inquiry: A Source Book of New Paradigm Research*, Wiley, Chichester.

Brown, R. H. (1977). *A Poetic for Sociology*, Cambridge University Press, Cambridge.

Brown, R. H. (1994). Reconstructing Social Theory after the Postmodern Critique. In (eds) Simons, H. W. and Billig, M., *After Postmodernism: Reconstructing Ideology Critique*, Sage, London.

Bunning, C. (1991). Turning experience into learning: the strategic challenge for individuals and organisations. *Training and Development in Australia*, **18**, 5–9.

Burchell, G. (1991). Peculiar Interests: Civil Society and Governing "the system of natural liberty". In (eds) Burchell, G., Gordon, C. and Miller, P., *The Foucault Effect: Studies in Governability*, Harvester, London.

Burns, T. and Stalker, G. M. (1961). *The Management Innovation*, Tavistock, London.

Burrell, G. and Morgan, G. (1979). *Sociological Paradigms and Organisational Analysis*, Heinemann, London.

Checkland, P. B. (1981). *Systems Thinking, Systems Practice*, Wiley, Chichester.

Checkland, P. B. (1995). Soft Systems Methodology and its Relevance to the

Development of Information Systems. In (ed.) Stowell, F., *Information Systems Provision: The Contribution of Soft Systems Methodology*, McGraw-Hill, Maidenhead.

Checkland, P. B. and Scholes, J. (1990). *Soft Systems Methodology in Action*, Wiley, Chichester.

Churchman, C. West. (1968a). *Challenge to Reason*, McGraw-Hill, New York.

Churchman, C. West. (1968b). *The Systems Approach*, Delacorte Press, New York.

Churchman, C. West. (1971). *The Design of Inquiring Systems, Basic Concepts of Systems and Organisation*, Basic Books, New York.

Churchman, C. West. (1979). *The Systems Approach and its Enemies*, Basic Books, New York.

Churchman, C. West. (1981). *Thought and Wisdom*, Intersystems Publications, Seaside, Ca.

Clegg, S. R. (1989). *Frameworks of Power*, Sage, London.

Coetzee, J. M. (1982). *Waiting for the Barbarians*, Penguin, New York.

Cohen, J. L. and Arato, A. (1994). *Civil Society and Political Theory*, MIT Press, Cambridge.

Cooper, R. and Burrell, G. (1988). Modernism, postmodernism and organisational analysis: an introduction. *Organisation Studies*, **9**, 91–112.

Cummings, S. (1994). An open letter to Total Systems Intervention (TSI) and friends: a postmodern remedy to make everybody feel better. *Systems Practice*, **7**, 575–588.

Czarniawska-Joerges, B. (1993). *The Three-Dimensional Organisation*, Studentlitteratur, Lund.

Dahl, R. (1961). *Who Governs? Democracy and Power in an American City*, Yale University Press, New Haven.

Dandridge, T. C. (1985). The Life Stages of a Symbol: When Symbols Work and When They Can't. In (eds) Frost, P.J., Moore, L.F., Louis, M.R., Lundberg, C. C. and Martin, J., *Organisational Culture*, Sage, London.

Davies, L. (1988). Understanding organisational culture: a soft systems perspective. *Systems Practice*, **1**, 11–30.

Denzin, N. K. (1991). *Images of Postmodern Society*, Sage, London.

Donnellon, A. and Kolb, D. M. (1994). Constructive for whom? The fate of diversity disputes in organisations. *Journal of Social Issues*, **50**, 139–155.

Donzelot, J. (1991). Pleasure in Work. In (eds) Burchell, G., Gordon, C. and Miller, P., *The Foucault Effect: Studies in Govermentality*, Harvester Wheatsheaf, Hertfordshire.

Dreyfus, H. L. and Rabinow, P. (1982). *Michel Foucault: Beyond Structuralism and Hermeneutics*, Harvester Press, Hemel Hempstead.

Driggers, P. F. (1977). Theoretical blockage: a strategy for the development of organisational theory. In (ed.) Benson, J. K., *Organisational Analysis: Critique and Innovation*, Sage, Beverly Hills, Ca.

Elstob, M. (1992). Creative Problem Solving. Robert L. Flood and Michael C. Jackson. *Kybernetes*, **21**, 62–63.

Espejo, R. and Harnden, R. (1989). *The Viable System Model: Interpretations and Applications of Stafford Beer's VSM*, Wiley, Chichester.

Espejo, R. and Schwaninger, M. (1993). *Organisational Fitness: Corporate Effectiveness Through Management Cybernetics*, Campus Verlag, New York.

Fairtlough, G. (1989). Systems practice from the start: some experiences in a biotechnology company. *Systems Practice*, **2**, 397–412.

Fairtlough, G. (1994). *Creative Compartments*, Adamantine, London.

Fals-Borda, O. (1991). Some Basic Ingredients. In (eds) Fals-Borda, O. and Rahman, M. A., *Action and Knowledge*, The Apex Press, New York.

Fals-Borda, O. (1996). Power/knowledge and emancipation, *Systems Practice*, **9**, 177–181.

Fals-Borda, O. and Rahman, M. A. (eds) (1991). *Action and Knowledge: Breaking the Monopoly with Participatory Action Research*, Intermediate Technology Pubs/Apex Press, New York.

Feyerabend, P. (1975). *Against Method. Outline of an Anarchistic Theory of Knowledge*, New Left Books, London.

Flood, R. L. (1990). *Liberating Systems Theory*, Plenum, New York.

Flood, R. L. (1991). Reconstructing the Management and Systems Sciences. In (eds) Flood, R. L. and Jackson, M. C., *Critical Systems Thinking: Directed Readings*, Wiley, Chichester.

Flood, R. L. (1993a). *Beyond TQM*, Wiley, Chichester.

Flood, R. L. (1993b). Practicing freedom: designing, debating and disemprisoning. *OMEGA*, **21**, 7–16.

Flood, R. L. (1994). An improved version of the process of Total Systems Intervention. *Systems Practice*, **8**, 329–334.

Flood, R. L. (1995a). *Solving Problem Solving*, Wiley, Chichester.

Flood, R. L. (1995b). *Implementing Local Area Policing in York Division: From Shift to Geographic Policing*, Centre for Systems Studies Press, University of Hull.

Flood, R. L. and Carson, E. R. (1993). *Dealing with Complexity: An Introduction to the Theory and Application of Systems Science*, Plenum, New York, 2nd edition.

Flood, R. L. and Isaac, M. (1993). A supplier development strategy for small and medium sized companies: The case of Cosalt Holiday Homes. *Int. J. Quality and Reliability Management*, **10**, 28–43.

Flood, R. L. and Jackson, M. C. (1991a). *Creative Problem Solving: Total Systems Intervention*, Wiley, Chichester.

Flood, R. L. and Jackson, M. C. (eds) (1991b). *Critical Systems Thinking: Directed Readings*, Wiley, Chichester.

Flood , R. L. and Romm, N. R. A. (1995a). Diversity Management: Theory in action. *Systems Practice*, **8**, 469–482.

Flood, R. L. and Romm, N. R. A. (1995b). Enhancing the process of methodology choice in Total Systems Intervention (TSI) and improving chances of tackling coercion. *Systems Practice*, **8**, 377–408.

Flood, R. L. and Ulrich, W. (1990). Testament to conversations on critical systems thinking between two systems practitioners. *Systems Practice*, **3**, 7–29. Reprinted in (eds) Flood, R. L. and Jackson, M. C. (1991). *Critical Systems Thinking: Directed Readings*, Wiley, Chichester.

Flood, R. L. and Zambuni, S. (1990). Viable Systems Diagnosis I: application with a major tourism services group. *Systems Practice*, **3**, 225–248.

Forester, J. (1987). The Policy Analysis – Critical Theory Affair: Wildavsky and Habermas as Bedfellows. In (ed.) Forester, J., *Critical Theory and Public Life*, MIT Press, Cambridge, Mass.

Forester, J. (1989). *Planning in the Face of Power*, University of California Press, London.

Foucault, M. (1973). *The Order of Things: An Archaeology of the Human Sciences*, Vintage, New York.

Foucault, M. (1980). *Power/Knowledge: Selected Interviews and Other Writings 1972–1977*. In (ed.) Gordon, C., Harvester Press, Brighton.

Foucault, M. (1984). Interviews. In (ed.) Rabinow, P., *The Foucault Reader*, Random House, New York.

Foucault, M. (1986). Disciplinary Power and Subjection. In (ed.) Lukes, S., *Power*, Basil Blackwell, Oxford.

Foucault, M. (1990). *Interviews and Other Writings, 1977–1984: Politics, Philosophy, Culture.* Edited with an introduction by Kritzman, L.D., Routledge, London.

Freire, P. (1985). *The Politics of Education: Culture, Power, and Liberation,* Bergin and Garvey, Mass.

Freud, S. (1973). Lecture 35. The question of Weltanschauung, *New Introductory Lectures of Psychoanalysis,* Pelican, Harmondsworth.

Freundlieb, D. (1989). Rationalism v irrationalism? Habermas's response to Foucault. *Inquiry,* **3**, 171–192.

Fuenmayor, R. (1991). The self-referential structure of an everyday-living situation: a phenomenological ontology for Interpretive Systemology. *Systems Practice,* **4**, 449–472.

Fuenmayor, R. (1995). The Will to Systems: From Making Sense to Enframing. In (eds) Ellis, K., Gregory, A., Mears-Young, B. R. and Ragsdell, G., *Critical Issues in Systems Theory and Practice,* Plenum, New York.

Fuenmayor, R. and Lopez-Garay, H. (1991). The scene for Interpretive Systemology. *Systems Practice,* **4**, 401–418.

Garfinkel, H. (1967). *Studies in Ethnomethodology,* Prentice-Hall, Englewood Cliffs, NJ.

Gergen, K. J. (1992). Organisation Theory in the Postmodern Era. In (eds) Reed, M. and Hughes, M., *Rethinking Organisation,* Sage, London.

Gergen, K. J. (1994). The Limits of Pure Critique. In (eds) Simons, H. W. and Billig, M., *After Postmodernism: Reconstructing Ideology Critique,* Sage, London.

Giddens, A. (1977). *Studies in Social and Political Theory,* Hutchinson, London.

Giddens, A. (1990). *The Consequences of Modernity,* Polity, Cambridge.

Giddens, A. (1994). *Beyond Left and Right: The Future of Radical Politics,* Polity, Cambridge.

Gouldner, A. W. (1954). *Patterns of Industrial Bureaucracy,* The Free Press, New York.

Gouldner, A. W. (1965). Explorations in Applied Social Science. In (eds) Gouldner, A. W. and Miller, S. *Applied Sociology,* The Free Press, New York.

Gouldner, A. W. (1973). *The Coming Crisis of Western Sociology,* Heinemann, London.

Gouldner, A. W. (1980). *The Two Marxisms,* Macmillan, London.

Green, P. (1995). *An Evaluation of Some of the Effects of Implementing Local Area Policing (LAP) in North Yorkshire,* Centre for Systems Studies Press, University of Hull.

Gregory, W. J. (1993). *Critical Systems Thinking and Pluralism: A New Constellation.* Ph.D. thesis, City University, London.

Gregory, W. J. and Romm, N. R. A. (1996). Towards Multi-agency Dialogue: Facilitation as Fair Education. In (eds) Gasparski, W. W., Mlicki, M. K., and Banathy, B. H., *Praxiology* (vol. 4), Transaction, New Brunswick.

Gregory, W. J., Romm, N. R. A. and Walsh, M. (1994). *The Trent Quality Initiative: A Multi-agency Evaluation of Quality Standards in the NHS,* Research Report, Centre for Systems Studies, University of Hull.

Gregory, W. J., Romm, N. R. A. and Walsh, M. (1995). Trent Health Authority. In Flood, R. L., *Solving Problem Solving,* Wiley, Chichester.

Gustavsen, B. (1992). *Dialogue and Development: Social Science for Social Action,* (vol. 1), Van Gorcum, Assen.

Gutmann, A. and Thompson, D. (1995). Moral disagreement in a democracy. *Social Philosophy & Policy,* **12**, 87–110.

Gutting, G. (1989). *Michel Foucault's Archaeology of Scientific Reason,* Cambridge University Press, Cambridge.

Habermas, J. (1969). A Positivistically Bisected Rationalism. In Adorno, T. W. *et al* (1969). *The Positivist Dispute in German Sociology,* Herman Luchterhand Verlag. English translation, 1976, Heinemann, London.

Habermas, J. (1971). *Knowledge and Human Interests*, Beacon Press, Boston.

Habermas, J. (1979). An interview with Jürgen Habermas, by Angelo Bolaffi. *Telos*, **39**, 163–172.

Habermas, J. (1981). Modernity versus postmodernity. *New German Critique*, **22**, 3–14.

Habermas, J. (1982). Reply to My Critics. In (eds) Thompson, J. B. and Held, D., *Habermas: Critical Debates*, Macmillan, London.

Habermas, J. (1984). *The Theory of Communicative Action* (vol. 1). *Reason and the Rationalisation of Society*, Beacon Press, Boston.

Habermas, J. (1986a). Hannah Arendt's Concept of Power. In (ed.) Lukes, S., *Power*, Basil Blackwell, Oxford.

Habermas, J. (1986b). *The Philosophical Discourse of Modernity*, Heinemann, London.

Habermas, J. (1987). *The Theory of Communicative Action* (vol. 2). *Lifeworld and System: A Critique of Functionalist Reason*, Beacon Press, Boston.

Habermas, J. (1989). *The Structural Transformation of the Public Sphere*, Polity, Cambridge.

Habermas, J. (1993). *Justification and Application: Remarks on Discourse Ethics*, Polity, Cambridge.

Hammer, M. and Champy, J. (1993). *Reengineering the Corporation: A Manifesto for Business Revolution*, Nicholas Brealey, London.

Hannigan, J. A. (1995). The postmodern city: a new urbanisation. *Current Sociology*, **43**, 152–217.

Hartsock, N. (1990). Foucault on Power: A Theory for Women? In (ed.) Nicholson, L. J., *Feminism/Postmodernism*, Routledge, New York.

Hassard, J. (1993). *Sociology and Organisation Theory: Positivism, Paradigms and Postmodernity*, Cambridge University Press, Cambridge.

Heckscher, C. (1994). Defining the Post-Bureaucratic Type. In (eds) Heckscher, C. and Donnellon, A., *The Post-Bureaucratic Organisation: New Perspectives on Organisational Change*, Sage, Thousand Oaks, Ca.

Heckscher, C. and Donnellon, A. (eds) (1994). *The Post-Bureaucratic Organisation: New Perspectives on Organisational Change*, Sage, Thousand Oaks, Ca.

Hofstede, G. (1994). *Uncommon Sense about Organisations*, Sage, London.

Hölscher, F. and Romm, N. R. A. (1987). Development as a Process of Consciousness. In (ed.) Coetzee, J. K., *Development is for People*, Macmillan, Johannesburg.

Hoy, D. C. (1986). Power, Repression, Progress: Foucault, Lukes, and the Frankfurt School. In (ed.) Hoy, D. C., *Foucault: A Critical Reader*, Basil Blackwell, Oxford.

Huyssen, A. (1990). Mapping the Postmodern. In (ed.) Nicholson, L.J., *Feminism/postmodernism*, Routledge, London.

Jackson, M. C. (1991). *Systems Methodology for the Management Sciences*, Plenum, New York.

Jackson, N. and Carter, P. (1991). In defence of paradigm incommensurability. *Organization Studies*, **12**, 109–127.

Jencks, C. (1977). *The Language of Postmodern Architecture*, Academy Editions, London.

Keat, R. and Urry, J. (1982) *Social Theory as Science*, Routledge and Kegan Paul, London.

Khandwalla, P. N. (1977). *The Design of Organisations*, Harcourt Brace Jovanovich, New York.

Klingel, S. and Martin, A. (eds) (1988). *A Fighting Chance: New Strategies to Save Jobs and Reduce Costs*, ILR Press, Cornell University.

Knights, D. and Vurdubakis, T. (1994). Foucault, Power, Resistance and All That. In (eds) Jermier, J. M., Knights, D. and Nord, W. R., *Resistance and Power in Organisations*, Routledge, London.

Knorr-Cetina, K. (1988). The Micro-social Order: Towards a Reconception. In (ed.) Fielding, N. G., *Actions and Structure: Research Methods and Social Theory*, Sage, London.

Konsynski, B. R. and Sviokla, J. J. (1994). Cognitive Reapportionment: Rethinking the Location of Judgement in Managerial Decision Making. In (eds) Heckscher, C. and Donnellon, A., *The Post-Bureaucratic Organisation: New Perspectives on Organisational Change*, Sage, London.

Krim, R. (1988). Managing to Learn: Action Inquiry in City Hall. In (ed.) Reason, P., *Human Inquiry in Action: Developments in New Paradigm Research*, Sage, London.

Kuhn, T. (1970) *The Structure of Scientific Revolutions*, University of Chicago Press, Chicago (2nd edition, enlarged).

Lartin-Drake, J. M. and Curran, C. R. (1996). All together now: the circular organisation in a university hospital. Part I – Planning and design. *Systems Practice*, **9** (issue 5, in press).

Lartin-Drake, J. M., Curran, C. R. and Kruger, N. R. (1996). All together now: the circular organisation in a university hospital. Part I – Implementation. *Systems Practice*, **9** (issue 5, in press).

Lash, S. and Urry, J. (1994). *Economies of Signs and Space*, London, Sage.

Lawrence, P. R. and Lorsch, J. W. (1967). *Organisation and Environment*, Irwin, Homewood, Ill.

Leroke, W. (1994). Transcending Sociology: The Emergence of Post-modern Social Theory. In (eds) Romm. N.R.A. and Sarakinsky, M., *Social Theory*, Heinemann, Johannesburg, 369–399.

Levin, M. (1994). Action Research and Critical Systems Thinking: two icons carved out of the same log. *Systems Practice*, **8**, 25–42.

Lewin, K. (1946). Action Research and minority problems. *Journal of Social Issues*, **2**, 34–36.

Lewin, K. (1952). Group Decision and Social Change. In (eds) Swanson, G. E., Newcomb, T. N. and Hartley, E. L., *Readings in Social Psychology*, Holt, New York.

Lopez-Garay, H. (1991). An interpretive-systematic study of the regional planning corporation of Los Andes in Venezuela. *Systems Practice*, **4**, 491–506.

Lopez-Garay, H. (1995). A Critical Appraisal of Organisational Studies from an Interpretive Systems Perspective. Paper presented in Mexico at *6th APROS (Asian Pacific Organisation Studies Research Group) International Colloquium*.

Lukes, S. (1974). *Power: A Radical View*, Macmillan, London.

Lundberg, C. C. (1985). On the Feasibility of Cultural Intervention in Organisations. In Frost, P. J., Moore, L.F., Louis, M.R., Lundberg, C. C. and Martin, J., *Organisational Culture*, Sage, London.

Lyotard, J. F. (1984). *The Postmodern Condition: A Report on Knowledge*, Manchester University Press, Manchester.

Lyotard, J. F. (1990). The Postmodern Condition. In (eds) Alexander, J. C. and Seidman, S., *Culture and Society: Contemporary Debates*, Cambridge University Press, Cambridge.

MacIntyre, A. (1981). *After Virtue: A Study in Moral Theory*, Duckworth, London.

Maghimbi, S. (1990a). *Rural Development Policy and Planning in Tanzania*, Ph.D. thesis, University of London.

Maghimbi, S. (1990b). The Abolition of Peasant Cooperatives and the Crisis in the Rural Economy in Tanzania. In (eds) Forster, P. G. and Maghimbi, S., *The Tanzanian Peasantry: Economy in Crisis*, Avebury, Aldershot.

Maghimbi, S. (1995). The Conflict Between the State and Grassroots-based Institutions in Tanzania's Rural Development. In (eds) Forster, P. G., and Maghimbi, S., *The Tanzanian Peasantry: Further Studies*, Avebury, Aldershot.

Magidson, J. (1992). Systems practice in several communities in Philadelphia. *Systems Practice*, **5**, 493–508.

Manier, E. (1969). The experimental method in biology. T. H. Morgan and the theory of the gene. *Synthese*, **20**, 185–205.

Mason, R. O. and Mitroff, R. R. (1981). *Challenging Strategic Planning Assumptions*, Wiley, New York.

McGill, I. and Beaty, L. (1992). *Action Learning: A Practitioner's Guide*, Kogan Page, London.

McKay, V. I. (1990). *A Sociological Study of "People's Education" in South Africa: a Humanist Evaluation*, Ph.D. thesis, University of South Africa.

McKay, V. I. and Romm, N. R. A. (1992). *People's Education in Theoretical Perspective*, Longman, Cape Town.

McKay, V. I. and Romm, N. R. A. (1995). The Practice of Discipline in Education. In (ed.) McKay, V. I., *A Sociology of Educating*, Heinemann, Johannesburg.

Merton, R. K. (1964). *Social Theory and Social Structure*, The Free Press, London.

McTaggart, R. (1991). Principles for Participatory Action Research. *Adult Education Quarterly*, **41**, 168–187.

Midgley, G. (1992). Pluralism and the legitimation of systems science. *Systems Practice*, **5**, 147–172.

Miles, R. E. and Snow, C. C. (1986). Organisations: new concepts for new forms, *California Management Review*, **28**.

Mintzberg, H. (1979). *The Structuring of Organisations*, Prentice-Hall, Englewood Cliffs, NJ.

Moggridge, A. and Reason, P. (1996). Human inquiry: Steps towards emancipatory practice. *Systems Practice*, **9**, 159–175.

Morgan, G. (1980). Paradigms, metaphors, and puzzle solving in organisation theory. *Administration Science Quarterly*, **25**, 605–621.

Morgan, G. (1984). Opportunities arising from paradigm diversity. *Administration and Society*, **16**, 306–327.

Morgan, G. (1989). *Creative Organisation Theory*, Sage, London.

Naisbitt, J. (1982). *Megatrends*, Random House, New York.

Nola, R. (1994). Post-modernism, a French cultural Chernobyl: Foucault on power/knowledge. *Inquiry*, **37**, 3–43.

Nonaka, I. and Takeuchi, H. (1995). *The Knowledge-Creating Company: How Japanese Companies Create the Dynamics of Innovation*, Oxford University Press, New York.

Norgaard, R. B. (1989). The case for methodological pluralism. *Ecological Economics*, **1**, 37–57.

Nurse, L. (1988). Theoretical pluralism in organisational analysis. *Administration and Society*, **20**, 92–108.

Ojo, O. J. B. (1983). Towards a Development Oriented Political Science Curriculum. In (ed.) Barongo, Y., *Political Science in Africa*, Zed Press, London.

Oliga, J. C. (1990). Power in organisations: a contingent, relational view. *Systems Practice*, **3**, 453–477.

Oliga, J. C. (1996). *Power, Ideology and Control*, Plenum, New York.

Parker, M. (1993). Life after Jean-François. In (eds) Hassard, J. and Parker, M., *Post-modernism and Organisations*, Sage, London.

Parsons, T. (1957). The distribution of power in American society. *World Politics*, **10**, 123–143.

Parsons, T. (1973). Social Classes and Class Conflict in the Light of Recent Sociological Theory. In (eds) Thompson, K. and Tunstall, J., *Sociological Perspectives*, Penguin, Harmondsworth.

Parsons, T. and Smelser, N. J. (1956). *Economy and Society*, The Free Press, Glencoe, Ill.

Payne, S. L. (1992). Critical Systems Thinking: a challenge or dilemma in its practice? *Systems Practice*, 5, 237–249.

Perrow, C. (1986). *Complex Organisations: A Critical Essay*, Random House, New York, 3rd edition.

Peters, T. and Waterman R. (1982). *In Search of Excellence*, Harper and Row, New York.

Picou, J. S., Wells, R. H. and Nyberg, K. L. (1978). Paradigms, theories, and methods in contemporary rural sociology. *Rural Sociology*, 43, 559–583.

Plato (1987). *The Republic*, Penguin Books, London.

Quine, W. V. (1964). *From a Logical Point of View*, Harvard University Press, Cambridge.

Quine, W. V. and Ullian, J. S. (1978). *The Web of Belief*, Random House, New York, 2nd edition.

Radnitsky, G. (1974). Preconceptions in Research: a study. *The Human Context*, 6, 1–63.

Rahman, M. A. (1991). The Theoretical Standpoint of PAR. In (eds) Fals-Borda, O. and Rahman, M. A., *Action and Knowledge*, The Apex Press, New York.

Rajan, V. (1993). *Rebuilding Communities*, Green Books, Dartington.

Readings, B. (1991). *Introducing Lyotard*, Routledge and Kegan Paul, London.

Reed, M. (1985). *Redirections in Organisational Analysis*, Tavistock, London.

Reed, M. and Hughes, M. (eds) (1992). *Rethinking Organisation*, Sage, London.

Reason, P. (1988). The Co-operative Inquiry Group. In (ed.) Reason, P., *Human Inquiry in Action*, Sage, London.

Reason, P. (1991). Power and conflict in multidisciplinary collaboration. *Complementary Medical Research*, 5, 144–150.

Reason, P. (1994). Human Inquiry as Discipline and Practice. In (ed.) Reason, P., *Participation in Human Inquiry*, Sage, London.

Revans, R. W. (1982). What is Action Learning? *Journal of Management Development*, 1.

Romm, N. R. A. (1991). *The Methodologies of Positivism and Marxism*, Macmillan, London.

Romm, N. R. A. (1994a). Symbolic Theory. In (eds) Romm, N. R. A. and Sarakinsky, M., *Social Theory*, Heinemann, Johannesburg.

Romm, N. R. A. (1994b). Continuing tensions between soft systems methodology and critical systems heuristics. *Working Paper* 5, Centre for Systems Studies, University of Hull.

Romm, N. R. A. (1995). Knowing as intervention: reflections on the application of systems ideas. *Systems Practice*, 8, 137–168.

Romm, N. R. A. (1996). A Dialogical Intervention Strategy for Development: Theoretical and Methodological Considerations. In (eds) Coetzee, J. K. and Graaff J., *Development and Reconstruction in the New South Africa*, International Thomson Publishing, Halfway House (South Africa).

Romm, N. R. A. and Romm, N. L. (1987). Militarizing tolerance: a strategy for creative entry into the 21st Century. *De Arte*, 36, 23–26.

Sayer, A. and Walker, R. (1992). *The New Social Economy*, Basil Blackwell, Cambridge, Mass.

Schön, D. A. (1983). *The Reflective Practitioner*, Basic Books, New York.

Schön, D. A. (1989). Supplement on Planning Education: Teaching Planning Practice.

Case study presented in Forester, J., *Planning in the Face of Power*, University of California Press, Berkeley.

Scott, R. W. (1992). *Organisations: Rational, Natural and Open Systems*, Prentice-Hall, Englewood Cliffs, NJ.

Selznick, P. (1948). Foundations of the Theory of Organisation. *American Sociological Review*, **13**, 25–35.

Shotter, J. (1993). *Cultural Politics of Everyday Life*, Open University Press, Buckingham.

Simons, H. W. and Billig, M. (eds) (1994). *After Postmodernism: Reconstructing Ideology Critique*, Sage, London.

Simons, J. (1995). *Foucault and the Political*, Routledge, London.

Smart, B. (1983). *Foucault, Marxism and Critique*, Routledge and Kegan Paul, London.

South Commission Report (1990). *The Challenge to the South*, Oxford University Press, New York.

Spaul, M. (1993). Critical Systems Thinking: Post-modernism and the Philosophy of Richard Rorty. In (eds) Stowell, F. A., West, D. and Howell, J., *Systems Science: Addressing Global Issues*, Plenum, New York.

Spaul, M. (1996). Critical Systems Thinking and "New Social Movements": a perspective from the theory of communicative action. *Systems Practice*, **9**, 317–332.

Swieringa, J. and Wierdsma, A. (1992). *Becoming a Learning Organisation; Beyond the Learning Curve*, Addison-Wesley, Wokingham.

Taket, A. (1992). Creative Problem Solving: Total Systems Intervention. Robert L. Flood and Michael C. Jackson. *Journal of the Operational Research Society*, **43**, 1013–1016.

Taket, A. and White, L. (1993). The death of the expert. *Journal of the Operational Research Society*, **45**, 733–748.

Topp, W. (1995). Southern Life Association. In Flood, R. L., *Solving Problem Solving*, Wiley, Chichester.

Ulrich, W. (1983). *Critical Heuristics of Social Planning: A New Approach to Practical Philosophy*, Haupt, Berne.

Ulrich, W. (1991). Critical Heuristics of Social Systems Design. In (eds) Flood, R. L. and Jackson, M. C., *Critical Systems Thinking: Directed Readings*, Wiley, Chichester.

Ulrich, W. (1994). Can we secure future-responsive management through Systems Thinking and Design? *Interfaces*, **24**, 26–37.

Vanderplaat, M. (1995). Beyond technique: Issues in evaluating for empowerment. *Evaluation*, **1**, 81–96.

Vickers, G. (1970). *Freedom in a Rocking Boat: Changing Values in an Unstable Society*, Basic Books, New York.

Vickers, G. (1987). *Policy Making, Communication and Social Learning*. Edited with an introduction by Adams, G. B., Forester, J. and Catron, B. L., Transaction, New Jersey.

Walker, J. (1990). Diagnosis and implementation: how a large cooperative employed a series of proposals for restructuring based upon the Viable System Model. *Systems Practice*, **3**, 441–452.

Weaver, W. (1948). Science and complexity. *American Science*, **36**, 536–544.

Weber, M. (1947). *The Theory of Social and Economic Organisation*, The Free Press, New York.

Weber, M. (1973). The Ideal Type. In (eds) Thompson, K. and Tunstall, J., *Sociological Perspectives*, Penguin, Harmondsworth.

Wexler, P. (1987). *Social Analysis of Education*, Routledge and Kegan Paul, London.

Whyte, W. F. (1943). *Street Corner Society*, University of Chicago Press, Chicago.

Whyte, W. F. (1972). *Organisation Man*, Simon and Schuster, New York.

Whyte, W. F. (1991a). Introduction. In (ed.) Whyte, W. F., *Participatory Action Research*, Sage, London.

Whyte, W. F. (1991b). *Social Theory for Action*, Sage, London.

Whyte, W. F. (1991c). Comparing PAR and Action Science. In (ed.) Whyte, W. F., *Participatory Action Research*, Sage, London.

Whyte, W. F. (1996). Emancipatory practice through the Sky River Project. *Systems Practice*, **9**, 151–157.

Whyte, W. F., Greenwood, D. J. and Lazes, P. (1991). Participatory Action Research: Through Practice to Science in Social Research. In (ed.) Whyte, W. F., *Participatory Action Research*, Sage, London.

Wolstenholme, E. (1993). *System Enquiry: A System Dynamics Approach*, Wiley, Chichester.

Woodward, J. (1958). *Management and Technology*, Her Majesty's Stationery Office, London.

Woodward, J. (1965). *Industrial Organisation: Theory and Practice*, Oxford University Press, London.

Wrong, D. H. (1995). *Power: Its Forms, Bases and Uses*, Transaction, New Brunswick.

Young, I. M. (1990). *Justice and the Politics of Difference*, Princeton University Press, New Jersey.

Zhu, Z. (1995). Government Policy/Decision Making: Dealing With Contestable Interests. In (ed.) Bergvall-Kareborn, B., *Systems Thinking, Government Policy and Decision Making*, Proceedings of the thirty-ninth Annual Meeting of the International Society for Systems Science.

Index

A

absolutism 55
Ackoff, RL 69, 87–91, 111, 128, 151, 215, 216, 218
Ackroyd, S 33
action learning 131–134
action learning, case study 132–133
action learning, discourse about consideredness 133–134
action research 130, 131, 132, 134–145, 154, 158, 161, 191
Action Science 140–145, 153, 158, 160
Action Science, case study 143–144
Action Science, discourse about consideredness 144–145
adhocracy 82, 94, 96
Ahrne, G 78, 87, 110, 111
Aldrich, HE 32, 33
Allied Health Company 149
Altieri, M 55
American Indian activists 193
apartheid 204, 233
Arato, A 73, 200
Arendt, H 195
Argyris, C 135, 140, 141, 144, 145, 153, 160
Ashley, D 23
assimilation 233
astuteness 74, 123, 171–172, 232
authentic people's movement 188
authority 79
autonomy, cybernetic 99

B

Babüroglu, ON 72
Bachrach, P 63, 66

Banner, DK 92
Baratz, MS 63, 66
barbarians 203–204
Barker, P 195, 220
Barnard, C 91
Bateson, W 30, 186
Bauman, Z 161
Bealer, RC 31
Beaty, L 132
Beer, S 66, 97, 215
Benhabib, S 72
Benton, T 23
Bertalanffy, L 38, 92
Bhaskar, R 25, 64, 66
Billig, M 8, 162
Bleicher, J 23
boards 87–90
Boddy, D 132
Bohr, N 29–30
Bourdieu, P 23
Boulding, K 38, 39
boundary judgements 123
Bowaters 132–133
Brand, A 200
Braun, G 191
Brent Spar 200
Brown, LD 183
Brown RH 34
Bunning, C 132
Burchell, G 203
bureaucracy 79–87, 90, 92, 111
bureaucracy, case study 81–84
bureaucracy, discourse about relevance 84–87
bureaucracy, mock 80
bureaucracy, paper 119
bureaucracy, punishment centre 80, 84

bureaucracy, representative 80
Burns, T 91, 92
Burrell, G 31, 164
Business Process Reengineering 112,
  113, 120–124
Business Process Reengineering, case
  study 121–122
Business Process Reengineering,
  discourse about relevance 122–124

C

Canadian social policy 192
Carson, ER 38
Carter, P 27, 32, 55, 71
Celltech 94–97
Centre for Systems Studies, Hull
  University xiii, 81, 179
Champy, J 120
Checkland, PB 69, 71, 90, 154–160,
  162–164
choice 8, 31, 45–46, 54–56, 111, 142
choice, enhancing the process of
  221–223
Churchman, CW 146
circular organisation 87–91
circular organisation, case study 88–90
circular organisation, discourse about
  relevance 90–91
circumstances, definition of 77
citizenry 123
Clegg, S 63–64, 73, 96
Coetzee, JM 203–204
Cohen, JL 73, 200
Collaborative Inquiry 184–188
Collaborative Inquiry, case study
  185–187
Collaborative Inquiry, discourse about
  astuteness 187–188
commensurability 5–8, 57, 198, 208
community organisation 104–106
community organisation, case study
  104–106
community organisation, discourse
  about relevance 106
compartmentation 93–96
complacency 233
complementarism 5–8, 11, 14–15, 17, 20,
  33, 37, 45, 47, 50, 54, 137, 213, 228
complementarity theory, Bohr 29
consensus 46, 48, 56, 89

contingency theory 92, 111
co-operative 101–103, 108–109, 190, 191,
  193
Cooper, R 164
cost-study groups 139
critical scientific rationalism 2
critical systemic modernism 41–47, 55
Critical Systems Heuristics 177–183, 221
Critical Systems Heuristics, case study
  179–181
Critical Systems Heuristics, discourse
  about astuteness 181–183
Critical Systems Thinking 161, 209
critique, process of 11
Cross, R 149
cultural renewal 109, 119
culture, corporate 106
Cummings, S 7, 8, 209
Curran, CR 88
cybernetics 37–39, 40, 42, 55, 116
Czarniawska-Joerges, B 68

D

Dahl, R 64
Dandridge, TC 68
Davies, L 104, 105, 106
debate, about 127–131
debate, adversarial 146
debate, problematising 170
debate management 127–168, 176, 208,
  212
decision making, considered 69–71, 232
defensive routines 142, 153, 160
defunctionalise, organisation 120
democratic hierarchy 87–91
Denzin, NK 73
Dept. Management Systems and
  Sciences 81–84
Derrida, J 64
design management 76–126, 176, 208,
  212
design, about 76–78
design, problematising 170
design, relevant 66–67, 232
Diagnostic Biotechnology Pte Ltd
  114–117
Dialogical Intervention Strategy
  174–177
Dialogical Intervention Strategy, case
  study 175–176

Dialogical Intervention Strategy,
  discourse about astuteness 176–177
dilemmas 10, 47, 49, 54–55, 166,
  209–212
disability, physical 233
disempowering relationships 71
diversity management 9, 14, 46, 49–50,
  53–57, 165–166, 194, 210, 211, 215,
  233
documentation 119
Donnellon, A 73, 96
Donzelot, J 115–116
double loop learning 9–10, 227–228
downsizing 121, 201
Dreyfus, HL 26
Driggers, PF 31

E
eclecticism 111, 207, 228–229
educational practices, vitalising
  173–183
emancipation 11, 46, 60, 103, 134, 160
emancipatory practice, enhancing
  207–224
empirical science 2, 21–22, 39
Elstob, M 43
Engels, F 3
Enlightenment 2–3, 17–18, 25
ennui 233
Espejo, R 97
executives, role of 91

F
Fairtlough, G xiii, 94–95
Fals-Borda, O 72, 188, 189
feminism 202
Feyerabend, P 24, 25, 39
Flood, RL 38, 41, 43–45, 47–50, 64, 66,
  73, 81, 82, 85, 112, 114, 116, 128, 146,
  149, 151, 152, 153, 160, 213
flat organisation 93, 97
force of reason 48–49
force of tactic 48–49
Forester, J 71, 72
Foucault, M 25, 26, 31, 32, 48, 49, 50, 56,
  64, 72, 73, 194, 195, 196, 198, 199, 201,
  202, 203, 220
freedom, forms of 51
Freire, P 72, 174

Freundlieb, D 27
Fuenmayor, R 196, 197

G
Gagné, TE 92
Garfinkel, H 155
General Systems Theory 38–39
Gergen, KJ 27, 32, 41, 72
Gestalt 39
Giddens, A 65, 192, 193, 194
Gordimer, N 204
Gouldner, AW 34, 63, 65, 80, 81, 83, 111,
  182, 210
Green, P 151
Greenpeace 164, 200
Gregory, WJ 179, 182, 219, 220
Gustavsen, B 154
Gutmann, A 71, 72
Gutting, G 195, 196

H
Habermas, J 20–23, 25, 26, 42, 46, 49, 50,
  55, 64, 71, 72, 73, 177, 194, 195, 196,
  198, 199, 200, 201, 220
Hammer, M 120
Hannigan, JA 107
Harndon, R 97
Hartstock, N 72, 202
Hassard, J 27, 32, 55
Heckscher, C 90, 96, 106, 110
Hendrix, J vi
Herschey Medical Centre 88–90
hierarchy, democratic 87–91
hierarchy, traditional 79–87, 90–91, 119
historical interpretation 195–197
Hofstede, G 66
Hölscher, F 174
Hoy, DC 195
homosexuality 202
Hughes, M 32
human experience 2
human reason 2
Huyssen, A 27
hybridisation of designs 111

I
ideal speech situation 21, 46
ideology critique 3

ideology managing system 105–106
image technology 121
imperialism 4–6, 37, 45, 228, 229
incommensurability 6–8, 19–20, 26, 33, 57, 58, 164, 198, 208
information science 97
inner city communities, Philadelphia 216–217
intelligence, cybernetic 97
Interactive Planning 90, 213, 215–218, 221
interests, might–right 172
Interpretive Analytics 48
Interpretive Systemology 196
interpretivism 21, 32, 40, 154, 155, 159, 196–197
intersubjective decision making 62, 64, 68–71, 73, 172
intrapsychic influences 140, 141, 144, 145, 153
irony 6, 34, 51
Isaac, M 112
ISO9000 112
isolationism 4–6, 37, 39, 40, 41, 45, 225
isomorphies 38–39

J
Jackson, MC 41, 43–45, 103, 104, 146, 212, 213
Jackson, N 27, 32, 55, 72
Jencks, C 107
job grouping 99
judgement, astute 72–74
judgement, responsible 46

K
Kafka 204
Kaizen 112
Khandwalla, PN 92, 111
Keat, R 23, 25
Kennedy, T 137
Klingel, S 137
Knights, D 63, 73
Knorr-Cetina, K 68
knowledge, experience-based 136–137
knowledge-power relations 72, 160, 172, 184, 188, 198, 215
knowledge and values 20–22
Kolb, DM 73

Konsynski, BR 97
Krim, R 183
Kuhn, T 18–20, 23, 62

L
Lash, S 107
Lartin-Drake, JM 89, 90
Lawrence, PR 77, 92
Lazes, P 138
Leroke, W 25, 26
Levin, B 204
Levin, M 161
Lewin, K 134, 135
Liberating Systems Theory 48–50
lifeworld and system 21–22, 46, 200, 201
Lim, JK 116
Local Area Policing 151–153
Local Systemic Intervention 43
Lopez-Garay, H 196, 197
Lorsch, JW 77, 92
Lukes, S 64, 71
Lundberg, CC 69
Lyotard, JF 25, 26, 56, 71, 73

M
MacIntyre, A 196, 197, 198
Maghimbi, S 72, 190, 191
Magidson, J 151, 216
Manier, E 30
Martin, A 137
Marx, Karl 3
Marxian conflictual theory 63, 65–66
Marxist nonrealism 25
Marylebone Health Centre 185
Mason, RO 146
McGill, I 132
McKay, V 72, 175–177
McKinsey and Company 138
measurement, viable system model 100, 101
Merton, RK 85
metatheory 14–15, 17–28, 29–35, 36–51
metaphor 32
Methodenstreit 22–23
Midgley, G 71
might–right management 62, 64, 68, 71–75, 123, 127, 128, 136, 153, 160, 168, 169–224
might–right, about 170–172

might–right, interests 172
Miles, RE 93
mind traps 128–129
Mintzberg, H 92, 111
mix and match 45, 219
Mitroff, RR 146
modernism 3, 14, 24–27, 37, 56, 161, 232
modernism, critical 72
modernism, critical systemic 41–47, 55
modernism, systemic 37, 40
Moggridge, A 183, 184, 187
moral judgements 34
Morgan, G 23, 30, 31, 32, 63

N
Naisbitt, J 93
narrative, grand 26–27
National Health Service, UK 179–181
natural sciences 29–30
natural and social sciences 20
nausea 233
Nazism 116
networking 93, 96
networks, peer 104
New Social Movements 200
no decisions 69–71, 129–130, 171
no structure 66–67, 77–78, 109, 170
Nonaka, I 94
Nola, R 73
Norgaard, RB 55
North Yorkshire Police 151–152
novel protest 203–204
Nurse, L 31
nurturing self-reliance 183–194

O
oblique intervention 73, 207–224
oblique intervention, examples of
    212–218
offensive model 200
Ojo, OJB 66
Oliga, JC 63–64, 65, 209, 210
Operational Research 145
Operational Research, soft 146
Orenstein, DM 23
organic organisation 91–97
organic organisation, case study 94–96
organic organisation, discourse about
    relevance 96–97

organisational design 78
organisational processes 78
outsourcing 121

P
paradigms 18–20, 30, 33, 57, 186
Parker, M 72
Parsonian collective theory 63, 65
Parsons, T 64, 65, 91
Participatory Action Research 136–140,
    141, 144, 158, 201
Participatory Action Research, case
    study 137–140
Participatory Action Research, discourse
    about consideredness 140
Payne, S 73, 209
People's Education Movement, South
    Africa 175–176
Perrow, C 85, 92
Peters, T 91
Picou, JS 23, 30
Plato 9
pluralism 64
Popper, K 22
positive welfare 193
postmodernism 14, 24–27, 37, 56, 72,
    157, 160, 194, 232
postmodern city 107–108
postmodern critique 3, 24, 47–51, 104,
    119
postmodern debate 161–166
postmodern debate, case study 162–164
postmodern debate, discourse about
    consideredness 164–166
postmodern organisation 106–110
postmodern organisation, case study
    108–109
postmodern organisation, discourse
    about relevance 109–110
postmodern urban lifestyle 108
postmodern world 6
power, arenas of discourse 62
power, circuits of 63
power, facilitative 64
power, fragility of 220
power, in reengineering 123–124
power, legitimate use of 195
power, typologies of 63–65
power and knowledge 26, 72, 160, 172,
    184, 188, 215

"power over" 65–75, 165–166, 232
"power to" 65–75, 136, 168, 232
power to make relevant design 66–68, 77–78
power to make considered decisions 69–71, 130–131, 136
power to transform relations 72–74, 170–171
pragmatism 4, 45, 111, 228, 229
Pride Coupon Program 217
professional expert 130–131, 136, 140, 145
profit 100–101, 201
protest 73, 190, 195, 198–204, 210
protest, might of strategy in 201–203
protest, novel 203–204
protest, political will to 202
protest, right in 199–201

Q
Quality Action Teams 113–114, 116
Quality Management 112–120, 124
Quality Management, case study 114–117
Quality Management, discourse about relevance 117–120
Quality Management, Total 112
Quality of Working Life 138
Quine, WV 24–25, 39

R
Rabinow, P 26
Radnitsky, G 55
Rahman, MA 72, 188, 189
Rajan, V 200
Ravn, I 72
Readings, B 26, 27
Reason, P 183, 184, 185, 186, 187
(re)consideration of social relationships 194–198
recursion, cybernetic 99, 102
Reed, M 32
reflexivity 34, 54, 170, 228–229
relativism 6–8, 20, 55
Revans, R 131, 132
Roman imperium 197
Romm, NL 72
Romm, NRA 23, 49, 68, 72, 73, 174, 176, 179, 182, 209, 220

Royal Sheffield Institute for Blind People and Visually Impaired Person's Group 180
rules of design 78

S
Sayer, A 66
Scholes, J 69, 90, 154–160, 162–164
Schön, DA 73, 135, 140, 141, 143, 144, 145, 153, 160
Schwaninger, M 97
Scott, RW 97
self-reflection 21, 32, 42
Self-reliant Participatory Action Research 188–194, 217
Self-reliant Participatory Action Research, case study 190–191
Self-reliant Participatory Action Research, discourse about astuteness 191–194
Selznick, P 91
Shell Group 157, 159, 162, 164, 200
Shotter, J 10, 72
Simons, HW 8, 162
Simons, J 195, 202, 203
single loop learning 9, 225–227
Smelser, NJ 91
Snow, CC 93
social sciences 33–35
Soft Systems Methodology 154–160, 180
Soft Systems Methodology, case study 157
Soft Systems Methodology, discourse about consideredness 158–160
Soft Systems Methodology, postmodern 157, 162–164
South Commission Report 191
Southern Life Association (Cape Town) 121–124
Spaul, M 27, 200, 201
Stalker, GM 91, 92
standards 6–9, 55, 78, 129, 170–171, 194
state coercion 203–204
Strategic Assumption Surfacing and Testing 146–154, 164
Strategic Assumption Surfacing and Testing, case study 149–152

Strategic Assumption Surfacing and
Testing, discourse about
consideredness 152–154
structuralism 62, 64, 65–68, 73, 172
superdecisions 69–70, 130, 171
superstructure 66–67, 77–78, 86, 87, 170
Sviokla, JJ 97
system and lifeworld 21–22, 46, 200, 201
System Dynamics 216
systemic interpretivism 40–41, 42, 55
systems approach 92
Systems Engineering 145
Systems Practice 85, 88, 97, 101, 104, 134, 137, 146
systems thinking 15, 36–51, 92
systems thinking, soft 146

T
Taket, A 27, 209
Takeuchi, H 94
task formation 99
tension 33, 34, 108, 109, 110, 145, 149, 163, 164, 166, 184, 233
theological speculation 2, 18
Thompson, D 71, 72
Topp, W 121–124
toleration 54
Total Quality Management 110
Total Systems Intervention 43–46, 49, 207
Trico Products Corporation 139–140, 168, 201
triple loop learning 9–10, 47, 49, 54, 60, 186, 208, 209, 220, 225–230

U
Ullian, JS 24
Ulrich, W 49, 72, 123, 160, 177–180, 211, 221
unity of science 38–39
Urry, J 23, 25, 107

V
values, shared 104

Vanderplaat, M 72, 192, 194
variety filter 99
vertical loading 99
Viable System Model 97–101, 213–215, 221
viable system organisation 97–104, 108–109, 117, 119
viable system organisation, case study 101–103
viable system organisation, discourse about relevance 103–104
Vickers, G 128, 129
violence 220
vitalising educational practices 173–183
Vurdubakis, T 63, 73

W
Walker, J 101, 102, 108
Walker, R 66
Walsh, M 179, 182
war 233
Waterman, R 91
Weaver, W 38
Weber, M 21, 79, 80, 83, 86
Wexler, P 34
White, L 27
Whyte, WF 86, 136, 137, 139, 140, 141
Wolstenholme, E 216
Woodward, J 92, 97
work groups, semi-autonomous 88
World One 232–234
World Two 232–234
Wrong, DH 65

X
Xerox Corporation 137–139, 168

Y
Young, IM 108, 110

Z
Zambuni, S 85, 213
Zhu, Z 65

Solving Problem Solving
A Potent Force for Effective Management

Robert L. Flood, University of Hull, UK

Solving Problem Solving identifies types of action to take when problem solving, establishes a problem solving system, and explains what is actually happening. In addition the book marks pitfalls to avoid, including a set of guidelines to use when choosing and using consultants.

The problem solving system presented in this book is called *Total Systems Intervention (TSI)*. *Solving Problem Solving* applies TSI to the business of management – an everday activity undertaken by millions of people throughout the world.

Case studies in the book report on problem solving with organisations based in Australia, Japan, Kenya, Singapore, South Africa, Taiwan, the UK, the USA and covers problem solving in a wide range of industries.

As *Robert Flood* says in his introduction:
"Over time, as you explore and put into practice the ideas and methods presented in this book, a fuller, deeper and richer understanding of problem solving will be accomplished. This is not a book to be read once and shelved forever. It is a book to be consulted again and again. The spine should get crumpled, the cover bashed up, the pages dog eared and annotated – then and only then, will this book have served its purpose".

0471 95590 6   June 1995   £22.50   HB